CONTENTS

☆ ☆ ☆

Introduction	ix
PLAYERS, A—Z	1
THE GAMES, I—XX	221
GAME RECORDS	243

★ ★ ★ ★ ★ ★ ★ ★ ★ ★

WHO'S WHO IN THE SUPER BOWLS

WHO'S WHO IN THE SUPER BOWLS

The Performance of Every Player in Super Bowls I to XX

MARK J. SABLJAK

MARTIN H. GREENBERG

DEMBNER BOOKS • New York

Dembner Books
Published by Red Dembner Enterprises Corp.,
80 Eighth Avenue, New York, N.Y. 10011
Distributed by W. W. Norton & Company, Inc.,
500 Fifth Avenue, New York, N.Y. 10110

Library of Congress Cataloging-in-Publication Data

Sabljak, Mark.
    Who's who in the Super Bowls.
        1. Super Bowl Game (Football)—Biography—Dictionaries.
    2. Football—United States—Biography—Dictionaries.
    I. Greenberg, Martin Harry. II. Title.
    GV956.2.S8S22 1986   796.332′7   86-6208
    ISBN 0-934878-80-3
    ISBN 0-934878-81-1 (pbk.)

Text design by Antler & Baldwin, Inc.

A special thanks to the sports staff of The Milwaukee Journal, for their help in researching this book, particularly columnist Bob Wolf, for the use of his extensive files and knowledge, and Bob Schwoch.

To my parents:
Thank you for getting me started.
To my boys, Matthew and Michael:
Thanks for keeping me going.

INTRODUCTION

"Anybody who has ever played in the Super Bowl has special memories," said Lynn Swann, whose special memories come from four dynamic Super Bowl appearances with the Pittsburgh Steelers. But what about pro football fans? We don't remember every play or player, but out of the twenty Super Bowls there are plenty of unforgettable moments, such as:

- The decking of Fred (The Hammer) Williamson, who spent a good deal of Super Bowl I pregame warning Green Bay Packer wide receivers of his viciousness.
- The vindication of Joe Namath, who spent most of his time prior to Super Bowl III guaranteeing victory for the New York Jets, and most of his time during the game securing it.
- The acrobatics of Steeler receivers Lynn Swann and John Stallworth, who seemed to spend half their game in midair.
- The frustration of the Minnesota Vikings, who made it to the Super Bowl four times and four times came up losers.
- The defense of the dynasties: the Cowboys and the Doomsday Defense; the Steelers and their Steel Curtain; the Dolphins and their No-Name Defense.
- The stalwart goal line stand of the 49ers against the Cincinnati Bengals in Super Bowl XVI.
- The overshadowing of Dan Marino by Joe Montana in Super Bowl XIX.
- The blast from the Windy City in the form of the Chicago Bears, led by Jim McMahon and William (The Refrigerator) Perry in Super Bowl XX.

These and many other moments that made arm chair quarterbacks crush their beer cans are recorded here in an easy-to-look-up format. Every pro who ever made a Super Bowl roster, the stars and bit players alike, is listed, along with his noteworthy activities and pertinent statistics. Height and weight listed for those players who appeared in more than one Super Bowl are taken from their first game roster.

In addition to the accomplishments of each individual, scoring and statistics are listed for each Super Bowl game. The final section lists the individual and team records for all Super Bowls combined.

Some outstanding defensive statistics are not listed because the NFL still terms defensive statistics as "unofficial" and they are not recorded in any significant source. Also, because of NFL style, a player's "substitute" status is not further defined, so a substitute could play on offense, defense, or special teams.

So now that you know all the rules, sit back, relax, and refresh your memory about the top players and the big plays. And maybe test yourself a bit on the contribution of some of the lesser-known players. And if you find yourself coming up a bit short on an answer, follow the advice of another sports figure, one not listed here, who said, "You could look it up."

☆ ☆ ☆

BUD ABELL

Kansas City Chiefs, linebacker, 6 feet 3, 220, Missouri. Played as a reserve in Super Bowl I.

JULIUS ADAMS

New England Patriots, defensive end, 6 feet 4, 263, Texas Southern. Started for the Patriots in Super Bowl XX at the age of 37. He made 2 solo tackles in his team's 46–10 drubbing at the hands of the Chicago Bears.

HERB ADDERLEY

Green Bay Packers and Dallas Cowboys, defensive back, 6 feet, 210, Michigan State. Played in four Super Bowls, two (SB I, SB II) as a member of the Packers and two (SB V, SB VI) as a member of the Cowboys. Started all four games he played in. In games played as a Packer, he also returned kickoffs (2 for 40 yards in SB I and 1 for 24 yards in SB II). In SB II, he scored a touchdown on a 60-yard return of an interception, to give the Packers a 32–7 lead.

Herb Adderley

1

GRADY ALDERMAN

Minnesota Vikings, tackle, 6 feet 2, 245, Detroit. Played in three Super Bowls with the Minnesota Vikings (SB IV, SB VIII, and SB IX). Started in SB IV and SB VIII and played as a reserve in SB IX. Of his team's 23–7 defeat to the Kansas City Chiefs in SB IV, he was quoted as saying, "They beat us on offense, they beat us on defense, and they beat us in every way."

LIONEL ALDRIDGE

Green Bay Packers, defensive end, 6 feet 4, 245, Utah State. Started for Packers in Super Bowls I and II.

CHARLES ALEXANDER

Cincinnati Bengals, running back, 6 feet 1, 221, Louisiana State. Started in the backfield for the Bengals in Super Bowl XVI. Rushed 5 times for 17 yards and caught 2 passes for 3 yards.

JIM ALLEN

Pittsburgh Steelers, defensive back, 6 feet 2, 194, UCLA. Played as a reserve in Super Bowls IX and X.

MARCUS ALLEN

Los Angeles Raiders, running back, 6 feet 2, 210, USC. Started in the offensive backfield in Super Bowl XVIII and was named the game's MVP. He gained 191 yards on 20 attempts, with a long run of 74 yards and 2 touchdowns. His rushing total set an SB record. He also caught 2 passes for 18 yards. Both of Allen's touchdowns were scored in the 3rd quarter. The first, a 5-yard run, climaxed a 70-yard drive and gave the Raiders a 27–9 lead. The second was of a more spectacular variety. With the Raiders ahead, 28–9, the Redskins were stopped deep in LA territory. On the first play from scrimmage, Allen took the ball and ran 74 yards for the touchdown, setting an SB record for a play from scrimmage. His average of 9.5 yards per carry also set an SB record for average gain.

NATE ALLEN

Minnesota Vikings, cornerback, 5 feet 11, 174, Texas Southern. Played as a substitute in Super Bowl XI.

HENRY ALLISON

Denver Broncos, tackle, 6 feet 3, 263, San Diego State. Played as a reserve in Super Bowl XII.

MACK ALSTON

Washington Redskins, tight end, 6 feet 2, 230, Maryland/Eastern Shore. Played as a reserve in Super Bowl VII.

LANCE ALWORTH

Dallas Cowboys, wide receiver, 6 feet, 180, Arkansas. Started for the Cowboys in Super Bowl VI. Caught 2 passes for 28 yards, including one for a touchdown. His touchdown, a 5-yard reception from Roger Staubach, capped a 76-yard Cowboy drive and actually proved the winning points, since it gave Dallas a 9–0 lead.

LYLE ALZADO

Denver Broncos and Los Angeles Raiders, defensive end, 6 feet 3, 260, Yankton. Started at the right end position for both the Broncos in Super Bowl XII and Raiders in SB XVIII. He played a key part in the Raiders' 38–9 victory over the Washington Redskins, as the defensive line held John Riggins of the Redskins to 64 yards rushing (the first time in 7 playoff games he had failed to reach 100 yards), forced 2 interceptions, and recorded 6 quarterback sacks.

ANTHONY ANDERSON

Pittsburgh Steelers, running back, 6 feet, 197, Temple. Used as a reserve in Super Bowl XIV but did not carry the ball.

BILL ANDERSON

Green Bay Packers, end, 6 feet 3, 216, Tennessee. Played as a reserve for the Packers in Super Bowl I.

DICK ANDERSON

Miami Dolphins, safety, 6 feet 2, 196, Colorado. Started at left safety position in Super Bowls VI, VII, and VIII. He was credited by Washington Redskins' quarterback Billy Kilmer as one of the reasons the Dolphins beat the Redskins in 1973, 14–7. "Their two safeties [Jake Scott and Anderson] are super athletes. They're the heart of the pass defense."

DONNY ANDERSON

Green Bay Packers, running back and punter, 6 feet 2, 210, Texas Tech. Used as a reserve for Packers in Super Bowl I and started in SB II, to replace glory-year stars Jim Taylor and Paul Hornung. In SB I, ran 4 times for 30 yards, returned a kickoff for 25 yards, and punted once for 43 yards. In SB II, he ran 14 times for 48 yards, scoring once, on a 2-yard plunge, to give the Packers a 22–7 lead over the Raiders. He also caught 2 passes for 18 yards and punted 6 times for an average of 39 yards.

FRED ANDERSON

Pittsburgh Steelers, defensive end and tackle, 6 feet 5, 235, Prairie View A & M. Played as a reserve in Super Bowl XIII.

KEN ANDERSON

Cincinnati Bengals, quarterback, 6 feet 3, 212, Augustana. Starting quarterback for the Bengals in Super Bowl XVI, a 26–21 defeat to the San Francisco 49ers. Set an SB record for completions by connecting on 25 passes in 34 attempts for 300 yards and 2 touchdowns. He also threw for 2 interceptions, the first of which set up the 49ers' first touchdown and ended a golden opportunity

Ken Anderson

for the Bengals. 49ers' Amos Lawrence had fumbled the opening kickoff and the Bengals recovered on their opponents' 26-yard line, but 6 plays later, Dwight Hicks (49er safety) intercepted a pass on his own 5, and the 49ers then drove 68 yards in 11 plays. Anderson ran for the Bengals' first touchdown, the 5-yard scoring play, pulling his team to within 13, at 20–7, and threw to Dan Ross for 2 more touchdowns before game's end.

LARRY ANDERSON

Pittsburgh Steelers, cornerback and kick returner, 5 feet 11, 177, Louisiana Tech. Played as a reserve in Super Bowls XIII and XIV at defensive position, but stood out as kick returner in SB XIV, a 31–19 victory over the Rams. After the Rams took a 7–3 lead, Anderson took the ensuing kickoff on his own 2, then returned it 45 yards, and Pittsburgh used the good field position to score and regain the lead at 10–7. With the Rams ahead, 13–10, Anderson took the 2nd-half kickoff 37 yards to his own 39, and five plays later Terry Bradshaw threw a 47-yard scoring pass to Lynn Swann to give Pittsburgh a 17–13 lead. He finished the game returning 5 kicks for 162 yards, setting several SB records in the process, including most yards gained in a single game. In SB XIII, he returned 3 kicks for 45 yards.

4

SCOTT ANDERSON

Minnesota Vikings, center, 6 feet 4, 234, Missouri. Played as a reserve in Super Bowl IX.

STUART ANDERSON

Washington Redskins, linebacker, 6 feet 1, 224, Virginia. Played as a reserve for Redskins in Super Bowl XVIII.

GEORGE ANDREWS

Los Angeles Rams, linebacker, 6 feet 3, 226, Nebraska. Played as a reserve for Rams in Super Bowl XIV, during which he came up with a big play as a member of the special teams. The Pittsburgh Steelers, after taking a 3–0 lead on a field goal, tried to pull a fast one on the Rams by having kicker Matt Bahr try an onsides kick. But Bahr got too much of the ball, and Andrews fell on it on his team's own 41. The Rams used the excellent field position to go on and score a touchdown.

TOM ANDREWS

Chicago Bears, center, 6 feet 4, 267, Louisville. Played as a reserve on offense for the Bears in Super Bowl XX.

GEORGE ANDRIE

Dallas Cowboys, defensive end, 6 feet 6, 250, Marquette. Started for Cowboys in Super Bowls V and VI. In SB V, twice figured in key plays. In the 1st half, he rushed and tackled Baltimore quarterback Johnny Unitas, who hurriedly threw a pass that was intercepted. Unitas ended up leaving the game with sore ribs. In the second half, his heavy rush forced Unitas' sub, Earl Morrall, to throw another interception.

FRED ARBANAS

Kansas City Chiefs, tight end, 6 feet 3, 240, Michigan State. Started for Chiefs in Super Bowls I and IV. His blocking was credited in SB IV as opening a hole through which Carl Garrett scored on a 5-yard run to give the Chiefs a 15–0 lead on the way to a 23–7 victory. In SB I, he caught 2 passes for 30 yards.

DAN ARCHER

Oakland Raiders, guard and tackle, 6 feet 5, 245, Oregon. Played as a reserve in Super Bowl II.

OTIS ARMSTRONG

Denver Broncos, running back, 5 feet 10, 197, Purdue. Starting running back for the Broncos in Super Bowl XII. He ran 7 times for 27 yards.

BOB ASHER

Dallas Cowboys, tackle, 6 feet 5, 250, Vanderbilt. Played as a reserve in Super Bowl V.

AL ATKINSON

New York Jets, linebacker, 6 feet 2, 230, Villanova. Started at middle linebacker in Super Bowl III. Early in the second period, with the Baltimore Colts deep in Jets' territory, Atkinson tipped a pass from Earl Morrall intended for Tom Mitchell alone in the end zone. Teammate Randy Beverly pulled in the ball, and the Colts were stopped from scoring. The Jets then went on to score their first touchdown of the game in a winning effort.

GEORGE ATKINSON

Oakland Raiders, safety, 6 feet, 185, Morris Brown. Started for the Raiders in Super Bowl XI. His aggressive style of play made him the target of much pregame controversy. He countered by saying, "I'm an aggressive player . . . but I'm not dirty. I play . . . against a lot of bigger guys. I have to play this way if I want to stay around."

DAN AUDICK

San Francisco 49ers, tackle, 6 feet 3, 253, Hawaii. Starting left tackle for the victorious 49ers in Super Bowl XVI.

OCIE AUSTIN

Baltimore Colts, defensive back, 6 feet 3, 200, Utah State. Played as a reserve in Super Bowl III.

JOHN AYERS

San Francisco 49ers, guard, 6 feet 5, 260, West Texas State. Started at the left guard position in Super Bowls XVI and XIX.

CHARLES BABB

Miami Dolphins, safety, 6 feet, 190, Memphis State. Played as a reserve in Super Bowls VII and VIII.

CHRIS BAHR

Oakland and LA Raiders, kicker, 5 feet 10, 175, Penn State. In Super Bowl XV, he made 2 of 3 field goals—from 46 and 35 yards—and kicked 2 point-after conversions. In SB XVIII, made his only field-goal attempt—from 21 yards—which turned out to be the final scoring of the game as the Raiders won, 38–9. He also made 5 point-after attempts. His point-after kicks tied career and game records. His brother Matt also played in the SB (see below).

MATT BAHR

Pittsburgh Steelers, 5 feet 10, 165, Penn State. In Super Bowl XIV, made his only field-goal attempt—from 41 yards—to open the game's scoring. A short kickoff after the field goal gave the LA Rams good field position from which they went on to score and take a 7–3 lead. He finished the game by making all 4 point-after attempts. Brother of Raiders' Chris Bahr (see above).

BILL BAIN

Los Angeles Rams, 6 feet 4, 270, USC. Played as a reserve for the Rams in Super Bowl XIV.

BILL BAIRD

New York Jets, defensive back, 5 feet 10, 180, San Francisco State. Starting right safety for the Jets in Super Bowl III. Only punt return of the day was a fair catch.

RALPH BAKER

New York Jets, linebacker, 6 feet 3, 235, Penn State. Starting left linebacker for the Jets in Super Bowl III. Recovered Matt Snell's fumble on the Colts' 33 on the first play from scrimmage in the 2nd half to set up a 32-yard field goal by Jim Turner, which gave the Jets a 10–0 lead.

RON BAKER

Philadelphia Eagles, guard, 6 feet 4, 250, Oklahoma State. Played as a reserve in Super Bowl XV.

LARRY BALL

Miami Dolphins, linebacker, 6 feet 6, 225, Louisville. Played as a reserve in Super Bowls VII and VIII.

SAM BALL

Baltimore Colts, tackle, 6 feet 4, 240, Kentucky. Starting right tackle for the Colts in Super Bowl III. Played as a reserve in SB V.

GARY BALLMAN

Minnesota Vikings, tight end, 6 feet 1, 215, Michigan State. DNP (on the roster but did not play) for Vikings in Super Bowl VIII.

JOHN BANASZAK

Pittsburgh Steelers, defensive end, 6 feet 3, 232, Eastern Michigan. Starting defensive right end for the Steelers in Super Bowls XIII and XIV. Played as a reserve in SB X. In SB XIII, helped stop Dallas' opening game drive, which went to the Steelers' 34, by recovering the ball on his own 47 after Dallas' Drew Pearson fumbled on an attempted double reverse play. Field position helped Pittsburgh to its first touchdown and victory. In SB XIV, made another key defensive play, dropping Rams' Squarterback Vince Ferragamo on the Steeler 27. On the next play—which turned out to be the last of the 1st half—the Rams kicked a field goal and went ahead, 13–10.

PETE BANASZAK

Oakland Raiders, running back, 5 feet 11, 200, Miami. Starting running back for the Raiders in Super Bowl II and a reserve in SB XI. In SB II, rushed 6 times for 16 yards and caught 4 passes for 69 yards. One reception, for 41 yards from Daryle Lamonica, helped set up the Raiders' final touchdown, a 23-yard pass from Lamonica to Bill Miller. In SB XI, despite coming off the bench, ran 10 times for 19 yards and 2 touchdowns. The first, a 1-yard run, put Oakland ahead, 16–0, over the Vikings. The second, a 2-yard run, put the Raiders ahead, 25–7. After each touchdown, threw the ball into the stands, and was quoted after the game as saying, "The first time, [Clarence] Davis said to me, 'Do something, you scored.' Throwing the ball was the only thing I could think of."

WARREN BANKSTON

Oakland Raiders, running back and tight end, 6 feet 4, 235, Tulane. Played as a reserve in Super Bowl XI.

BRUCE BANNON

Miami Dolphins, linebacker, 6 feet 3, 225, Penn State. Played as a reserve in Super Bowl VIII.

BENNY BARNES

Dallas Cowboys, corner back, 6 feet 1, 185, Stanford. Started at left cornerback for the Cowboys in Super Bowls XII and XIII and played as a reserve in SB X. In SB XII, intercepted one pass. In SB XIII, was involved in one of the most controversial plays in SB history. Early in the 4th quarter, with the Cowboys trailing, 21–17, was covering Lynn Swann on a pass play. Barnes and Swann collided, and field judge Fred Swearingen called a tripping violation on Barnes, putting the ball on the Cowboys' 23. The call brought protests from the Cowboys and was the object of much postgame conversation, particularly since the Steelers went ahead to score a touchdown and take a 28–17 lead on the way to a 35–31 victory.

Barnes was quoted after the game: "Swann ran right up my back. When I saw the flag, I knew it was on him. I couldn't believe the call. Maybe Swearingen needs glasses."

JEFF BARNES

Oakland and LA Raiders, linebacker, 6 feet 2, 215, California. Played as a reserve in Super Bowls XV and XVIII.

RODRIGO BARNES

Oakland Raiders, linebacker, 6 feet 1, 215, Rice. Played as a reserve in Super Bowl XI.

BILL BARNETT

Miami Dolphins, nose tackle and defensive end, 6 feet 4, 260, Nebraska. Played as a reserve for the Dolphins in Super Bowl XIX.

MALCOM BARNWELL

Los Angeles Raiders, wide receiver, 5 feet 11, 185, Virginia Union. Starting wide receiver in Super Bowl XVIII.

DON BASS

Cincinnati Bengals, wide receiver and tight end, 6 feet 2, 220, Houston. Played as a reserve in Super Bowl XVI.

MIKE BASS

Washington Redskins, corner back, 6 feet, 190, Michigan. Starting right corner back in Super Bowl VII. Was involved in one of the most memorable plays in SB history—kicker Garo Yepremian's kick-turned-pass. The Dolphins led, 14–0, late in the game, when a drive was stopped, and Yepremian trotted out to attempt a 41-yard field goal. Yepremian's kick, however, went squarely into the charging Bill Brundige. Yepremian, instead of falling on the ball, picked it up and attempted a forward pass, which took off feebly and was batted into the hands of Bass, who ran 49 yards for a Washington touchdown.

Bass was quoted after the game: "I heard the thump when the ball was blocked. And it's my job to get the ball when it's blocked. Then I saw Garo with the ball, and I knew from our years in Detroit that he wasn't going to run with it. He picked up the ball, and it slipped out of his hand when he tried to throw it. When he tried to get it back, he kinda batted it into the air. That's when I got it. Somebody threw a good block on [Earl] Morrall, and that opened up the way for me."

BOB BAUMHOWER

Miami Dolphins, nose tackle, 6 feet 5, 260, Alabama. Started in Super Bowls XVII and XIX for the Dolphins at nose tackle.

AUTRY BEAMON

Minnesota Vikings, safety, 6 feet 1, 190, East Texas State. Played as a reserve in Super Bowl XI.

JOHN BEASLEY

Minnesota Vikings, tight end, 6 feet 3, 230, California. Starting tight end in Super Bowl IV. Caught 2 passes for 41 yards, the longest for 26 yards.

TOM BEASLEY

Pittsburgh Steelers, defensive tackle, 6 feet 5, 253, Virginia Tech. Played as a reserve in Super Bowls XIII and XIV.

PETE BEATHARD

Kansas City Chiefs, quarterback, 6 feet 2, 210, USC. Came in as a backup to Len Dawson in Super Bowl I and completed 1 pass in 5 attempts for 17 yards. Also ran once for 14 yards.

BOBBY BELL

Kansas City Chiefs, linebacker, 6 feet 4, 228, Minnesota. Started at left linebacker in Super Bowls I and IV.

THEO BELL

Pittsburgh Steelers, wide receiver and kick returner, 6 feet, 180, Arizona. Replaced starter Lynn Stallworth, who went out with leg cramps, in Super Bowl XIII. Caught 2 passes for 21 yards and returned 4 punts for 27 total yards. In SB XIV, was a substitute at the wide receiver position and also returned 2 punts for 17 yards.

CEASER BELSER

Kansas City Chiefs, safety, 6 feet, 212, Arkansas/Pine Bluff. Played as a reserve in Super Bowl IV.

GUY BENJAMIN

San Francisco 49ers, quarterback, 6 feet 3, 210, Stanford. Did not play in Super Bowl XVI.

WOODY BENNETT

Miami Dolphins, running back, 6 feet 2, 222, Miami. Played as a reserve in Super Bowl XVII, then took over the starting fullback position early in the 1984 season and became the Dolphins' leading rusher that season. He was a starter in SB XIX against the SF 49ers but made only 3 carries for 7 yards, as the Dolphins finished the game with only a net of 25 yards rushing.

CHARLES BENSON

Miami Dolphins, defensive end, 6 feet 3, 267, Baylor. Played as a reserve in Super Bowl XIX.

DUANE BENSON

Oakland Raiders, linebacker, 6 feet 2, 215, Hamline. Played as a reserve in Super Bowl II.

BILL BERGEY

Philadelphia Eagles, linebacker, 6 feet 3, 245, Arkansas State. Started at inside linebacker in Super Bowl XV.

BOB BERRY

Minnesota Vikings, quarterback, 5 feet 11, 185, Oregon. A backup quarterback, Berry did not play in any of the three Super Bowls he was on the roster for— SB VII, SB IX, and SB XI.

LARRY BETHEA

Dallas Cowboys, defensive tackle, 6 feet 5, 254, Michigan State. Played as a reserve in Super Bowl XIII.

DOUG BETTERS

Miami Dolphins, defensive end, 6 feet 7, 260, Nevada—Reno. Started at left end for the Dolphins in Super Bowls XVII and XIX.

RANDY BEVERLY

New York Jets, defensive back, 5 feet 11, 198, Colorado State. He accounted for two of the Jets' 4 interceptions in their stunning upset of the Baltimore Colts in Super Bowl III. After recovering a fumble deep in Jets' territory, the Colts moved to the Jets' 6-yard line early in the 2nd quarter and were about to score the first points of the game. On third down and 4, Colts' quarterback Earl Morrall fired down the middle toward tight-end Tom Mitchell in the end zone, but Jets' linebacker Al Atkinson got a hand on the ball, and Beverly made a diving interception in the end zone. Before the game, Beverly was hoping "I won't look like a clown out there." He ended another Colts drive in the 4th quarter with his second interception.

VERLON BIGGS

New York Jets and Washington Redskins, defensive end, 6 feet 4, 268, Jackson State. Starting right end for the Jets in Super Bowl III and the Redskins in SB VII.

FRED BILETNIKOFF

Oakland Raiders, flanker and wide receiver, 6 feet 1, 190, Florida State. Started at flanker in Super Bowl II and at wide receiver in SB XI—in which he was named the game's MVP. Biletnikoff's performance differed greatly in the two games, as did his team's final results.

In SB II, he caught only 2 passes for 10 yards, as the Raiders were throttled by the Green Bay Packers, 33–14, in Miami. Nine years later, across the country in Pasadena, California, Biletnikoff caught only 4 passes for 79 yards and did not score, yet his catches put the Raiders in position for 3 touchdowns. His key contribution probably came early in the 4th quarter. The game's momentum appeared to be changing, the Vikings pulling to within 12 points of the leading Raiders, at 19–7. Ken Stabler threw a 48-yard pass to Biletnikoff, who was stopped at the 2-yard line. Pete Banaszak then took the ball into the end zone, and the Raiders had a 26–7 lead.

His teammate, Stabler, talked of his MVP selection: "Freddie

12

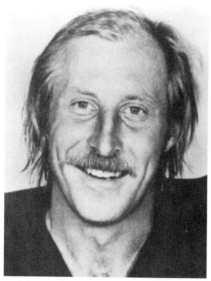

Fred Biletnikoff

started to cry. He's a very emotional fellow. The other players were hugging him and shaking his hand. Photographers were snapping his picture, and the game was still going on. It was a great experience to see something like that because he deserved it so much."

DENNIS BIODROWSKI

Kansas City Chiefs, guard, 6 feet 1, 225, Memphis State. Played as a reserve in Super Bowl I.

RODGER BIRD

Oakland Raiders, defensive back and kick returner, 5 feet 11, 195, Kentucky. In Super Bowl II, he played as a reserve on defense, but also fielded 2 punts and ended

up making a key mistake. Near the end of the 1st half, after the Raiders had pulled to within 6 points of the Packers, at 13–7, Bird called for a fair catch on a punt from Donny Anderson, then fumbled the ball. The Packers recovered in Raiders' territory with 23 seconds remaining in the half. Don Chandler ended up converting a 43-yard field goal, as the Packers went on to a 33–14 victory.

DAN BIRDWELL

Oakland Raiders, defensive tackle, 6 feet 4, 250, Houston. Started at left tackle for the Raiders in Super Bowl II. He talked about the Packers' offensive line before the game, saying, "The Packers have been playing together for so long that they don't have to hold illegally. If one guy breaks down, another helps out. It's second nature to them."

RICHARD BISHOP

Miami Dolphins, nose tackle, 6 feet 1, 265, Louisville. On the roster, but did not play in Super Bowl XVII.

DON BLACKMON

New England Patriots, linebacker, 6 feet 3, 235, Tulsa. Started at the right linebacker position for the Patriots in Super Bowl XX. In the unofficial defensive statistics, was credited with 7 tackles, best on the Patriots' squad for the game. He was also credited with forcing a fumble by Walter Payton of the Chicago Bears on the second play from scrimmage that was recovered by New England's Larry McGrew on the Bears' 19. The recovery led to a 36-yard field goal by Tony Franklin, to give the Patriots a short-lived 3–0 lead.

RICHARD BLACKMORE

Philadelphia Eagles, corner back, 5 feet 10, 174, Mississippi State. Played as a reserve for the Eagles in Super Bowl XV.

ALOIS BLACKWELL

Dallas Cowboys, running back, 5 feet 10, 195, Houston. Played as a reserve in Super Bowl XIII, but did not carry the ball.

GLENN BLACKWOOD

Miami Dolphins, safety, 6 feet, 186, Texas. Starting strong safety for the Dolphins in Super Bowls XVII and XIX. His brother Lyle also played in the SB (see below).

LYLE BLACKWOOD

Miami Dolphins, safety and kick returner, 6 feet 1, 188, Texas

Christian. Starting free safety for the Dolphins in Super Bowls XVII and XIX. In SB XVII, he returned 2 kickoffs for a total of 32 yards. He fumbled once, but recovered the ball. He also came up with 1 interception, when the Washington Redskins attempted a trick play in the 4th quarter. John Riggins faked a run and lateraled the ball to quarterback Joe Theismann, who tried to throw deep downfield to Charlie Brown. But Blackwood was waiting and intercepted the ball on his own 1. Brother of the Dolphins' Glenn Blackwood (see above).

JOE BLAHAK

Minnesota Vikings, corner back and safety, 5 feet 10, 188, Nebraska. On the roster, but did not play in Super Bowl IX.

MATT BLAIR

Minnesota Vikings, linebacker, 6 feet 5, 229, Iowa State. His special-teams play helped give Vikings fans something to cheer about in Super Bowl IX. Early in the 4th quarter, with the Vikings trailing, 9–0, and the Pittsburgh Steelers preparing to punt, Blair broke through the line and blocked Bobby Walden's punt. With the ball rolling in the end zone, Terry Brown recovered for the touchdown. Fred Cox missed the point-after attempt, however, and the Vikings were held scoreless the rest of the game.

GEORGE BLANDA

Oakland Raiders, kicker and quarterback, 6 feet 3, 215, Kentucky. One of pro football's all-time stars, Blanda went into Super Bowl II at the age of 40. He did not play at quarterback, but went into the game as the AFL's leading scorer for the season. He kicked 2 extra points, but missed a 47-yard field-goal attempt.

ROCKY BLEIER

Pittsburgh Steelers, running back, 5 feet 11, 210, Notre Dame. Started in the backfield in four Steeler appearances—Super Bowls IX, X, XIII, and XIV—all of which were victories. Bleier, a Vietnam War hero who had been awarded the Purple Heart, was among the most popular of the colorful Pittsburgh Steeler stars of the mid 1970s.

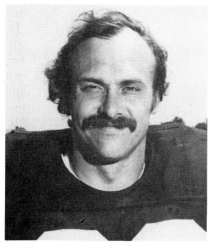

Rocky Bleier

Despite carrying the ball 44 times for 144 yards in his 4 appearances, Bleier's biggest play may have come while playing on a special team. In SB XIII, the Steelers built what seemed to be a commanding 35–17 lead with just over 6 minutes left before the Dallas Cowboys mounted a thrilling rally. It started with an 89-yard drive that ended with a 7-yard touchdown pass from Roger Staubach to Billy Joe DuPree. On the ensuing kickoff, Rafael Septien squibbed the kick, the Steelers' Tony Dungy bobbled the ball, and the Cowboys' Dennis Thurman recovered on the Dallas 48. Nine plays later, the Cowboys scored again, on Staubach's 4-yard pass to Butch Johnson.

Septien was sure to attempt the onsides kick again, so Bleier was one of the Steelers' sure-handed players inserted onto the receiving team. The ball headed toward Bleier, who positioned himself, fell on it—and clinched the victory. "I was trying to anticipate what Septien would do," Bleier said. "If he kicked it hard and tried to bounce it off me, I was going to let it go through to Sidney Thornton rather than risk a fumble. But he decided to dribble the ball . . . so I was able to get it."

Bleier's only touchdown in SB play had come earlier in that game, on a 7-yard pass from Terry Bradshaw that gave the Steelers a 21–14 lead.

Bleier's game-by-game SB statistics: SB IX, 17 rushing attempts for 65 yards, 2 receptions for 11 yards, 1 fumble; SB X, 15 rushing attempts for 51 yards; SB XIII, 2 rushing attempts for 3 yards, 1 reception for 7 yards and his touchdown; and SB XIV, 10 rushing attempts for 25 yards.

MEL BLOUNT

Pittsburgh Steelers, corner back, 6 feet 3, 205, Southern University. Starting right corner back for the Steelers in four Super Bowls—SB IX, SB X, SB XIII, and SB XIV. Blount accounted for 2 interceptions. In SB XIII, he ended a Dallas Cowboys' drive late in the first half and deep in Steeler territory, picking off Roger Staubach's pass intended for Drew Pearson and running the ball back 13 yards to his own 29. Later Staubach was to say, "Of all the passes I've ever thrown, this one will haunt me the longest." Blount's other interception came in SB IX.

DWAINE BOARD

San Francisco 49ers, defensive end, 6 feet 5, 250, North Carolina A&T. Started at the right defensive end position in both Super Bowls XVI and XIX. Board recorded a key sack in SB XIX. The Miami Dolphins had come to life in the closing minutes of the 1st half, moving up from a 28–10 deficit to 28–16. But in the first series of plays of the 3rd quarter, Board caught Dolphins' quarter-back Dan Marino behind the line of scrimmage for a 9-yard loss on third down, Miami was forced to punt and the 49ers drove to within field-goal range. Ray Wersching's kick gave San Francisco a 31–16 lead on the way to a 38–16 victory.

KIM BOKAMPER

Miami Dolphins, defensive end, 6 feet 6, 250, San Jose State. Starting right end for the Dolphins in Super Bowls XVII and XIX. Bokamper was involved in what Washington Redskins' quarter-back Joe Theismann called "the biggest play of the game" in SB XVII. After trailing, 17–10, at half-time, the Redskins had closed to 17–13 when Theismann dropped back to pass on his own 18. But just after the ball left his finger-tips, Bokamper reached up and tipped the ball, which went straight up in the air. Just as Bokamper was about to pull the ball in, Theismann jumped forward and slapped the ball to the ground.

Bokamper, distraught that he was not able to catch the ball and possibly return it for a touch-down, said, "I just came upfield on my guy and got an opportunity to get my hand up and tip it. The ball went straight up. Theismann wasn't anywhere in sight. Then just as it came down in my hands he punched it right through."

16

RIK BONNESS

Oakland Raiders, linebacker, 6 feet 3, 220, Florida State. Played as a reserve in Super Bowl IX.

DAVE BOONE

Minnesota Vikings, defensive end, 6 feet 3, 248, Eastern Michigan. While on the Vikings' roster, he did not play in Super Bowl IX.

EMERSON BOOZER

New York Jets, running back, 5 feet 11, 202, Maryland/Eastern Shore. One of three players from Maryland/Eastern Shore on the Jets' Super Bowl III championship team, along with defensive backs Earl Christy and John Sample. Started in the backfield for the Jets and carried 10 times for 19 yards. Boozer made himself a bit of pregame publicity when he and three other teammates—Joe Namath, Jim Hudson, and roomate Matt Snell—did not show for the official media picture day. Boozer later said, "We heard it [the phone] ringing, and we ignored it. We thought it was just another silly call."

MARK BORTZ

Chicago Bears, guard, 6 feet 6, 269, Iowa. Started at the offen-sive left guard position for the Bears in Super Bowl XX.

JEFF BOSTIC

Washington Redskins, center, 6 feet 2, 245, Clemson. Starting center for the Redskins in Super Bowls XVII and XVIII and a member of the Washington offensive line, affectionately nicknamed the Hogs.

JIM BOWMAN

New England Patriots, safety, 6 feet 2, 210, Central Michigan. Played as a reserve for the Patriots in Super Bowl XX.

KEN BOWMAN

Green Bay Packers, center, 6 feet 3, 230, Wisconsin. He played as a reserve in Super Bowl I and started in the center position in SB II.

CHARLES BOWSER

Miami Dolphins, linebacker, 6 feet 3, 222, Duke. He was a starter in Super Bowl XIX, after playing as a reserve in SB XVII.

BOB BOYD

Baltimore Colts, defensive back, 5 feet 10, 192, Oklahoma.

He was a starter in the backfield for the Colts in Super Bowl III.

ORDELL BRAASE

Baltimore Colts, defensive end, 6 feet 4, 245, South Dakota. On defense, he started in the right end position in Super Bowl III.

ED BRADLEY

Pittsburgh Steelers, linebacker, 6 feet 2, 239, Wake Forest. He played as a reserve for the Steelers in Super Bowls IX and X.

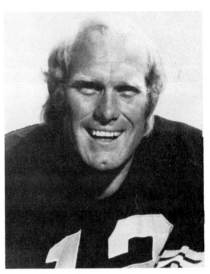

Terry Bradshaw

MORRIS BRADSHAW

Oakland Raiders, wide receiver, 6 feet 1, 195, Ohio State. Was inserted as a reserve in Super Bowls XI and XV, but did not catch a pass.

TERRY BRADSHAW

Pittsburgh Steelers, quarterback, 6 feet 3, 218, Louisiana Tech. Shortly before Super Bowl XIII, Bradshaw was accused—by Thomas (Hollywood) Henderson, the linebacker for the Dallas Cowboys, the Steelers' opponent—of not being able to spell the word *cat* "if given the C and A."

But Bradshaw had the last laugh by leading his team to a 35–31 victory—one of 4 he would head up for the Steelers in the SB, winning two MVP awards in the process and throwing 4 touchdown passes for a record that still stands.

Bradshaw struck three times in the 1st half, the first after the Steelers recovered a Dallas fumble. The drive nearly stalled twice, but Bradshaw threw 2 key third-down completions of 12 yards to John Stallworth and 10 yards to Randy Grossman. On the next play, from the Dallas 28, Bradshaw hit Stallworth in the end zone.

Dallas came back to take a 14–7 lead, but Bradshaw threw 2 more touchdown passes before the half ended, to put the Steelers ahead, 21–14, at the end of the period.

Bradshaw completed the Pittsburgh scoring with an 18-yard pass to Lynn Swann in the final quarter, following another

Steeler fumble recovery, to give the Steelers a 35–17 lead, before the Cowboys rallied for 2 touchdowns.

In all, Bradshaw was 17 of 30 for 318 yards—a record until 1985—and he was named the game's MVP. Afterward, Bradshaw couldn't help gloating: "Go ask Henderson if I was dumb today."

Bradshaw's SB legend wasn't completed, though. In SB XIV he rallied his team from a 13–10 halftime deficit to a 31–19 victory over the Los Angeles Rams. Bradshaw helped the Steelers regain the lead twice, first with a 47-yard toss to Swann and again, with the Steelers trailing, 19–17, with a 73-yard pass to Stallworth—a play that the Steelers practiced 8 times during SB week and which never had worked before. By game's end, Bradshaw had completed 14 of 21 passes for 309 yards and 3 interceptions and was again named the MVP.

Bradshaw's first SB appearance was as a fifth-year player in SB IX—the Steelers' debut in the contest. After the 1st half yielded only 2 points on a Pittsburgh safety, Pittsburgh took advantage of a Minnesota fumble on the 2nd half kickoff to recover the ball and score. Bradshaw clinched the victory with a 4-yard pass to Larry Brown, who had caught a 30-yard pass earlier in the drive.

SB X, Bradshaw's second, ended with another victory, but also with Bradshaw flat on his back. With Pittsburgh leading, 15–10, and the ball at third-and-4 on the Steelers' 36, Bradshaw completed a 64-yard touchdown pass to Swann, the game's MVP, to give Pittsburgh its winning points.

The Cowboys had blitzed on the play, though, and Bradshaw was hit by Cliff Harris just as he released the ball. He was dropped on the spot, unconscious, then was revived and taken off the field.

Despite a concussion, he told reporters later, "I didn't see him [Swann] catch the ball. I didn't know it was a touchdown until I came to in the locker-room and somebody told me."

Bradshaw's total Super Bowl statistics included 49 receptions in 84 attempts for a percentage of 58.3 and 932 yards—an average gain of 11.10 yards—along with 9 touchdowns and 4 interceptions. He also carried the ball 14 times for 53 yards.

MIKE BRAGG

Washington Redskins, punter, 5 feet 11, 186, Richmond. Punted 5 times for 156 yards in Super Bowl VII.

CLIFF BRANCH

Oakland and Los Angeles Raiders, wide receiver, 5 feet 11, 170, Colorado. The speedy wide receiver has played in three Super Bowls for the Raiders—SB XI, SB XV, and SB XVIII—all of them

19

Cliff Branch

victories. He tied the SB record for most touchdown receptions in a game with 2 in SB XV. A starter in SB XI, he caught 3 passes for 20 yards, the longest 10 yards.

In SB XV, Jim Plunkett's 2-yard pass to Branch opened the game's scoring as the Raiders went on to beat the Philadelphia Eagles, 27–10. The Raiders began the scoring drive after linebacker Rod Martin intercepted a Ron Jaworski pass and returned it 17 yards to the Eagles' 30. After 3 running plays and an Eagles penalty, the Raiders had the ball on the 19 when Plunkett connected with Branch on a 14-yard pass to put the ball on the 5. On third-and-goal from the 2, Plunkett found Branch alone in the end zone.

Branch's second touchdown in the game came in the 3rd period, as the Raiders took the opening kickoff and proceeded to drive down the field. With a second down on the Eagles' 29, Plunkett threw toward the goal line and Branch. For a second it appeared as if the Eagles' rookie cornerback, Roynell Young, would intercept, but Branch stepped in front of him and took the ball for the touchdown.

In SB XVIII, branch caught 6 passes for 94 yards, the longest 50. The 50-yarder came in the 2nd quarter and helped set up Branch's third SB touchdown. With the ball on the Raider 35, Plunkett hit Branch, who had split the double coverage of Anthony Washington and Curtis Jordan, and the ball ended up on the Redskins' 15. After a short running play, Plunkett again connected with Branch, this time for 12 yards and the touchdown. The Raiders led, 14–0, on the way to a 38–9 rout of the Redskins.

Branch's SB total of 14 receptions stands third in the Super Bowl list for most in a career, behind Lynn Swann's 16 and Chuck Foreman's 15. His two receiving touchdowns in SB XV put him in a six-way tie for most touchdowns received in a game.

ZEKE BRATKOWSKI

Green Bay Packers, quarterback, 6 feet 3, 200, Georgia. The backup for Bart Starr, who was named MVP in both Super Bowls I and II, Bratkowski played in each game in the final minutes. In SB I, he attempted 1 pass, which was incomplete. In SB II, he did not attempt a pass.

JIM BREECH

Cincinnati Bengals, kicker, 5 feet 6, 161, California. He converted on all 3 point-after attempts for the Bengals in Super Bowl XVI. But after Breech's third, which brought the Bengals to within 5 points, at 26–21, with less than 2 minutes remaining, his onsides kick attempt was pulled in by the San Francisco 49ers' Dwight Clark and the 49ers held on to win. Breech did not attempt a field goal in the game.

LOUIS BREEDEN

Cincinnati Bengals, corner back, 5 feet 11, 185, North Carolina Central. Breeden was starting left corner back for the Bengals in Super Bowl XVI.

BOB BREUNIG

Dallas Cowboys, linebacker, 6 feet 2, 227, Arizona State. Breunig played as a reserve in Super Bowl X, and started at the right linebacker position in SB XII and SB XIII. In SB XII, his defensive play helped the Cowboys take a 10–0 lead over the Denver Broncos. Breunig tipped a pass from Broncos quarterback Craig Morton, which Cowboys' cornerback Aaron Kyle caught and re-

turned 19 yards to the Denver 35. Six plays later, the Cowboys kicked a field goal.

LARRY BRINSON

Dallas Cowboys, running back and kick returner, 6 feet, 214, Florida. He played on special teams in Super Bowls XII and XIII. In SB XII, he returned 1 kickoff for 22 yards. In SB XIII, he returned 2 for 41 yards, with the longest 25.

MARLIN BRISCOE

Miami Dolphins, wide receiver, 5 feet 11, 178, Nebraska/Omaha. He played as a reserve in Super Bowl VII and started at that position in SB VIII, during which he caught 2 passes for 19 yards.

PETE BROCK

New England Patriots, center, 6 feet 5, 275, Colorado. Started on offense at center for the Patriots in Super Bowl XX.

LARRY BROOKS

Los Angeles Rams, defensive tackle, 6 feet 3, 254, Virginia State/Petersburg. Started at the defensive right tackle position for the Rams in Super Bowl XIV.

PERRY BROOKS

Washington Redskins, defensive tackle, 6 feet 3, 265, Southern University. He played as a reserve in Super Bowls XVII and XVIII.

JAY BROPHY

Miami Dolphins, linebacker, 6 feet 3, 233, Miami. Started as inside linebacker for the Dolphins in Super Bowl XIX, during which he recorded his top statistical game of his rookie season with 12 stops, including 5 solo tackles and 7 assists.

AARON BROWN

Kansas City Chiefs, defensive end, 6 feet 5, 265, Minnesota. Brown played as a reserve in Super Bowl I and started at the right defensive end position for the Chiefs in SB IV. With 4 minutes left in SB IV and the Chiefs leading the Minnesota Vikings, 23–7, Brown put Vikings' quarterback Joe Kapp out of the game with a hard but clean tackle that hurt Kapp's left shoulder and arm—an injury later diagnosed as a severe bruise.

BILL BROWN

Minnesota Vikings, running back, 5 feet 11, 230, Illinois. Brown started in the backfield for the Vikings in Super Bowl IV, then played as a reserve in SB VIII and SB IX. In SB IV, he rushed 6 times for 26 yards and caught 3 passes for 11 yards. In SB VIII, he ran once for 2 yards and caught 1 pass for 9 yards. In SB IX—the last game of his career which he played as a 36-year-old—Brown fumbled the 3rd quarter kickoff, which the Pittsburgh Steelers recovered on the Vikings' 30. The Steelers used the break to score the game-winning touchdown, a 12-yard run by Franco Harris that gave Pittsburgh a 9–0 lead.

BOB BROWN

Green Bay Packers, defensive end, 6 feet 5, 270, Arkansas/Pine Bluff. Brown played as a reserve in Super Bowls I and II.

BUD BROWN

Miami Dolphins, safety, 6 feet, 194, Southern Mississippi. Played as a reserve for the Dolphins in Super Bowl XIX.

CHARLIE BROWN

Washington Redskins, wide receiver, 5 feet 10, 179, South Carolina State. Brown started at the wide receiver position for the Redskins in Super Bowls XVII and XVIII. Brown, along with fellow wide receiver Alvin Garrett, made up the Smurfs, tagged with the nickname because of their relatively small size.

In SB XVII, Brown teamed with Garrett to help the Redskins tie the score at 10–10 late in the 1st half. Both wide receivers ran to the right, Brown picked off defensive coverage and Garrett caught quarterback Joe Theismann's 4-yard pass for the touchdown. Brown ended up scoring a touchdown of his own that gave the Redskins their final points in a 27–17 victory. On third down and 9, with the ball on the Miami 18, Theismann connected with Brown, who was tackled on the 9. Three plays later, Theismann again hit Brown, this time for 6 points and the touchdown.

Brown finished SB XVII with 6 receptions for 60 yards.

In SB XVIII, the Smurfs were held in check by the LA Raiders' defense. However, Brown caught 3 passes for 93 yards, the longest 60 yards.

DAVE BROWN

Pittsburgh Steelers, defensive back and punt returner, 6 feet 1, 200, Michigan. He returned 3 punts for a total of 14 yards in Super Bowl X, fumbling once.

EDDIE BROWN

Los Angeles Rams, safety and kick returner, 5 feet 11, 190, Tennessee. Playing in a reserve position as a fifth defensive back in Super Bowl XIV, Brown intercepted Terry Bradshaw's pass in-

tended for Jim Smith. Brown then lateraled the ball to Pat Thomas, who took the ball to his own 39. The Rams, leading 19–17 at the time, failed to score with the possession. Brown also returned 1 punt for 4 yards.

GUY BROWN

Dallas Cowboys, linebacker, 6 feet 4, 215, Houston. Played as a reserve in Super Bowls XI and XIII.

LARRY BROWN

Pittsburgh Steelers, tight end and tackle, 6 feet 4, 229, Kansas. Played in four Super Bowls, starting in Super Bowls IX and X, and playing as a reserve in SB XIII and SB XIV.

Brown and quarterback Terry Bradshaw combined for 2 key plays in the Steelers' 16–6 victory over the Minnesota Vikings in SB IX. After the Vikings scored to pull within 3 points, with 10:33 remaining, the Steelers took possession at their own 34. On third-and-2, Bradshaw went long to Brown, who pulled in a 30-yard completion, putting the ball on the Vikings' 28. After a couple of running plays, Bradshaw faced another third down, this time at the 5. And Bradshaw found Brown in the end zone with a pass for the touchdown.

Of the play, Bradshaw said Brown made a smart move: "He

stopped after running toward the corner of the end zone, then started again. That made the middle linebacker [Jeff Siemon] commit himself, and I drilled the ball to Larry." Brown finished the game with 3 receptions for 49 yards.

In SB X, Brown caught 1 pass for 7 yards. He was moved to a tackle position, at which he played in SB XIII and SB XIV.

LARRY BROWN

Washington Redskins, running back, 5 feet 11, 195, Kansas State. Went into Super Bowl VII as the Redskins' leading rusher during the regular season, but—like the rest of his teammates—was smothered by the Miami Dolphins' defense. Brown ended up rushing 22 times for 72 yards and catching 5 passes for 26. Trailing 14–7, the Redskins took over the ball at their own 30 with 1:14 left. Billy Kilmer's first 2 passes went incomplete, then Brown caught a third, but was thrown for a 4-yard loss. On fourth down, Kilmer himself was thrown for a loss, and the Dolphins won.

MARK BROWN

Miami Dolphins, linebacker, 6 feet 2, 225, Purdue. Started at an inside linebacker position for the Dolphins in Super Bowl XIX. He was credited with 8 tackles and 2 assists.

TERRY BROWN

Minnesota Vikings, safety, 6 feet 2, 205, Oklahoma State. Played as a reserve in Super Bowls VIII and IX. Brown scored the Vikings' only touchdown in SB IX, recovering a blocked punt in the end zone. With the Pittsburgh Steelers ahead, 9–0, the Vikings drove deep into Pittsburgh territory, only to lose the ball on a fumble. The Steelers could not move the ball, and on fourth down, Bobby Walden went back to punt. But linebacker Matt Blair broke through the line and blocked Walden's kick, which Brown recovered in the end zone.

THOMAS BROWN

Philadelphia Eagles, defensive end, 6 feet 4, 240, Baylor. Played as a reserve for the Eagles in Super Bowl XV.

TIM BROWN

Baltimore Colts, running back and kick returner, 5 feet 11, 200, Ball State. In Super Bowl III, he returned 4 punts for 34 yards, with 21 the longest, and returned 2 kickoffs for 46 yards, with 25 the longest.

TOM BROWN

Green Bay Packers, defensive back, 6 feet 1, 195, Maryland.

Started at the left safety position for the Packers in Super Bowls I and II. Brown took partial blame for the Oakland Raiders' 2 touchdowns in SB II, a 23–14 victory. With the Packers leading, 13–0, in the 1st half, Raiders' split end Bill Miller slipped behind Brown in the end zone and Daryle Lamonica connected for a 23-yard touchdown pass. "I was supposed to take Miller deep, but I played him too soft," Brown said. "Dave Robinson dropped back as far with him as he could, and I should have taken him. But I didn't." Oakland's final touchdown, in the 4th quarter, was another Lamonica-to-Miller pass, again for 23 yards, with Miller again slipping behind Brown.

WILLIE BROWN

Oakland Raiders, defensive back, 6 feet 1, 190, Grambling. Despite a 9-year interval, Brown started in the defensive backfield for the Raiders in Super Bowls II and XI, at the ages of 27 and 36. In the 4th quarter of SB XI, with the Raiders leading the Minnesota Vikings, 26–7, Brown intercepted a pass from Fran Tarkenton and ran 75 yards for a touchdown to put the game out of reach.

ROSS BROWNER

Cincinnati Bengals, 6 feet 3, 261, Notre Dame. Started at the right defensive end position for the Bengals in Super Bowl XVI.

DAVE BROWNING

Oakland Raiders, defensive end, 6 feet 5, 245, Washington. Started at the right defensive end position for the Raiders in Super Bowl XV.

BOB BRUDZINSKI

Los Angeles Rams and Miami Dolphins, linebacker, 6 feet 4, 231, Ohio State. Played in three Super Bowls with two different teams. With the Rams from 1977, he started at the right linebacker position in SB XIV. He left the Rams during the 1980 season after a contract dispute and was traded to the Dolphins before the 1981 season. For the Dolphins, he started at the left linebacker position in both SB XVII and SB XIX.

BILL BRUNDIGE

Washington Redskins, defensive tackle, 6 feet 5, 270, Colorado. A starter at the left defensive tackle position for the Redskins in Super Bowl VII, he blocked Garo Yepremian's attempted 42-yard field goal, which Yepremian then picked up and threw. Washington's Mike Bass picked off the feeble pass and ran 49 yards for the Redskins' only touchdown of the game.

BOB BRUNET

Washington Redskins, running back, 6 feet 1, 205, Louisiana Tech. Played as a reserve for the Redskins in Super Bowl VII.

BOBBY BRYANT

Minnesota Vikings, corner back and kick returner, 6 feet 1, 170, South Carolina. Started at the right corner back position for the Vikings in Super Bowls VIII and XI. In SB VIII, he signaled for a fair catch on his lone punt return.

CULLEN BRYANT

Los Angeles Rams, running back, 6 feet 1, 234, Colorado. A starter at the fullback position for the Rams in Super Bowl XIV, he scored the game's first touchdown, on a 1-yard plunge, which gave the Rams a 7–3 lead over the Pittsburgh Steelers with 12:16 left in the 1st quarter. He finished the game with 6 rushes for 30 yards and also caught 3 passes for 21 yards.

BUCK BUCHANAN

Kansas City Chiefs, defensive tackle, 6 feet 7, 287, Grambling. Started at the defensive right tackle position for the Chiefs in both Super Bowls I and IV.

ED BUDDE

Kansas City Chiefs, guard, 6 feet 5, 260, Michigan State. Started at the offensive left guard position for the Chiefs in Super Bowls I and IV.

BILL BUDNESS

Oakland Raiders, linebacker, 6 feet 2, 215, Boston University. Played as a reserve for Raiders in Super Bowl II.

GEORGE BUEHLER

Oakland Raiders, guard, 6 feet 2, 270, Stanford. Started at the offensive right guard position for the Raiders in Super Bowl XI.

BART BUETOW

Minnesota Vikings, tackle, 6 feet 5, 250, Minnesota. On the roster for the Vikings for Super Bowl XI, he did not play.

MAURY BUFORD

Chicago Bears, punter, 6 feet 1, 181, Texas Tech. In Super Bowl XX, Buford punted only 4 times, recording 173 total yards and a long of 52 yards. He had to kick only once in the 1st half, and did not punt again until the 4th quarter.

GLENN BUJNOCH

Cincinnati Bengals, guard, 6 feet 6, 258, Texas A & M. On the roster for the Bengals in Super Bowl XVI, but did not play.

NORM BULAICH

Baltimore Colts, running back, 6 feet 1, 218, Texas Christian. Started in the backfield for the Colts in Super Bowl V. He rushed 18 times for a total of 28 yards, with his longest run 8 yards. He also caught one pass for 5 yards.

Dan Bunz

JOHN BUNTING

Philadelphia Eagles, linebacker, 6 feet 1, 220, North Carolina. Started at the left outside linebacker position for the Eagles in Super Bowl XV.

DAN BUNZ

San Francisco 49ers, linebacker, 6 feet 4, 225, Long Beach State. A reserve for the 49ers in Super Bowl XVI, he started at the left linebacker position in SB XIX. In SB XVI, he played a key role in what was one of the most important defensive series in SB history. Trailing, 20–7, the Cincinnati Bengals seemed to have the momentum behind them in the 2nd half, as they drove to the SF 3-yard line, where they were first-and-goal. On first down, Pete Johnson carried to the 1. Johnson carried again but came up with no gain. Then, on third down, Ken Anderson passed to Charles Alexander in the right flat, but Bunz came up fast, put his arms around the receiver's waist, and wrestled him to the ground before he could cross the goal line. On fourth down, Johnson again was given the ball, and he headed toward the center of the line. But Bunz and Jack Reynolds met him and held him to no gain.

NICK BUONICONTI

Miami Dolphins, linebacker, 5 feet 11, 220, Notre Dame. One of the best known of the Dolphins of

27

Nick Buoniconti

ter luck the next two SB games, beating Washington and Minnesota. In SB VII, with the Dolphins leading 7–0, the Redskins began a drive that appeared as if it would give the team their first points. But with 2 minutes remaining, Buoniconti picked off a Billy Kilmer pass on the Dolphins' 41 and ran it back to the Washington 27. In SB VIII, again with his team ahead, this time, 17–0, late in the 2nd quarter, Buoniconti stopped a Viking drive by hitting ball carrier Oscar Reed, who fumbled. Miami's Jake Scott recovered the ball on his own 6.

the mid-1970s, he started at linebacker for the team in three straight Super Bowls—SB VI, SB VII, and SB VIII.

Buoniconti's first SB stood in contrast to his next two appearances. In SB VI, the Dallas Cowboys had great success in "handling" Buoniconti, according to Cowboy Coach Tom Landry, whose team piled up 352 total yards, including 252 rushing, to Miami's 185 total yards. After the game, Buoniconti was quoted as saying: "Everything went foggy, I don't remember how or when they scored."

The Dolphins had much bet-

CHRIS BURFORD

Kansas City Chiefs, end, 6 feet 3, 220, Stanford. Starting right end for the Chiefs in Super Bowl I. He caught 4 passes for 67 yards in the game.

GARY BURLEY

Cincinnati Bengals, defensive end, 6 feet 3, 274, Pittsburgh. Played as a reserve for the Bengals in Super Bowl XVI.

GEORGE BURMAN

Washington Redskins, center and guard, 6 feet 3, 255, Northwestern. Played as a reserve in Super Bowl VII.

BLAIR BUSH

Cincinnati Bengals, center, 6 feet 3, 252, Washington. Starting center for the Bengals in Super Bowl XVI.

KEVIN BUTLER

Chicago Bears, kicker, 6 feet 1, 204, Georgia. Tied a Super Bowl record held by four others (Don Chandler, Roy Gerela, Chris Bahr, and Ray Wersching) for most point-after touchdowns in a game with 5 in SB XX. Butler also kicked 3 field goals. His first, a 28-yarder, helped the Bears come back to even with the New England Patriots, at 3–3, with 9:20 left in the 1st quarter. His second, a 24-yarder with 1:21 left, put the Bears ahead for good, 6–3. He kicked a third, also from 24 yards, with time elapsed in the first half, to give the Bears a 23–3 lead.

DAVE BUTZ

Washington Redskins, defensive tackle, 6 feet 7, 295, Purdue. Started at left tackle for the Redskins in Super Bowls XVII and XVIII. In his second appearance, Butz came up with a key fumble recovery. With the Dolphins ahead, 7–0, and driving, Redskin defensive end Dexter Manley charged in on Miami quarterback David Woodley and hit him so hard he fumbled. Butz recovered the ball and the drive was over.

DARRYL BYRD

Los Angeles Raiders, linebacker, 6 feet 1, 220, Illinois. Played as a reserve for the Raiders in Super Bowl XVIII.

☆ ☆ ☆

BRIAN CABRAL

Chicago Bears, linebacker, 6 feet 1, 224, Colorado. A substitute in Super Bowl XX, he made 2 tackles.

LEE ROY CAFFEY

Green Bay Packers, linebacker, 6 feet 3, 250, Texas A. & M. Started at right linebacker for the Packers in Super Bowls I and II. Along with teammates Ray Nitschke and Dave Robinson, made up the linebacker trio that Len Dawson of the Kansas City Chiefs, opposing quarterback in SB I, called the best he'd seen all season.

TONY CALDWELL

Los Angeles Raiders, linebacker, 6 feet 1, 225, Washington. Played as a reserve for the Raiders in Super Bowl XVIII.

RICH CAMARILLO

New England Patriots, punter, 5 feet 11, 185, Washington. Camarillo was kept busy by the Patriots' inept offense in Super Bowl XX, punting 6 times for a total of 263 yards, a 43.8 yard average, and a long punt of 62 yards, which set a SB record.

GLENN CAMERON

Cincinnati Bengals, linebacker, 6 feet 2, 228, Florida. Starter at the right linebacker position in Super Bowl XVI.

JOE CAMPBELL

Oakland Raiders, defensive end and nose tackle, 6 feet 6, 250, Maryland. Played as a reserve in Super Bowl XV.

BILLY CAMPFIELD

Philadelphia Eagles, running back, 6 feet, 205, Kansas. Names that otherwise might be forgotten get a bit more glory in the Super Bowl, particularly when they handle the opening kickoff. Campfield, a third-year player, took the opening kickoff of SB XV and returned it to his own 24-yard line. In all, he handled 5 for 87 yards, with his longest return 21 yards.

BILLY CANNON

Oakland Raiders, tight end, 6 feet 1, 215, Louisiana State. Starting right end for the Raiders in Super Bowl II. He finished with 21 receptions for 25 yards.

WARREN CAPONE

Dallas Cowboys, linebacker, 6 feet 1, 218, Louisiana State. Played as a reserve for the Cowboys in Super Bowl X.

DICK CAPP

Green Bay Packers, tight end, 6 feet 3, 235, Boston College. After being cut by the Boston Patriots of the AFL in 1966, Capp was as surprised as anyone when he was activated by the Packers a day before SB II. Just before the end of the 1st half, Capp figured into the game. Green Bay punted, and the Oakland Raiders' Rodger Bird called for a fair catch on his own 45-yard line. But he dropped the ball, Capp fell on it, and the Packers got close enough to score again, on a 43-yard field goal by Don Chandler, to lead, 16–7, at halftime.

GLENN CARANO

Dallas Cowboys, quarterback, 6 feet 3, 202, Nevada/Las Vegas. On the Cowboys' roster, Carano did not play in Super Bowl XIII.

HAROLD CARMICHAEL

Philadelphia Eagles, wide receiver, 6 feet 8, 225, Southern University. A starter at wide receiver for the Eagles in Super Bowl XV, he caught 5 passes for 83 yards, his longest 29 yards. He was also called for an illegal motion penalty in the 1st half that nullified an apparent 40-yard touchdown pass from Ron Jaworski to Rodney Parker.

REG CAROLAN

Kansas City Chiefs, tight end, 6 feet 6, 238, Idaho. A reserve for the Chiefs in Super Bowl I, he caught 1 pass for 7 yards in the game.

BRIAN CARPENTER

Washington Redskins, corner back, 5 feet 10, 167, Michigan. Played as a reserve for the Redskins in Super Bowl XVIII.

JOE CARTER

Miami Dolphins, running back, 5 feet 11, 198, Alabama. Played as a reserve for the Dolphins in Super Bowl XIX, but did not carry the ball. He was credited with forcing a fumble on a kickoff near the end of the 1st half that led to a Dolphins' field goal. 49ers' Guy McIntyre, a guard, picked up the bouncing kickoff and, urged by teammates, ran with it. Carter hit him hard, the ball was jarred loose, and Dolphin teammate Jim Jensen recovered it at the 49ers' 12-yard line. Uwe von Schamann hit a 30-yard field goal with 4 seconds left that pulled the Dolphins to within 12 points, at 28–16.

MIKE CARTER

San Francisco 49ers, nose tackle, 6 feet 2, 281, Southern Methodist. Played as a reserve for the 49ers in Super Bowl XIX.

RUBIN CARTER

Denver Broncos, nose tackle, 6 feet, 254, Miami. Started at nose tackle for the Broncos in Super Bowl XII. He was credited with a fumble recovery in the game.

DAVE CASPER

Oakland Raiders, tight end, 6 feet 4, 228, Notre Dame. Started at tight end for the Raiders in Super Bowl XI. He caught 4 passes for 70 yards, with one touchdown—the Raiders' first of the game. With Oakland leading, 3–0, the Raiders drove from their own 36-yard line. Casper caught a 19-yard pass from Ken Stabler during the drive. Stabler ended the drive with a 1-yard pass to Casper.

RICH CASTER

Washington Redskins, tight end, 6 feet 5, 230, Jackson State. Listed on the Redskins' roster for Super Bowl XVII, but did not play.

MATT CAVANAUGH

San Francisco 49ers, quarterback, 6 feet 2, 212, Pittsburgh. A backup, Cavanaugh did not play in Super Bowl XIX.

JIMMY CEFALO

Miami Dolphins, wide receiver, 5 feet 11, 188, Penn State. Started at wide receiver in Super Bowl XVII, then played as a reserve in SB XIX. In SB XVII, he caught 2 passes, one for the game's opening touchdown. On the Dolphins' second possession of the game, with the ball on the Miami 24-yard line at second-and-6, Miami quarterback David Woodley connected with a wide open Cefalo on his own 45-yard line, and Cefalo then outraced Redskins' safety Tony Peters to the goal line. In all, the play covered 76 yards. His other reception was for 6 yards. In SB XIX, he caught one pass for 14 yards.

MARIO CELOTTO

Oakland Raiders, linebacker, 6 feet 3, 225, USC. Played as a reserve for the Raiders in Super Bowl XV.

BOB CHANDLER

Oakland Raiders, wide receiver, 6 feet 1, 180, USC. Starting wide receiver for the Raiders in Super Bowl XV. He caught 4 passes for 77 yards, the longest for 32 yards. That play helped a Raider drive that ended with a 29-yard touchdown pass from Jim Plunkett to Cliff Branch, giving Oakland a 21–3 lead over the Philadelphia Eagles.

DON CHANDLER

Green Bay Packers, kicker, 6 feet 2, 210, Florida. Handled both the placekicking and punting duties for the Packers in Super Bowl I, and the placekicking duties in SB II. In his first SB appearance, Chandler converted on 5 point-after-touchdowns, and punted 3 times for an average of 43.3 yards.

His second SB set several records, some of which stand today. He kicked 3 point-after-touchdowns and 4 field goals to finish with 15 points. That stood as a single game scoring record until Roger Craig scored 18 points in SB XIX. His 4 field goals—from 39, 20, 43, and 31 yards—still stand as a record, although the record was tied by Ray Wersching of the SF 49ers in SB XVI.

After SB II, Chandler said, "I knew this would be my last game as a Packer. . . . It was time to get to know my kids, build up my business and plant some family roots. . . . Thankfully, this game was going to wrap up my best season in football."

MIKE CHARLES

Miami Dolphins, defensive end, 6 feet 4, 283, Syracuse. Played as a reserve for the Dolphins in Super Bowl XIX.

BARNEY CHAVOUS

Denver Broncos, defensive end, 6 feet 3, 250, South Carolina State. Started at the defensive left end position for the Broncos in Super Bowl XII.

AL CHESLEY

Philadelphia Eagles, linebacker, 6 feet 3, 240, Pittsburgh. Played as a reserve for the Eagles in Super Bowl XV.

RAYMOND CHESTER

Oakland Raiders, tight end, 6 feet 4, 235, Morgan State. Starting tight end for the Raiders in Super Bowl XV. He caught 2 passes for 24 yards, with the longest for 16 yards.

JOHN CHOMA

San Francisco 49ers, guard and tackle, 6 feet 6, 261, Virginia. Played as a reserve for the 49ers in Super Bowl XVI.

TODD CHRISTENSEN

Oakland Raiders and Los Angeles Raiders, tight end and running back, 6 feet 3, 220, Brigham Young. Played as a reserve in Super Bowl XV, then started for the Raiders at the tight end position in SB XVIII.

EARL CHRISTY

New York Jets, defensive back and kick returner, 5 feet 11, 195, Maryland/Eastern Shore. Played as a reserve and on special teams for the Jets in Super Bowl III. Returned one kickoff for 25 yards.

NEIL CLABO

Minnesota Vikings, punter, 6 feet 2, 200, Tennessee. In Super Bowl XI he punted 7 times for 265 yards, or an average of 37.9 yards, with a long punt of 46 yards.

JIM CLACK

Pittsburgh Steelers, guard and center, 6 feet 3, 250, Wake Forest. Starting left guard for the Steelers in both Super Bowls IX and X.

DWIGHT CLARK

San Francisco 49ers, wide receiver, 6 feet 4, 210, Clemson. Starting wide receiver for the 49ers in both Super Bowls XVI and XIX. In SB XVI, he caught 4 passes for 45 yards, the longest 17 yards. He had key receptions in two early San Francisco scoring drives. In the 2nd quarter, with the 49ers on the Cincinnati 43 and facing a third-and-6, Joe Montana hit Clark with a 12-yard completion for a first down. The 49ers ended the drive with a touchdown for a 14–0 lead. Late in the 1st half, Clark caught passes of 17 and 10 yards—the latter on a key third-down play—to aid another drive, which helped San Francisco take a 20–0 lead into the locker-

Dwight Clark

though listed on the 49ers roster for Super Bowl XIX, he did not play in the game.

MIKE CLARK

Dallas Cowboys, kicker, 6 feet 1, 205, Texas A&M. Clark handled the placekicking duties for the Cowboys in Super Bowls V and VI. In SB V, against the Baltimore Colts, Clark gave the Cowboys early leads of 3–0 and 6–0 with field goals of 14 and 30 yards. They were the only 2 field goals he attempted in the game. He also kicked a point-after-touchdown in the second quarter, as the Cowboys led at the half, 13–6. In SB VI, Clark again got the scoring going with a 9-yard field goal with 1:23 left in the first quarter—his only attempt of the game. He finished the game kicking 3 point-after-touchdowns.

room at halftime. Clark ended the Cincinnati Bengals' final hopes of winning the game when he pulled in an onsides kick attempt with less than 20 seconds remaining, and the 49ers ran out the clock to win, 26–21.

In SB XIX, Clark caught 6 passes for 77 yards, including a long pass of 33 yards.

KEN CLARK

Los Angeles Rams, punter, 6 feet 2, 197, St. Mary's (Halifax, N.S.). Clark handled the Rams' punting duties in Super Bowl XIV and ended up punting 5 times for 220 yards, an average of 44 yards, including a long kick of 59 yards.

STEVE CLARK

Miami Dolphins, defensive end, 6 feet 4, 255, Utah. Listed on the Dolphins' roster for Super Bowl XVII, but did not play.

MARIO CLARK

San Francisco 49ers, corner back, 6 feet 2, 195, Oregon. Al-

KEN CLARKE

Philadelphia Eagles, nose tackle, 6 feet 2, 260, Syracuse. Played as a reserve for the Eagles in Super Bowl XV.

RAYMOND CLAYBORN

New England Patriots, corner back, 6 feet, 186, Texas. Started at the right corner back position for the Patriots in Super Bowl XX. Clayborn recovered a fumble by the Chicago Bears' Matt Suhey on the Bears' 47-yard line, ending a Chicago possession in the 1st half.

MARK CLAYTON

Miami Dolphins, wide receiver, 5 feet 9, 175, Louisville. The Dolphins went into Super Bowl XIX against the San Francisco 49ers possessing a potent passing attack, with Clayton and fellow wide receiver Mark Duper the main targets for quarterback Dan Marino. In the game, Clayton caught 6 passes for 92 yards, with his longest reception 27 yards, but the Dolphins lost, 38–16, and Coach Don Shula said his offense had played its "poorest game of the year."

BERT COAN

Kansas City Chiefs, running back and kick returner, 6 feet 4, 220, Kansas. Played as a reserve for the Chiefs in Super Bowl I. Coan carried the ball 3 times for a total of 1 yard and caught 1 pass for 5 yards. He also returned 4 kicks for 87 total yards, with his longest return 31 yards.

KEN COFFEY

Washington Redskins, safety, 6 feet, 190, Southwest Texas State. A first-year player, Coffey won the starting position at strong safety for the Redskins in Super Bowl XVIII.

LARRY COLE

Dallas Cowboys, defensive end, 6 feet 4, 224, Hawaii. Along with five Cowboy teammates, Cole tied the Super Bowl record for service, playing in five SBs during his career. He was the starting left end for the Cowboys in SB V and SB VI, then started at right tackle in SB X and left tackle in SB XIII. Cole played as a reserve in SB XII. Individually, he was credited with a fumble recovery in SB VI.

ROBIN COLE

Pittsburgh Steelers, linebacker, 6 feet 2, 220, New Mexico. Played as a reserve in Super Bowl XIII, then started at the right linebacker position in SB XIV. Cole was credited with a key sack late in the first half of SB XIV. With the Steelers and LA Rams tied, 10–10, a Ram interception gave them the ball on the Steeler 39. But Cole dropped quarterback Vince Ferragamo for a 10-yard loss on first down. Los Angeles ended up kicking a field goal to lead, 13–10, at halftime.

TERRY COLE

Baltimore Colts and Miami Dolphins, running back, 6 feet 1, 220, Indiana. Played as a reserve for both the Colts, in Super Bowl III, and the Dolphins, in SB VI, but did not record any individual statistics.

MONTE COLEMAN

Washington Redskins, linebacker, 6 feet 2, 235, Central Arkansas. Played as a reserve for the Redskins in both Super Bowls XVII and XVIII.

MIKE COLLIER

Pittsburgh Steelers, running back and kick returner, 5 feet 11, 200, Morgan State. He returned one kickoff for 25 yards in Super Bowl X.

TONY COLLINS

New England Patriots, running back, 5 feet 11, 212, East Carolina. Started in the Patriots' backfield in Super Bowl XX. The Patriots' frustration with the Chicago Bears defense showed up in the team's total of only 11 rushing attempts. Collins had 3 of his team's attempts, finished with a net gain of 4 yards and an average of 1.3 yards per attempt. He also caught 2 passes for 19 yards, including a long one of 11 yards.

CRIS COLLINSWORTH

Cincinnati Bengals, wide receiver, 6 feet 5, 192, Florida. A starter for the Bengals in Super Bowl XVI, he ended up leading the team in yards gained by receiving with 107 yards on 5 receptions, including a long gain of 49 yards. Collinsworth fumbled once during a Bengals' drive. On the SF 49ers' 27, quarterback Ken Anderson connected on a 19-yard pass to Collinsworth, who fumbled the ball when he was hit by corner back Eric Wright. Reserve defensive back Lynn Thomas recovered for the 49ers. Collinsworth's 49-yard reception came during the 3rd period, on a third-and-23, and it put the Bengals on the SF 14. The Bengals, however, did not score, as the 49ers staged their dramatic goal-line stand.

CRAIG COLQUITT

Pittsburgh Steelers, punter, 6 feet 2, 182, Tennessee. Colquitt handled the Steelers' punting duties in successful Super Bowls XIII and XIV. In SB XIII, he punted 3 times for 129 yards, for an average of 43 yards and a long of 52 yards. In SB XIV he punted only twice, for 85 yards, or a 42.5 yard average with a long punt of 50 yards.

NEAL COLZIE

Oakland Raiders, corner back and kick returner, 6 feet 2,

205, Ohio State. A reserve in Super Bowl XI, Colzie returned 4 punts for 43 yards. His longest return—for 25 yards—put the ball on the Minnesota Vikings' 35-yard line. The Raiders used the good field position to score a touchdown and took a 16–0 lead in the 2nd quarter.

RICHARD (DICK) CONN

Pittsburgh Steelers, safety, 6 feet, 185, Georgia. Conn, a rookie, played as a reserve in Super Bowl IX.

DAN CONNERS

Oakland Raiders, linebacker 6 feet 1, 230, Miami. Conners started at middle linebacker for the Raiders in Super Bowl II. Jimmy (the Greek) Snyder called Conners "a 1-point player." Unfortunately, he was matched against the Packers' Ray Nitschke, a 3-point player in the Greek's eyes.

EARL COOPER

San Francisco 49ers, running back and tight end, 6 feet 2, 227, Rice. Cooper started the 49ers' first Super Bowl, SB XVI, as a fullback, then played as a reserve, listed as a tight end, in SB XIX. In SB XVI, he caught an 11-yard touchdown pass from quarterback Joe Montana to send the 49ers ahead, 14–0. In all, Cooper caught 2 passes for 15 yards and carried the ball 9 times for 34 yards.

JIM COOPER

Dallas Cowboys, tackle and guard, 6 feet 5, 252, Temple. Played as a reserve for the Cowboys in both Super Bowls XII and XIII.

WALT COREY

Kansas City Chiefs, linebacker, 6 feet 1, 233, Miami. Played as a reserve for the Chiefs in Super Bowl I.

FRANK CORNISH

Miami Dolphins, defensive lineman, 6 feet 3, 285, Grambling. Played as a reserve in Super Bowl VI.

FRANK CORRAL

Los Angeles Rams, kicker, 6 feet 2, 220, UCLA. Corral made both of his field-goal attempts and 1 point-after-touchdown in the Ram's defeat in Super Bowl XIV. Corral's field goals—from 31 and 45 yards, the second with seconds to play in the 1st half—helped the Rams to a 13–10 lead at halftime.

STEVE COURSON

Pittsburgh Steelers, guard, 6 feet 1, 260, South Carolina. Played as a reserve for the Steelers in Super Bowls XIII and XIV.

JIM COVERT

Chicago Bears, tackle, 6 feet 4, 271, Pittsburgh. Starting left tackle for the Bears in Super Bowl XX.

FRED COX

Minnesota Vikings, kicker, 5 feet 10, 200, Pittsburgh. Cox played in four Super Bowls for the Vikings—SB IV, SB VIII, SB IX, and SB XI—yet scored only 4 points, despite being the team's regular placekicker in all four games. In SB IV, he made his only point-after-attempt, but missed on his only field-goal attempt. In SB VIII, he made his only point-after-touchdown and did not attempt a field-goal. In SB IX, he missed both a point-after attempt and field-goal attempt. The field-goal attempt came early in the 2nd quarter, with the game scoreless. Cox's kick from 39 yards went wide to the right. He missed the point-after attempt, following Terry Brown's recovery of a blocked punt in the end zone, which brought the Vikings to within 3, at 9–6, in the 3rd quarter. His kick hit the left upright. And in SB XI, he made both his point-after attempts, but did not attempt a field goal.

ROGER CRAIG

San Francisco 49ers, running back, 6 feet, 220, Nebraska. Craig, who started at running back for the 49ers in Super Bowl XIX, had a performance that would have won him an MVP award in most years. He carried the ball 15 times for 58 yards and 1 touchdown and caught the ball 7 times for 77 yards and 2 touchdowns. His touchdowns came on an 8-yard pass from Joe Montana—who was voted the game's MVP—to give the 49ers a 14–10 lead, on a 2-yard run to give the 49ers a 28–10 lead, and on a 16-yard pass from Montana for the game's final points, giving the 49ers a 38–16 lead.

STEVE CRAIG

Minnesota Vikings, tight end, 6 feet 3, 231, Northwestern. Played as a reserve in Super Bowls IX and XI, but was not credited with any individual statistics.

PAUL CRANE

New York Jets, linebacker and center, 6 feet 2, 205, Alabama. Played in the offensive line as a reserve for the Jets in Super Bowl III.

SMILEY CRESWELL

New England Patriots, defensive end, 6 feet 4, 251, Michigan State. Played as a reserve for the Patriots in Super Bowl XX.

NOLAN CROMWELL

Los Angeles Rams, safety, 6 feet 1, 197, Kansas. Started at free safety for the Rams in Super Bowl XIV. By his own admission, missed on an interception attempt in the 3rd quarter that could have led to a touchdown. With the ball on the Pittsburgh Steeler 44-yard line, Terry Bradshaw launched a bomb for Lynn Swann. Cromwell positioned himself, but let the ball go through his hands. At the time, the Rams were leading, 19–17.

PETE CRONAN

Washington Redskins, linebacker, 6 feet 2, 238, Boston College. Played as a reserve for the Redskins in Super Bowls XVII and XVIII.

RANDY CROSS

San Francisco 49ers, guard, 6 feet 3, 250, UCLA. Started at the right-guard position for the 49ers in both Super Bowls XVI and XIX.

DOUG CRUSAN

Miami Dolphins, tackle, 6 feet 4, 250, Indiana. Started at left tackle for the Dolphins in Super Bowl VI, then played as a reserve in SB VII and SB VIII.

TOMMY CRUTCHER

Green Bay Packers, linebacker, 6 feet 3, 230, Texas Christian. Played as a reserve for the Packers in Super Bowls I and II.

LARRY CSONKA

Miami Dolphins, running back, 6 feet 2, 237, Syracuse. The Miami Dolphins' formula for winning Super Bowl VIII was simple—Csonka, Csonka, and Csonka. The bruising back carried the ball 33 times for a record 145

Larry Csonka

40

yards in the Dolphins' 24–7 victory over the Minnesota Vikings and was named the game's MVP. The figures are even more impressive when you consider the Dolphins needed to throw the ball only 7 times in the game, and that the Vikings as a team gained only 72 yards rushing.

A key Viking strategy, it was thought, was not letting the Dolphins get ahead—for then Csonka traditionally took over. It was not to be. On the opening kickoff, the Dolphins drove 62 yards, and Csonka carried the ball the final 5.

The Dolphins scored again on their second possession, then took a 17–0 lead in the 2nd quarter, as Csonka carried 5 times in a drive that ended with Garo Yepremian's 28-yard field goal. The Dolphins added their final points in the 3rd quarter with Csonka running it in from the 2.

After the game, Miami Coach Don Shula said of Csonka, "He's a throwback to the old days. He likes to get down in the dirt. He's not comfortable until he gets his nose cut, and the blood is dripping across his mouth."

Csonka had tasted failure and success in his two previous SB appearances. In SB VI, Csonka gained only 40 yards on 9 carries and caught 2 passes for 18 yards as the Dolphins were beaten by the Dallas Cowboys, 24–3. Csonka, who had not fumbled all season, let a handoff slip off his fingers on the Dolphins' second possession, the Cowboys recovered and used the turnover to take a 3–0 lead with a field goal late in the 1st quarter.

Csonka's contributions in SB VII were much more significant, and the Dolphins ended up beating the Washington Redskins, 14–7. Csonka led Miami in rushing with 15 carries for 112 yards and also caught 1 pass for a loss of 1 yard. His SB totals were 57 carries for 297 yards and 2 touchdowns, with 3 receptions for 17 yards.

CURLEY CULP

Kansas City Chiefs, defensive tackle, 6 feet 1, 265, Arizona State. Starting left tackle for the Chiefs in Super Bowl IV. His playing helped the Chiefs hold the Minnesota Vikings to 67 yards rushing.

BENNIE CUNNINGHAM

Pittsburgh Steelers, tight end, 6 feet 5, 247, Clemson. Starting tight end for the Steelers in Super Bowl XIV, he was listed on the Steelers' roster but did not play in SB XIII. IN SB XIV, he caught 2 passes for 21 yards, both in a drive that ended with Franco Harris' 1-yard run to give the Steelers a 10–7 lead in the second quarter.

GARY CUOZZO

Minnesota Vikings, quarterback, 6 feet 1, 195, Virginia. Cuozzo replaced starting quarterback Joe Kapp in the 4th quarter of Super Bowl IV after Kapp, badgered the entire game by the Kansas City Chiefs' defense, was tackled hard by Aaron Brown and had to leave the game. The Chiefs led at the time, 23–7, and Cuozzo did not have any more success than Kapp, completing only 1 of 3 pass attempts for 16 yards and having 1 pass intercepted.

BILL CURRY

Green Bay Packers and Baltimore Colts, center, 6 feet 2, 235, Georgia Tech. Curry started at center for the Packers in Super Bowl I, then started at the same position for the Colts in SB III and SB V. He left the Packers after being placed on the NFL expansion list in 1967, chosen by the New Orleans Saints, then traded to the Colts when he said he would retire rather than play for New Orleans.

ISAAC CURTIS

Cincinnati Bengals, wide receiver, 6 feet 1, 192, San Diego State. The starting wide receiver in Super Bowl XVI, Curtis had 3 receptions for 42 yards, including a long play of 21 yards. Curtis had a key 13-yard reception—a play on which a face mask penalty was called—that put the ball on the San Francisco 49ers' 11-yard line as the Bengals drove for their first touchdown in the 3rd quarter after falling behind, 20–0, at halftime.

MIKE CURTIS

Baltimore Colts, linebacker, 6 feet 2, 232, Duke. Started at the left linebacker position in Super Bowl III and at the middle linebacker position in SB V, the first official "Super Bowl"—the fifth in the series whose formal name had previously been "the NFL-AFL World Championship Game"—a game which was quickly nicknamed the "Stupor Bowl" and the "Blooper Bowl." Curtis made what his coach, Don McCafferty, called the "turning point of the game." In the 4th quarter, with the score tied, 13–13, Dallas Cowboy quarterback Craig Morton's high pass toward running back Dan Reeves bounced off Reeves' hands and was picked off by Curtis, who ran 13 yards to the Dallas 28. With 59 seconds left, the Colts tried 2 running plays, then put in Jim O'Brien, who kicked a 32-yard field goal to win the game.

☆ ☆ ☆

DAVE DALBY

Oakland and Los Angeles Raiders, center, 6 feet 3, 250, UCLA. Starting center for the Raiders in 3 Super Bowls—SB XI, SB XV, and SB XVIII.

CARROLL DALE

Green Bay Packers and Minnesota Vikings, wide receiver, end, 6 feet 2, 200, Virginia Tech. Started for the Packers in Super Bowls I and II and for the Vikings in SB VIII. In SB I, Dale caught 4 passes for 59 yards with a long play of 25, but an apparent 64-yard touchdown pass from Bart Starr in the 2nd quarter was called back because left tackle Bob Skoronski was ruled to be in motion.

In SB II, Dale caught 4 passes for 43 yards with a long play of 17 yards, which was a key play in a Packer drive that led to a field goal and a 6–0 lead over Oakland in the 2nd quarter.

Dale was not credited with any individual statistics in SB VIII.

MIKE D'AMATO

New York Jets, defensive back, 6 feet 2, 204, Hofstra. Played as a reserve for the Jets in Super Bowl III.

GEORGE DANEY

Kansas City Chiefs, guard, 6 feet 4, 240, Texas/El Paso. Played as a reserve for the Chiefs in Super Bowl IV.

BEN DAVIDSON

Oakland Raiders, defensive end, 6 feet 7, 265, Washington. Starting right defensive end for the Raiders in Super Bowl II. Davidson had played with the Packers, which led to much pre-game publicity.

BRUCE DAVIS

Oakland and Los Angeles Raiders, guard and tackle, 6 feet 6, 280, UCLA. Played as a reserve in Super Bowl XV, then started at left tackle in SB XVIII and was part of the offensive line, which helped running back Marcus Allen to a record 191 yards rushing.

CHARLIE DAVIS

Pittsburgh Steelers, defensive tackle, 6 feet 1, 265, Texas Christian. One of three Steelers with the last name Davis on the 1974–'75 roster, he played as a reserve in Super Bowl IX.

CLARENCE DAVIS

Oakland Raiders, running back, 5 feet 11, 195, USC. Started in the backfield for the Raiders in Super Bowl XI and rushed 16 times for 137 yards. A 35-yard gain—his longest of the day—at the end of the 1st quarter got the Raiders out of a hole deep in their own territory and put them on their way to a drive that ended with a 24-yard field goal by Errol Mann to put Oakland ahead, 3–0.

DOUG DAVIS

Minnesota Vikings, tackle, 6 feet 4, 255, Kentucky. On the Vikings' roster for Super Bowl IV, he did not play.

JAMES DAVIS

Los Angeles Raiders, corner back, 6 feet, 190, Southern University. Played as a reserve for the Raiders in Super Bowl XVIII.

JOHNNY DAVIS

San Francisco 49ers, running back, 6 feet 1, 235, Alabama. A reserve in Super Bowl XVI, Davis rushed two times for 5 yards.

KYLE DAVIS

Dallas Cowboys, center, 6 feet 4, 240, Oklahoma. Played as a reserve for the Cowboys in Super Bowl X.

MIKE DAVIS

Oakland and LA Raiders, safety, 6 feet 3, 200, Colorado. Starting strong safety for the Raiders in both Super Bowls XV and XVIII. In SB XVIII, Davis delivered one of 6 Raider sacks of Washington quarterback Joe Theismann. In the 4th quarter, with the Redskins first-and-goal at the Raider 8, Davis blind-sided Theismann, who was setting up to pass, and the ball was jarred loose. LA's Rod Martin recovered the ball.

OLIVER DAVIS

Cincinnati Bengals, safety, 6 feet 1, 205, Tennessee. Played as a reserve for the Bengals in Super Bowl XVI.

SAM DAVIS

Pittsburgh Steelers, guard, 6 feet 1, 255, Allen. A reserve in Super Bowls IX and X, Davis started at the left guard position for the Steelers in SB XIII and SB XIV.

STEVE DAVIS

Pittsburgh Steelers, running back, 6 feet 1, 218, Delaware State. Played as a reserve for the Steelers in Super Bowl IX.

WILLIE DAVIS

Green Bay Packers, defensive end, 6 feet 3, 245, Grambling. The starting defensive left end for the Packers in Super Bowls I and II. Davis, and the rest of his defensive teammates, came back from a lackluster performance in the 1st half of SB I to smother Len Dawson and his Kansas City Chiefs, holding the Chiefs to 58 yards in the 2nd half. "We weren't nearly so cautious," Davis said. "We also sent in the linebackers more than usual, and that paid off. I had tried to be too careful with Dawson in the 1st half. A couple of times I had him back there, but I tried to make too sure, and he got the ball away." At one point early in the 3rd quarter, Davis, along with Henry Jordan, rushed Dawson, and his pass was intercepted by Willie Wood, who returned it to the Chiefs' 5-yard line. Elijah Pitts scored on the next play, and the Chiefs were finished.

LEN DAWSON

Kansas City Chiefs, quarterback, 6 feet, 190, Purdue. Dawson had two distinctly different Super Bowl appearances, coming up a loser in SB I against the Green Bay Packers, then being named the MVP in SB IV in a winning effort against the Minnesota Vikings.

Dawson's second appearance was newsworthy before he ever stepped on the field—the 34-year-old, in his thirteenth year in pro football, had spent much of the pregame period fending off reports linking him with gambling. It had been a bad enough year already. During the Chiefs' regular

Len Dawson

45

season Dawson had sustained a knee injury that kept him out of 6 games and had suffered the death of his father. Then in early January, Dawson's name was mentioned along with other players as part of a federal investigation into sports gambling.

But once he stepped onto the field, there was no doubt Dawson was in form, directing the Chiefs' offense on a game plan that included the short pass and run. The Chiefs scored the first 4 times they had the ball—driving the first 3 times deep into Minnesota Viking territory and allowing Jan Stenerud to kick field goals of 48, 32, and 25 yards. After Stenerud's third field goal, the Vikings' Charlie West fumbled the kickoff, Remi Prudhomme recovered for the Chiefs at the Viking 19-yard line, and the Chiefs went on to score again, on Mike Garrett's 5-yard run, to lead 16–0 at halftime. Dawson gave the Chiefs their final points in the 3rd quarter, completing a 46-yard pass to wide receiver Otis Taylor.

In all, Dawson completed 12 of 17 passes for 142 yards and 1 interception. He also ran 3 times for 11 yards.

"I don't think the victory vindicated anything," Dawson said after the game. "Unfortunately, the gambling report put a great deal of stress and strain on me, and more so on my family. But I asked the Good Lord to give me strength and courage to play my best, and I asked him to let the sun shine on my teammates today."

Dawson was never charged with any offense and the investigation was dropped.

In SB I, Dawson was criticized, rather than honored. He completed 16 of 27 passes for 211 yards and 1 touchdown, but an interception early in the 3rd quarter, which was run back 50 yards by Willie Wood, helped the Packers break the game open, and he was harried most of the 2nd period by the Packer defense. In that game, Dawson also ran 3 times for 24 yards. His touchdown pass came in the first half, a 7-yarder to Curtis McClinton.

LIN DAWSON

New England Patriots, tight end, 6 feet 3, 240, North Carolina State. Dawson started at tight end for Super Bowl XX, but had to be carried off the field with a ruptured tendon in his left knee. He received the injury while running to catch a pass on the Patriots' first play from scrimmage.

FRED DEAN

San Francisco 49ers, defensive end, 6 feet 2, 230, Louisiana Tech. Starting left linebacker for the 49ers in Super Bowl XVI and a reserve in SB XIX. No relation to the player by the same name on the Washington Redskins roster for SB XVII. Dean was a trade acquisition of the 49ers in 1981, one of several additions credited with helping the team rise to the top of the NFL.

FRED DEAN

Washington Redskins, guard, 6 feet 3, 255, Texas Southern. Starting right guard for the Redskins in Super Bowl XVII and a member of the Hogs, the Washington offensive line that led the way to John Riggins' MVP performance.

VERNON DEAN

Washington Redskins, corner back, 5 feet 11, 178, San Diego State. Starting right corner back for the Redskins in Super Bowl XVII and a reserve in SB XVIII. In SB XVII, Dean got his fingers on the ball twice, for 2 key tips. The first, in the 2nd quarter, prevented David Woodley from completing a pass to Jimmy Cefalo on the 3. The Dolphins settled for a field goal and a 10–3 lead. The second again involved Cefalo. Dean tipped a long pass from Woodley, which was then picked off by the Redskins' Mark Murphy.

JACK DELOPLAINE

Pittsburgh Steelers, running back and kick returner, 5 feet 10, 205, Salem. A reserve for the Steelers in Super Bowl XIII, he was not credited with any individual statistics.

BOB DeMARCO

Miami Dolphins, center, 6 feet 2, 250, Dayton. Starting center for the Dolphins in Super Bowl VI.

VERN DEN HERDER

Miami Dolphins, defensive end, 6 feet 6, 250, Central Iowa. Den Herder, a 22-year old rookie in Super Bowl VI, played in four SBs, including SB VII, SB VIII, and his final, SB XVII, as a 33-year old veteran of 12 NFL seasons.

MARK DENNARD

Miami Dolphins, center, 6 feet 1, 252, Texas A&M. Played as a reserve for the Dolphins in Super Bowl XVII.

PRESTON DENNARD

Los Angeles Rams, wide receiver, 6 feet 1, 185, New Mexico. Starting wide receiver and deep threat for the Rams in Super Bowl XIV. He caught 2 passes for 32 yards.

DOUG DENNISON

Dallas Cowboys, running back, 6 feet, 195, Kutztown State. Dennison ran 5 times for 16 yards and caught 1 pass for 6 yards in a reserve role in Super Bowl X. As a reserve in SB XII, he was not credited with any individual statistics.

RICHARD DENT

Chicago Bears, defensive end, 6 feet 5, 263, Tennessee State. Dent started Super Bowl XX on his back, then ended up its MVP. Dent was put down by the New England Patriots' tackle, Brian Holloway, early in the game. "I had never been hit like that before," Dent said afterward. "The first lick is what you need. It gets you going."

Did it ever. Take the Patriots' second possession. On third-and-10, Dent and teammate Wilbur Marshall got to New England quarterback Tony Eason for a 10-yard loss, forcing a punt. Take the Patriots' fourth possession. On first down, Dent hit Craig James, he fumbled, and the Bears recovered on the Patriots' 10-yard line. Two plays later, they scored a touchdown to go ahead, 13–3.

Take the rest of the 1st half: Dent stops James for no gain, Dent bats down a Steve Grogan pass, you get the picture. In all, Dent finished with 2 tackles, 1 assist, 1½ sacks, and 1 batted pass. Not bad for a player who had threatened weeks previously that he would not play in the SB unless his contract was renegotiated.

But later, Dent admitted, "I wouldn't have . . . passed up an opportunity like this. It's not often you get one."

Richard Dent

Dent's MVP award marked only the fourth time a defensive player earned the honor, with Randy White and Harvey Martin of the Dallas Cowboys the last to win the award, sharing it for SB XII.

RICH DIANA

Miami Dolphins, running back, 5 feet 9, 220, Yale. A rookie, Diana played as a reserve in Super Bowl XVII.

PAUL DICKSON

Minnesota Vikings, defensive tackle, 6 feet 5, 250, Baylor. Played as a reserve for the Vikings in Super Bowl IV.

CLINT DIDIER

Washington Redskins, tight end, 6 feet 5, 240, Portland State. A reserve in both Super Bowls XVII and XVIII, Didier was not credited with any individual statistics in his first performance, but was one of few Redskins to have a good game in their 38–9 defeat by the LA Raiders in SB XVIII. In that game, he caught 5 passes for 65 yards.

BUCKY DILTS

Denver Broncos, punter, 5 feet 9, 190, Georgia. Handled the punting duties for the Broncos in Super Bowl XII, punting 4 times for 153 yards, or an average of 38.2. His longest punt was for 46 yards.

TONY DiMIDIO

Kansas City Chiefs, tackle, 6 feet 3, 250, West Chester State. Played as a reserve for the Chiefs in Super Bowl I.

TOM DINKEL

Cincinnati Bengals, linebacker, 6 feet 3, 237, Kansas. Played as a reserve for the Bengals in Super Bowl XVI.

MIKE DITKA

Dallas Cowboys, tight end, 6 feet 3, 225, Pittsburgh. Who was

Mike Ditka

the first man to have played in the Super Bowl and then directed a team to victory as a coach? You might name Tom Flores of the Oakland Raiders, who was on the KC Chiefs roster for SB IV. But Flores did not play in that game, and it was Ditka, whose Chicago Bears won Super Bowl XX, who has claimed the honor.

Ditka played as a reserve in SB V, then started SB VI and caught 2 passes for 28 yards, including the Cowboys' final touchdown in a 24–3 victory over Miami. Chuck Howley's interception gave the Cowboys the ball on the Dolphins' 9-yard line early in the 4th quarter. Three plays later, Ditka caught a 7-yard pass from Roger Staubach to finish the game's scoring.

HEWRITT DIXON

Oakland Raiders, running back, 6 feet 1, 220, Florida A&M. A starting back for the Raiders in Super Bowl II, Dixon led his team in rushing with 12 carries for 54 yards including a long play of 14 yards. He also caught 1 pass for 3 yards. After the Raiders fell behind, 13–0, Dixon's running helped the team drive to its first touchdown.

JOHN DOCKERY

New York Jets, defensive back, 6 feet, 186, Harvard. Dockery played as a reserve in Super Bowl III.

JACK DOLBIN

Denver Broncos, wide receiver, 5 feet 10, 183, Wake Forest. A starting wide receiver for the Broncos in Super Bowl XII, Dolbin caught 2 passes for 24 yards, but was involved in the Broncos' 1st-half march of mistakes: 4 interceptions and 3 lost fumbles. Dolbin caught a 15-yard pass from quarterback Craig Morton, then fumbled. The ball was recovered by the Dallas Cowboys' Randy Hughes.

PAT DONOVAN

Dallas Cowboys, tackle, 6 feet 4, 250, Stanford. A reserve in Super Bowl X, Donovan started at the right tackle position in SB XII and at the left tackle position in SB XIII.

THOM DORNBROOK

Pittsburgh Steelers, center and guard, 6 feet 2, 240, Kentucky. A rookie, Dornbrook played as a reserve in Super Bowl XIV.

TONY DORSETT

Dallas Cowboys, running back, 5 feet 11, 192, Pittsburgh. Dorsett, a starter in both Super Bowls XII and XIII, went out of SB XII with a knee injury, but still led his team in rushing, with 15 carries for 66 yards. He also caught 2 passes for 11 yards. He scored the game's first touchdown, after an interception gave the Cowboys the ball on the Denver Broncos' 25-yard line. Five plays later, Dorsett took the ball in from the 3.

Dorsett again led the Cowboys in rushing in SB XIII, with 96 yards on 16 carries, and also had 5 receptions for 44 yards. He was a big factor in the Cowboys' first possession, carrying 3 times in 4 Cowboy plays for 38 yards, to put the ball on the Pittsburgh Steelers' 34. But the Cowboys fumbled away the ball on a double reverse play.

REGGIE DOSS

Los Angeles Rams, defensive end, 6 feet 4, 267, Hampton Insti-

tute. Played as a reserve for the Rams in Super Bowl XIV.

BOYD DOWLER

Green Bay Packers, end, 6 feet 5, 225, Colorado. Dowler started Super Bowl I, but had a short stay on the field. On the second play of the game, a running play by teammate Elijah Pitts, Dowler attempted to block out KC Chiefs' linebacker E. J. Holub and reinjured a shoulder. He did not play again, and was replaced by Max McGee, who ended up scoring 2 touchdowns.

Dowler had much better luck in SB II. After the Packers took an early 6–0 lead on a pair of field goals, Bart Starr took advantage of close coverage by Oakland Raider corner backs Kent McCloughan and Willie Brown for a long touchdown. Dowler ran inside McCloughan and was beyond the last defender when he pulled in the ball, finishing with a 62-yard touchdown play. "I just bulled by McCloughan," he said. "He was playing me tight, and he bumped me, and I ran through him. . . . When I got by him, there was no one left to stop me."

He finished the game with 2 receptions for 71 yards.

WALT DOWNING

San Francisco 49ers, center and guard, 6 feet 3, 254, Michi-

gan. A fourth-year player, he was a reserve in Super Bowl XVI.

RICK DRUSCHEL

Pittsburgh Steelers, guard and tackle, 6 feet 2, 248, North Carolina State. Played as a reserve for the Steelers in Super Bowl IX.

FRED DRYER

Los Angeles Rams, defensive end, 6 feet 6, 230, San Diego State. Starting right end for the Rams in Super Bowl XIV, in which Los Angeles became the Pittsburgh Steelers' fourth victim in as many championship games. Afterward, Dryer was quoted as saying, "Nobody in this locker-room is bitter.

Fred Dryer

. . . We had the chance to be great, and we didn't quite make it. The Steelers are the champs, great champs, and I respect them."

DAVE DUERSON

Chicago Bears, safety, 6 feet 1, 203, Notre Dame. Starting strong safety for the Bears in Super Bowl XX. In unofficial defensive statistics, was credited with 4 tackles. After the game, he said all that had to be said of this lopsided contest: "We knew we were the better team."

A. J. DUHE

Miami Dolphins, linebacker, 6 feet 4, 248, Louisiana State. A starter at inside linebacker in Super Bowl XVII, he played as a reserve in SB XIX. Came up with an interception in SB XVII, picking off a Joe Theismann pass intended for Don Warren on the Washington 47 in the 3rd quarter.

DOUG DUMLER

Minnesota Vikings, center, 6 feet 3, 245, Nebraska. Played as a reserve in Super Bowl XI for the Vikings.

JIM DUNCAN

Baltimore Colts, corner back and kick returner, 6 feet 2, 200, **Maryland/Eastern Shore.** Duncan was involved in 3 key plays in the 2nd half of the error-filled Super Bowl V. He fumbled the opening kickoff, and the Dallas Cowboys' Richmond Flowers recovered on the Baltimore 31. Dallas drove to the Colts' 1, but Duane Thomas fumbled, and Duncan recovered the ball on the 1. Then, in the 4th quarter, Duncan deflected a Craig Morton pass; it was intercepted by Rick Volk, and 2 plays later, the Colts tied the game, 13–13, on Tom Nowatzke's 2-yard run with 6:35 left.

TONY DUNGY

Pittsburgh Steelers, safety, 6 feet, 190, Minnesota. A reserve in Super Bowl XIII, his special-teams play included forcing a fumble and bobbling the ball himself. After the Steelers took a 28–17 lead, the Cowboys' Randy White, a defensive tackle, came up with the kickoff, was hit by Dungy, and fumbled. Pittsburgh's Dennis Winston recovered, and Terry Bradshaw connected with Lynn Swann to give the Steelers a 35–17 lead. After the Cowboys pulled to within 11, at 35–24, Dungy bobbled the onside kickoff, the Cowboys recovered, then scored the game's final touchdown with less than a minute remaining.

GARY DUNN

Pittsburgh Steelers, defensive tackle, 6 feet 3, 247, Miami. Played as a reserve for the Steelers in Super Bowl XIII and started in SB XIV at defensive right tackle.

MARK DUPER

Miami Dolphins, wide receiver, 5 feet 9, 185, Northwestern Louisiana. Duper was on the Dolphins' roster but did not play in Super Bowl XVII because of ankle and hamstring injuries that slowed his rookie season. In SB XIX, he started at wide receiver position, but like teammate Mark Clayton—the Marks Brothers—was stymied by the SF 49ers' defense. Duper caught only 1 pass for 11 yards in the game.

BILLY JOE DuPREE

Dallas Cowboys, tight end, 6 feet 4, 228, Michigan State. A reserve in Super Bowl X, DuPree started for the Cowboys in SB XII and SB XIII. On special teams, in SB X, he helped the Cowboys take an early 7–0 lead when he tackled Pittsburgh punter Bobby Walden on the Steeler 29-yard line after Walden bobbled a low snap.

In SB XII, DuPree contributed to a mistake-filled 1st half by fumbling away a completed pass on the Denver Broncos' 12-yard line. He did catch 4 passes for 66 yards in the game. In SB XIII, he helped the Cowboys' late rally, catching a 7-yard touchdown pass from Roger Staubach to pull Dallas to within 11 points of the Pittsburgh Steelers, at 35–24, with 2:27 remaining in the game. DuPree ended up with 2 passes for 17 yards in the game.

☆ ☆ ☆

WALT EASLEY

San Francisco 49ers, running back, 6 feet 1, 226, West Virginia. On the 49ers' roster for Super Bowl XVI, he did not play in the game.

TONY EASON

New England Patriots, quarterback, 6 feet 4, 212, Illinois. When fans talk about players who had frustrating Super Bowls, Eason's name will have to come up. Eason missed 5 games in the middle of the '85 season with a shoulder separation, then came back after an injury to back up Steve Grogan and led the team to upset victories over the LA Raiders and Miami Dolphins in the AFC playoffs.

But in SB XX, Eason fell victim to the Chicago Bears smothering defense, and lasted only until 5:08 remained in the 1st half, when he was pulled in favor of Grogan, as the Bears led, 20–3. In that time, Eason did not complete one pass in 6 attempts and fumbled once. Even the Patriots' 3 points came more by defensive play, a result of a Walter Payton fumble on the Bears' 19 and the Patriots' Larry McGrew's recovery. Eason tried 3 straight passes, all incomplete, and finally settled for Tony Franklin's 36-yard field goal. The Patriots' next two possessions were indicative of the kind of day he was to have: incomplete pass, incomplete pass, sack, punt, then, on the next possession, no gain on a running play, and a sack and fumble, recovered by the Bears.

After the game, Patriots' Coach Raymond Berry said, "Replacing a quarterback is the hardest decision a coach has to make. Both Tony Eason and Steve Grogan, by their tremendous performance this year, got us to the Super Bowl. . . . [But] if one is off a little in the ball game, I feel I've got to try the other one."

Eason was less than happy

with the decision, and afterward said, "How did I feel? You can say I was slightly shocked. . . . As for the Bears, they're the best I've seen."

RON EAST

Dallas Cowboys, defensive tackle, 6 feet 4, 242, Montana State. Played as a reserve for the Cowboys in Super Bowl V.

DAVE EDWARDS

Dallas Cowboys, linebacker, 6 feet 1, 225, Auburn. Started at left linebacker for the Cowboys in three Super Bowls—SB V, SB VI, and SB X.

GLEN EDWARDS

Pittsburgh Steelers, safety and kick returner, 6 feet, 185, Florida A&M. Starting right safety for the Steelers in Super Bowls IX and X. His interception, in the final minutes of SB X, preserved the Steelers' 21–17 victory over the Dallas Cowboys. The Cowboys, trailing by 4 points, had driven to the Pittsburgh 38-yard line. Roger Staubach threw 2 incomplete passes, then attempted to connect with Drew Pearson. But Edwards picked the ball off in the end zone and returned it to his own 33 before time ran out. Edwards also returned 2 punts for 17 yards.

EDDIE EDWARDS

Cincinnati Bengals, defensive end, 6 feet 5, 257, Miami. Starting left defensive end for the Bengals in Super Bowl XVI.

HERMAN EDWARDS

Philadelphia Eagles, corner back, 6 feet, 190, San Diego State. Starting right corner back for the Eagles in Super Bowl XV. Edwards was burned for the longest pass play in SB history in the 1st quarter against the Oakland Raiders. With the Raiders ahead, 7–0, but pinned deep in their own territory, quarterback Jim Plunkett, on third-and-4, passed in the direction of running back Kenny King. Edwards seemed to be in position for an interception, but the ball went untouched into the hands of King at the 20. King sprinted down the sideline for the touchdown.

RON EGLOFF

Denver Broncos, tight end, 6 feet 5, 227, Wisconsin. Played as a reserve for the Broncos in Super Bowl XII.

MIKE EISCHEID

Oakland Raiders and Minnesota Vikings, punter, 6 feet, 190, Upper Iowa. Handled the punting duties for the Raiders in

Super Bowl II, then for the Vikings in SB VIII and SB IX. His statistics: SB II, 6 punts for a 44 yard average and a long of 55 yards; SB VIII, 5 punts for 42.2 yard average and a long of 48; and SB IX, 6 punts for a 37.2 yard average and a long of 42.

CARL ELLER

Minnesota Vikings, defensive end, 6 feet 6, 250, Minnesota. Starting left end for the Vikings in 4 Super Bowls—SB IV, SB VIII, SB IX, and SB XI. Eller was one of the mainstays of the Vikings' celebrated defensive front four. Yet it was his fate to come up a loser 4 times in SB play. For the first two SBs, the Vikings' defense was a hard-charging bunch. But by SB IX, the Vikings' defense had aged. Eller himself was 32. And after the fourth defeat, 32–14, by the Oakland Raiders, he attempted to shrug it off by saying, "It's not the end of the world. Personally, I don't feel down."

JOHN ELLIOTT

New York Jets, defensive tackle, 6 feet 4, 249, Texas. Starting right tackle for the Jets in Super Bowl III.

LENVIL ELLIOTT

San Francisco 49ers, running back, 6 feet, 210, Northeast Mis- souri State. On the 49ers' roster for Super Bowl XVI, he did not play.

KEN ELLIS

Los Angeles Rams, cornerback, 5 feet 11, 180, Southern University. Listed on the Rams' roster for Super Bowl XIV, he did not play in the game.

RIKI ELLISON

San Francisco 49ers, linebacker, 6 feet 2, 220, USC. Started at a linebacker position for the 49ers in Super Bowl XIX.

DAVE ELMENDORF

Los Angeles Rams, safety, 6 feet 1, 196, Texas A. & M. The starting strong safety for the Rams in Super Bowl XIV, he came up with one interception, late in the 1st half, of a Terry Bradshaw pass. Elmendorf returned the ball 10 yards to the Steelers' 39, but the Rams ended up settling for a 31-yard field goal by Frank Corral to give them a 13–10 lead at halftime. However, late in the game, Elmendorf and teammate Rod Perry let John Stallworth get behind them. Bradshaw hit Stallworth with a play that covered 73 yards and put the Steelers ahead to stay, 24–19.

LARRY EVANS

Denver Broncos, linebacker, 6 feet 2, 218, Mississippi College. Played as a reserve for the Broncos in Super Bowl XII.

NORM EVANS

Miami Dolphins, tackle, 6 feet 5, 252, Texas Christian. Starting right tackle for the Dolphins in Super Bowls VI, VII, and VIII. Part of the offensive front line that led the way for celebrated running backs Larry Csonka and Mercury Morris. Of him, line coach Monte Clark said, "Evans is an expert at knowing the details of his assignment. He makes it a point to know his duties better and study harder and know more detail than the next guy. He fights, and he scratches, and he digs; any way that will help him win."

REGGIE EVANS

Washington Redskins, running back, 5 feet 11, 201, Richmond. Played as a reserve in Super Bowl XVIII.

☆ ☆ ☆

KEITH FAHNHORST

San Francisco 49ers, tackle, 6 feet 6, 263, Minnesota. Starting right offensive tackle for the 49ers in both Super Bowls XVI and XIX.

PAUL FAIRCHILD

New England Patriots, guard, 6 feet 4, 270, Kansas. Played as a reserve for the Patriots in Super Bowl XX.

MIKE FANNING

Los Angeles Rams, defensive tackle, 6 feet 6, 248, Notre Dame. Fanning started at left defensive tackle for the Rams in Super Bowl XIV.

MIKE FANUCCI

Washington Redskins, defensive end, 6 feet 4, 225, Arizona State. Played as a reserve for the Redskins in Super Bowl VII.

GARY FENCIK

Chicago Bears, safety, 6 feet 1, 196, Yale. Fencik started at free safety for the Bears in Super Bowl XX. In the unofficial defensive statistics, he was credited with 2 tackles and 1 assist.

MANNY FERNANDEZ

Miami Dolphins, defensive tackle, 6 feet 2, 248, Utah. The starting defensive left tackle in Super Bowls VI, VII, and VIII, he won great praise for his final two appearances, both in Dolphin victories. In SB VI, he prevented the Dallas Cowboys, leading 24–3, from gaining a bigger victory than they did by recovering a fumble by the Cowboys' Calvin Hill on the Miami 1-yard line.

In SB VII, he stopped a Washington Redskins' drive at the beginning of the 3rd period, sacking quarterback Billy Kilmer on a third down deep in Miami territory, forcing Washington to attempt a field goal, which it ended up missing. In the game, the Dolphins held the vaunted Redskins' running game to 141 yards. Washington guard John Wilbur said later, "I really believed we could run on them. But, hell, it seemed that Manny Fernandez was all over the place."

Fernandez had another big day in SB VIII, against the Minnesota Vikings. "It was our lines against their lines," he said afterward. "Well, their Purple People Eaters certainly didn't eat any people today. Our offense just carved them up."

VINCE FERRAGAMO

Los Angeles Rams, quarterback, 6 feet 3, 207, Nebraska. After four players had started at quarterback for the Rams during the regular season, it was Ferragamo who emerged as the Rams starter in their 31–19 defeat by Pittsburgh in Super Bowl XIV. Ferragamo, who was expected by some to fold under the pressure of the big game, ended up completing 15 passes in 25 attempts for 212 yards with 1 interception but no touchdowns. He also ran once for 7 yards.

After the Steelers rallied to take a 24–19 lead, Ferragamo led the Rams back, taking the team to the Steeler 32-yard line. On first down, Ferragamo threw into a crowd, intending the ball for Ron Smith, but the Steelers' Jack Lambert pulled the ball in.

"Maybe I could have dumped off that pass Lambert intercepted," Ferragamo said later, "but I had made the decision to go deep."

The Steelers were still impressed by Ferragamo. "He must have a taken a cool pill," said Steeler safety Donnie Shell.

PAT FISCHER

Washington Redskins, corner back, 5 feet 9, 170, Nebraska. Starting left corner back for the Redskins in Super Bowl VII. The victim of the Miami Dolphins' first touchdown, he was covering wide receiver Howard Twilley, who had received a 28-yard scoring pass from Bob Griese. Twilley ran inside, then outside on his pattern, and turned Fischer completely around. "He went so far inside I couldn't believe he was coming back out," Fischer said afterward.

JOHN FITZGERALD

Dallas Cowboys, center, 6 feet 5, 250, Boston University. A reserve in Super Bowl VI, Fitzgerald started at center for the Cowboys in SB X, SB XII, and SB XIII. He was credited with fumble recoveries in the early stages of both SB X and SB XII.

JIM FLANIGAN

Green Bay Packers, linebacker, 6 feet 3, 240, Pittsburgh. Flanigan played as a reserve for the Packers in Super Bowl II.

MARV FLEMING

Green Bay Packers and Miami Dolphins, tight end, 6 feet 4, 235, Utah. Fleming became the first player in NFL history to play in five Super Bowl games, setting a mark that has since been tied by six players—Larry Cole, Cliff Harris, D. D. Lewis, Charlie Waters, and Rayfield Wright, (all Dallas Cowboys), and Preston Pearson, who was with the Baltimore Colts, Pittsburgh Steelers, and Dallas Cowboys.

Fleming started in SB I and SB II with Green Bay and played SB VI, SB VII, and SB VIII with the Dolphins, the last as a reserve.

He recorded all but one of his 7 receptions in the first two games, finishing with 7 receptions for 84 yards. He did not score.

In SB I, Fleming finished with 2 receptions for 22 yards, one an 11-yarder from Bart Starr in a Packer drive that ended with Jim Taylor's 14-yard touchdown run, giving Green Bay the win over the KC Chiefs, 14–7.

In SB II, Fleming ended up with 4 receptions for 35 yards. His final reception, a 27-yarder, came in SB VI. In SB VII, Fleming did not catch a pass, although in the 3rd quarter he had what could

have been his first SB touchdown, which was taken away when Brig Owens intercepted a pass from Bob Griese in the end zone.

TOM FLORES

Kansas City Chiefs, quarterback, 6 feet 1, 202, Pacific. Flores, who did not play in Super Bowl IV, later returned to the game as coach of the Oakland and LA Raiders.

RICHMOND FLOWERS

Dallas Cowboys, safety, 6 feet, 180, Tennessee. A reserve for the Cowboys in Super Bowl V, he recovered a fumble by Jim Duncan of the Baltimore Colts on the opening kickoff of the 2nd half on the Colts' 31-yard line. The Cowboys, however, failed to score.

STEVE FOLEY

Denver Broncos, corner back, 6 feet 2, 190, Tulane. Foley, the starting right corner back for the Broncos in Super Bowl XII, was the object of a trick play which all but put the game away for the Dallas Cowboys.

In the 4th quarter, with the Cowboys on the Denver 29-yard line, Dallas wide receiver Golden Richards faked a block, as if it were a running play, then sped by Foley. Meanwhile, running back Robert Newhouse took the ball as if he were going to run, then fired to Richards in the end zone. Foley dived for the ball, but could not get to it.

"I made it look like I was going to block Foley," Richards said, "but when I tried to go around him, he knew. I had to go the opposite way I wanted to go."

The touchdown gave the Cowboys a 27–10 lead, which they held until the end of the game.

Chuck Foreman

TIM FOLEY

Miami Dolphins, corner back, 6 feet, 194, Purdue. Started at left corner back for the Dolphins in Super Bowl VI and played as a reserve in SB VIII.

CHUCK FOREMAN

Minnesota Vikings, running back, 6 feet 2, 216, Miami. The Vikings lost the Super Bowl three times with Foreman in the backfield—SB VIII, SB IX, and SB XI. A dynamo during the regular season, in SB play, although Foreman carried the ball a total of 36 times, he gained only 80 total yards, a 2.2-yard average, with a long run of only 12 yards. He did have 15 receptions for 139 yards, for a 9.3 average. However, he never scored a point in the SB.

In SB VIII, the Vikings' offense revolved around Foreman—then a rookie—who had gained 801 yards rushing and 362 pass-ing during the season. But he finished the game carrying only 7 times for 18 yards as the Vikings totaled 72 yards rushing. He also caught 5 passes for 27 yards.

In SB IX, with the Vikings trailing the Pittsburgh Steelers, 9–0, in the 4th quarter, Foreman fumbled on the Pittsburgh 7, and the Steelers' Joe Greene recovered the ball. Foreman finished with 12 carries for 18 yards and 5 receptions for 50 yards.

Before SB XI, Foreman probably got more publicity for his pregame interviews, griping about the Vikings' failure to renegotiate his contract, than he did for any actual game action. His statistics for SB XI included 17 carries for 44 yards and 5 receptions for 62 yards.

Although Foreman never showed his true form in Super Bowl play, his quarterback teammate, Fran Tarkenton, called him the most valuable in the league.

ROY FOSTER

Miami Dolphins, guard and tackle, 6 feet 4, 275, USC. A reserve in Super Bowl XVII, Foster started at left guard for the Dolphins in SB XIX, winning the job after a career-ending eye injury to Dolphins' star Bob Kuechenberg.

DOUG FRANCE

Los Angeles Rams, tackle, 6 feet 5, 268, Ohio State. France started at left tackle for the Rams in Super Bowl XIV.

RUSS FRANCIS

San Francisco 49ers, tight end, 6 feet 6, 242, Oregon. Francis, obtained from the New England Patriots in a 1982 trade, started at the tight-end position for the 49ers in Super Bowl XIX. For Francis, it was the type of game he likes to play: "Ideally, if I can catch the ball a few times in a game and block a lot, I'd be very happy. In my mind, that is how the tight end position is supposed to be played." That's how he played it in the SB, catching 5 passes for 60 yards and throwing at least 1 key block, which allowed Roger Craig to score on an 8-yard pass from Joe Montana to take a 14–10 lead over the Miami Dolphins.

JOHN FRANK

San Francisco 49ers, tight end, 6 feet 3, 225, Ohio State. Frank was injured in the 49ers' NFC championship game with the Chicago Bears, and did not play in Super Bowl XIX.

ANDRA FRANKLIN

Miami Dolphins, running back, 5 feet 10, 225, Nebraska. A backfield starter for the Dolphins in Super Bowl XVII, he led his team in rushing with 16 carries for 49 yards.

TONY FRANKLIN

Philadelphia Eagles and New England Patriots, kicker, 5 feet 8, 182, Texas A&M. Franklin, who kicked barefoot, handled the placekicking duties for two losers—the Eagles in Super Bowl XV and the Patriots in SB XX.

In SB XV, Franklin was 1 of 2 in field-goal attempts, while making his lone point-after attempt. He kicked a 30-yard field goal in the 2nd quarter for the Eagles' first points, as they trailed 14–3. But he failed to put his team any closer later in the period, when his 28-yard attempt with 54 seconds left was blocked by Ted Hendricks.

Franklin did not have to do much work in SB XX. After giving the Patriots a 3–0 lead with only

1:19 elapsed with a 36-yard field goal, he did not attempt another field goal, and did not have to attempt a point-after until the 4th quarter. The Patriots still trailed, 44–10, after the kick.

GUY FRAZIER

Cincinnati Bengals, linebacker, 6 feet 2, 215, Wyoming. Frazier played as a reserve for the Bengals in Super Bowl XVI.

LESLIE FRAZIER

Chicago Bears, corner back, and kick returner, 6 feet, 187, Alcorn State. The Bears' starting right corner back in Super Bowl XX, he went out in the 2nd quarter on an attempted reverse play. Frazier took the ball from Keith Ortego, who was returning the punt. Frazier injured his knee on the play and afterward limped off the field. The play was called back because Ortego had signaled for a fair catch.

WAYNE FRAZIER

Kansas City Chiefs, center, 6 feet 3, 245, Auburn. The starting center for the Chiefs in SB I.

ANDY FREDERICK

Dallas Cowboys and Chicago Bears, tackle, 6 feet 6, 241, New Mexico. Played as a reserve for the Cowboys in Super Bowls XII and XIII and for the Bears in SB XX.

TONI FRITSCH

Dallas Cowboys, kicker, 5 feet 7, 195, no college. Fritsch, a native of Vienna who did not play collegiate football in the United States, made his only field-goal attempt and 2 point-after-touchdowns in Super Bowl X. His field goal, from 36 yards, gave the Cowboys a 10–7 lead in the 2nd quarter.

IRVING FRYAR

New England Patriots, wide receiver and kick returner, 6 feet, 200, Nebraska. Although he had a cut tendon in his right little finger, suffered the week before in the AFC championship game, Fryar ended up playing reserve wide receiver and handling the team's punt returns. Fryar caught 2 passes for 24 yards and returned 2 punts for a total of 22 yards.

JEAN FUGETT

Dallas Cowboys, tight end and wide receiver, 6 feet 3, 226, Amherst. Starting tight end for the Cowboys in Super Bowl X, he caught 1 pass for 9 yards. The reception gave the Cowboys a first down in a drive that ended with

Toni Fritsch's 36-yard field goal, as Dallas took a 10–7 lead in the first half.

JEFF FULLER

San Francisco 49ers, safety, 6 feet 2, 216, Texas A. & M. The rookie played nearly all of Super Bowl XIX as the "nickel" linebacker in the 49ers defense.

MIKE FULLER

Cincinnati Bengals, safety, 5 feet 10, 182, Auburn. Played as a reserve for the Bengals in Super Bowl XVI.

STEVE FULLER

Chicago Bears, quarterback, 6 feet 4, 195, Clemson. Fuller, who started 5 games for the Bears during the regular season, relieved starter Jim McMahon after Chicago had taken a 44–3 lead over the New England Patriots in Super Bowl XX. He ended up with no completions in 4 attempts and 1 run for 1 yard.

JOHN (FRENCHY) FUQUA

Pittsburgh Steelers, running back, 5 feet 11, 200, Morgan State. Fuqua played as a substitute in Super Bowl X, but did not record any individual statistics.

STEVE FURNESS

Pittsburgh Steelers, defensive tackle and defensive end, 6 feet 4, 255, Rhode Island. Furness started at defensive right tackle for the Steelers in Super Bowl XIII and came up with a key sack. With the Steelers leading, 7–0, Dallas drove to the Pittsburgh 39. But Furness got to quarterback Roger Staubach for a 12-yard loss. Another sack, and the Cowboys were forced to punt. Furness also played as a reserve in SB IX, SB X, and SB XIV.

★ ★ ★

FRANK GALLAGHER

Minnesota Vikings, guard, 6 feet 2, 245, North Carolina. The starting right guard for the Vikings in Super Bowl VIII.

RON GARDIN

Baltimore Colts, corner back and kick returner, 5 feet 11, 180, Arizona. Gardin had 3 fair catches for 4 punt returns for the Colts in Super Bowl V. On his other return, Gardin fumbled on his own 9-yard line, and the ball was recovered by the Dallas Cowboys. The Colt defense held, though, and the Cowboys ended up with a 14-yard field goal by Mike Clark.

ALVIN GARRETT

Washington Redskins, wide receiver, 5 feet 7, 178, Angelo State. Garrett played in both Super Bowls XVII and XVIII for the Redskins, starting at wide receiver in the first and playing as a reserve in the second.

Garrett, the original Smurf because of his size, scored a touchdown in SB XVII, a Redskins' victory. After the Miami Dolphins had jumped to a 10–3 lead, Garrett's 4-yard touchdown pass from Joe Theismann tied the game with less than 2 minutes remaining in the 1st half. He also helped the Redskins come back from another deficit in the 2nd half with a 44-yard run on a reverse that put the ball on the Dolphins' 9-yard line. In all, Garrett finished with 2 receptions for 13 yards and his single rushing attempt.

In SB XVIII, Garrett caught 1 pass for 17 yards.

CARL GARRETT

Oakland Raiders, running back and kick returner, 5 feet 10, 205, New Mexico Highlands. A substitute in Super Bowl XI, Garrett carried four times for 19 yards and also returned 2 kickoffs for 47 yards, with his longest 24 yards.

MIKE GARRETT

Kansas City Chiefs, running back and kick returner, 5 feet 9, 195, USC. Garrett saw a good deal of action, as he started in the backfield for the Chiefs in Super Bowl I, and carried 6 times for 17 yards. Garrett also had 3 receptions for 28 yards. He also handled kickoff returns, with 2 catches and 17 yards, and punt returns, with 2 catches for 43 yards, with a long of 23 yards.

Garrett also started for the Chiefs in SB IV, carrying 11 times for 39 yards and 1 touchdown, and catching 2 passes for 25 yards. He returned 1 punt for no yardage. Garrett scored the Chiefs' first touchdown in the game, from 5 yards out, helping the team to a 16–0 lead at halftime. After the Chiefs' victory, Garrett got up on a platform for a TV interview and said, "Just want to say I remember what Vince Lombardi said three years ago about us—that we're not as good as a lot of teams in the NFL. Love ya, Vince."

REGGIE GARRETT

Pittsburgh Steelers, wide receiver, 6 feet 1, 172, Eastern Michigan. A reserve in both Super Bowls IX and X, Garrett did not record any individual statistics.

WALT GARRISON

Dallas Cowboys, running back, 6 feet, 205, Oklahoma State. Garrison started for the Cowboys in Super Bowls V and VI. In SB V, despite coming into the game with a swollen right ankle, a twisted right knee, and a chipped collarbone, Garrison led the team in rushing, carrying the ball 12 times for 65 yards and catching 2 passes for 19 yards. But one pass got away. Leading 13–6, the Cowboys were in their own territory when Craig Morton's pass bounced off Garrison's hands, and Rich Volk intercepted. The Colts then proceeded to tie the game, on the way to a victory.

The Cowboys came away winners in Garrison's second SB, as he rushed 14 times for 74 yards and also caught 2 passes for 11

Walt Garrison

yards. His rushing played a key part in the Cowboys' second touchdown, which put the team up, 17–3.

DENNIS GAUBATZ

Baltimore Colts, linebacker, 6 feet 2, 232, Louisiana State. Starting middle linebacker for the Colts in Super Bowl III.

WILLIE GAULT

Chicago Bears, wide receiver and kick returner, 6 feet 1, 183, Tennessee. Gault, a world-class sprinter, started Super Bowl XX for the Bears and caught 4 passes for 129 yards, including a 60-yard reception.

Willie Gault

On the Bears' second possession, with New England ahead, 3–0, Gault caught a 43-yard pass from Jim McMahon to put the ball on the Patriots' 23. The Bears ended the drive with a 28-yard field goal by Kevin Butler.

Gault's 60-yard reception came on the Bears' first play of the 2nd half and moved the ball from the Chicago 4 to the New England 36. The drive ended with Mc-Mahon's 1-yard plunge and the Bears leading, 30–3.

SHAUN GAYLE

Chicago Bears, corner back, 5 feet 11, 193, Ohio State. Gayle played as a reserve in Super Bowl XX.

DENNIS GENTRY

Chicago Bears, running back, 5 feet 8, 181, Baylor. A reserve, Gentry carried the ball 3 times for 15 yards and also caught 2 passes for 41 yards in Super Bowl XX.

ROY GERELA

Pittsburgh Steelers, kicker, 5 feet 10, 185, New Mexico State. Gerela handled the Steelers' placekicking duties in Super Bowls IX, X, and XIII. Gerela's first SB appearance started on an off-note, as he missed a 37-yard field-goal attempt, then was unable to try for his second as an errant

Roy Gerela

snap from center was picked up by holder Bobby Walden, who wound up with a 7-yard loss. Then, on the 2nd-half kickoff, Gerela squibbed the kick. But the Minnesota Vikings' Bill Brown couldn't hold on to the ball, and Pittsburgh recovered, scoring the game's first touchdown.

Gerela ended up SB IX none for 2 in field-goal attempts and 2 for 2 in point-after attempts. He came out of SB X with a pair of .500 performances, making 2 of 4 field-goal attempts and 1 of 2 point-after attempts. After missing field-goal attempts of 36 and 33 yards earlier in the game, Gerela gave the Steelers a 12–10 lead with a 36-yarder with 8:14 remaining in the game. Just mintutes later, an interception set up another field goal, this time from 18 yards with 6:37 left.

In SB XIII, Gerela was none for 1 in field-goal attempts, but made all 5 point-after attempts—to tie an SB record. His career total of 8 point-after-touchdowns also tied an SB record set by Don Chandler of the Green Bay Packers.

RICK GERVAIS

San Francisco 49ers, safety, 5 feet 11, 190, Stanford. Played as a reserve in Super Bowl XVI.

LOUIE GIAMMONA

Philadelphia Eagles, running back and kick returner, 5 feet 9, 180, Utah State. Giammona played as a substitute in Super Bowl XV and carried the ball once for 7 yards.

NICK GIAQUINTO

Washington Redskins, running back, 5 feet 11, 204, Connecticut. Gianquinto played as a reserve in both Super Bowls XVII and XVIII, with a pair of receptions for 21 yards in SB XVIII.

ERNEST GIBSON

New England Patriots, corner back, 5 feet 10, 185, Furman. Played as a reserve in Super Bowl XX.

JON GIESLER

Miami Dolphins, tackle, 6 feet 5, 260, Michigan. Giesler started at left tackle for the Dolphins in Super Bowls XVII and XIX.

JOE GILLIAM

Pittsburgh Steelers, quarterback, 6 feet 2, 187, Tennessee State. Gilliam was one of Terry Bradshaw's backups in both Super Bowls IX and X, but did not play in either game.

JOHN GILLIAM

Minnesota Vikings, wide receiver and kick returner, 6 feet 1, 195, South Carolina State. Gilliam, a starter in Super Bowls VIII and IX, had a 65-yard run with the opening kickoff of the 2nd half in SB VIII nullified because of a clipping penalty. He did return 2 for a total of 41 yards and caught 4 passes for 44 yards. In SB IX, Gilliam caught 1 pass for 16 yards, on the Vikings' first possession.

JON GILLIAM

Kansas City Chiefs, center, 6 feet 2, 240, East Texas State. Played as a reserve in Super Bowl I.

GALE GILLINGHAM

Green Bay Packers, guard, 6 feet 3, 250, Minnesota. Gillingham played as a reserve in Super Bowl I and then started at left guard in SB II.

In his first game, he was involved in one of the most bizarre plays of the game, which ended with the Kansas City Chiefs' Fred (The Hammer) Williamson carried off the field. In pregame interviews Williamson had taunted the Packers, threatening to lower his "hammer" on any wide receiver who came his way. But in the 4th quarter, Gillingham, in for Fuzzy Thurston at left guard, led a sweep in front of Packer back Donny Anderson. Gillingham recounted the play: "I pulled out to lead the sweep, with Donny Anderson carrying behind me. I saw Williamson coming at me like a wild man, and I knew he was going to try to take me out of the play, leaving Anderson unprotected for somebody else. To my surprise, he came barreling at me real low, and I simply picked my knee up a little, and he caught it flush on the head. Then Anderson went over the top, and all three of us just lay there for a while. Donny and I got up slowly, and Williamson didn't get up at all."

HUBERT GINN

Miami Dolphins and Oakland Raiders, running back and kick returner, 5 feet 10, 188, Florida A&M. Ginn played for the Dolphins in Super Bowls VI and VII and for the Raiders in SB XI. In SB VI, he returned 1 kickoff for 32 yards. In SB XI, he carried the ball 2 times for 9 yards.

TOM GLASSIC

Denver Broncos, guard, 6 feet 4, 248, Virginia. Starting left guard for the Broncos in Super Bowl XII.

IRV GOODE

Miami Dolphins, center and guard, 6 feet 5, 262, Kentucky. Played as a reserve in Super Bowl VIII.

TOM GOODE

Baltimore Colts, center, 6 feet 3, 245, Mississippi State. Played as a reserve in Super Bowl V.

CHARLES GOODRUM

Minnesota Vikings, tackle and guard, 6 feet 3, 256, Florida A&M. Goodrum played as a reserve in Super Bowl VIII, started at left tackle in SB IX and at left guard in SB XI.

CORNELL GORDON

New York Jets, defensive back, 6 feet, 187, North Carolina A&T. Gordon played as a reserve for the Jets in Super Bowl III.

LARRY GORDON

Miami Dolphins, linebacker, 6 feet 4, 230, Arizona State. Starting right linebacker for the Dolphins in Super Bowl XVII.

JIM GRABOWSKI

Green Bay Packers, running back, 6 feet 2, 215, Illinois. As a rookie in Super Bowl I, Grabowski played as a reserve and carried twice for 2 yards. He also fumbled once. Grabowski was injured and did not play in SB II.

RANDY GRADISHAR

Denver Broncos, linebacker, 6 feet 3, 231, Ohio State. Starting right inside linebacker for the Broncos in Super Bowl XII.

BOB GRANT

Baltimore Colts, linebacker, 6 feet 2, 225, Wake Forest. Played as a reserve in Super Bowl V.

DARRYL GRANT

Washington Redskins, defensive tackle, 6 feet 2, 265, Rice. Grant started at defensive left tackle for the Redskins in both Super Bowls XVII and XVIII.

JOHN GRANT

Denver Broncos, nose tackle, 6 feet 3, 246, USC. Played as a reserve for the Broncos in Super Bowl XII.

LARRY GRANTHAM

New York Jets, linebacker, 6 feet, 212, Mississippi. Grantham, who made the transition to the Jets from the New York Titans, started Super Bowl III as right linebacker.

GORDON GRAVELLE

Pittsburgh Steelers and Los Angeles Rams, guard and tackle, 6 feet 5, 250, Brigham Young. Gravelle started at right tackle for the Steelers in Super Bowls IX and X and played as a reserve for the Rams in SB XIV.

TOM GRAVES

Pittsburgh Steelers, linebacker, 6 feet 3, 228, Michigan State. Played as a reserve for the Steelers in Super Bowl XIV.

DAVE GRAYSON

Oakland Raiders, defensive back, 5 feet 10, 185, Oregon. Played as a reserve for the Raiders in Super Bowl II.

CLEVELAND GREEN

Miami Dolphins, tackle, 6 feet 3, 262, Southern University. Green played as a reserve in Super Bowl XVII, then cracked the starting lineup at the right tackle position in SB XIX.

CORNELL GREEN

Dallas Cowboys, 6 feet 3, 208, Utah State. Starting left safety for the cowboys in Super Bowls V and VI. He was credited as part of the Cowboys' coverage that held the Miami Dolphins' vaunted passing game to 105 yards in SB VI.

DARRELL GREEN

Washington Redskins, corner back and kick returner, 5 feet 8, 170, Texas A&I. Starting left corner back for the Redskins in Super Bowl XVIII, Green also handled punt return duties with 1 return for 34 yards.

JOE (MEAN JOE) GREENE

Pittsburgh Steelers, defensive tackle, 6 feet 4, 275, North Texas State. Probably the most famous member of the Steelers' outstanding defensive front line, the Steel Curtain. Mean Joe started at left tackle for Pittsburgh in Super

Joe Greene

Bowls IX, X, XIII, and XIV and was arguably the best defensive tackle in pro football in the 1970s.

Just how did Greene get that nickname? According to his own version, Greene already had it before the incident that made it stick. It was a game against the New York Giants, in which Fran Tarkenton was at quarterback. "I kept chasing him and chasing him," Greene said, "and I didn't get him. When I finally hit him, I didn't realize that he had thrown the ball about five seconds before. . . . Yeah, I got flagged for it and got escorted off the field. . . . But 'Mean' has been good to me."

So who do Mean Joe and his Steelers meet in their first Super Bowl? Tarkenton and the Minnesota Vikings. There's little doubt who won. The Steeler defense harried Tarkenton the entire game, and he finished completing only 11 of 26 passes for 102 yards with 3 interceptions and 4 deflected passes. Greene came up with 1 interception and 1 fumble recovery in the game.

L. C. GREENWOOD

Pittsburgh Steelers, defensive end, 6 feet 6, 245, Arkansas/Pine Bluff. Greenwood was a key part of the Steelers' Steel Curtain defense, starting at left end for the Steelers in Super Bowls IX, X, XIII, and XIV. The Steelers' first victory may have been the defense's finest, as Pittsburgh held the Minnesota Vikings to the fewest total yards in SB history—a total of 119 with only 17 yards rushing.

L. C. Greenwood

After the game, Greenwood said, "I think we played as well as we could. We concentrated on stopping the run, then the pass." In SB X, Greenwood had 3 of 7 Steeler sacks against the Dallas Cowboys.

FORREST GREGG

Green Bay Packers and Dallas Cowboys, tackle, 6 feet 4, 250, Southern Methodist. The starting right tackle for the Packers in Super Bowls I and II, he came back to coach the Cincinnati Bengals to SB XVI. Gregg did not play in SB VI for the Cowboys.

BILL GREGORY

Dallas Cowboys, defensive tackle, 6 feet 5, 255, Wisconsin. Played as a reserve for the Cowboys in Super Bowls VI, X, and XII.

BOB GRIESE

Miami Dolphins, quarterback, 6 feet 1, 190, Purdue. Griese led the Dolphins to two Super Bowl victories—after a disappointment in his first appearance, in SB VI. In that game, Griese completed only 12 of 23 passes for 134 yards, fumbled once and had 1 pass intercepted. The interception, in the 4th quarter, ended all hope for the Dolphins as Chuck Howley picked off a pass at midfield, and the Dallas Cowboys

Bob Griese

were able to score the game's final touchdown.

Griese, however, came right back to take the team to victories in SB VII and SB VIII. In SB VII, Griese drove the Dolphins 63 yards the third time they had the ball, getting on the scoreboard with a 28-yard pass to Howard Twilley. Griese finished with 8 completions in 11 attempts for 88 yards, with 1 interception.

Griese got the Dolphins off to a fast start in SB VIII, and the Minnesota Vikings were never able to catch up. Griese drove the Dolphins 62 yards and 56 yards the first 2 times they had the ball, with Larry Csonka scoring from 5 yards out and Jim Kiick from 1 yard to build a 14–0 lead. Griese finished with 6 completions in 7 attempts for 73 yards.

Yet while Griese's SB passing totals may not seem flashy in comparison to others, he is given credit for leading the Dolphins' outstanding running game. Bill McPeak, the Dolphins' offensive backfield coach, said, "Bob is like a surgeon. Not only does he throw the ball well and at the right time, he knows about defenses and blocking angles and how to run the running game most effectively."

ARCHIE GRIFFIN

Cincinnati Bengals, running back and kick returner, 5 feet 9, 184, Ohio State. Griffin, a reserve in Super Bowl XVI, was credited with 1 kickoff return for no gain and 1 rushing attempt for 4 yards. His return actually cost the Bengals 3 points, as the ball touched his hands, then bounced to his team's 4-yard line where it was recovered by the 49ers, who kicked a field goal to go ahead, 20–0, with just seconds left in the 1st half. Griffin's brother Ray also played in the SB (below).

RAY GRIFFIN

Cincinnati Bengals, corner back, 5 feet 10, 186, Ohio State. In Super Bowl XVI, Griffin saw action as a reserve on defense. Brother of the Bengals' Archie.

BOB GRIM

Minnesota Vikings, wide receiver, 6 feet, 195, Oregon State. Played as a reserve for the Vikings in both Super Bowls IV and XI.

RUSS GRIMM

Washington Redskins, center and guard, 6 feet 3, 273, Pittsburgh. Starting left guard for the Redskins in Super Bowls XVII and XVIII.

RON GROCE

Minnesota Vikings, running back, 6 feet 2, 211, Macalester. Groce played as a reserve in Super Bowl XI, but did not record any individual statistics.

STEVE GROGAN

New England Patriots, quarterback, 6 feet 4, 210, Kansas State. Grogan, who started in the place of injured teammate Tony Eason for six games during the season, was himself placed on the injured reserve list with 4 games left in the regular season with a fractured tibia and sprained ligament in his left leg.

Grogan's return to action, however, led to no dramatic story. He replaced Eason with a little over 5 minutes remaining in the 1st half of Super Bowl XX, with the Chicago Bears leading, 20–3. Grogan had no better luck against the Bears' defense, completing only 17 of 30 attempts for 177 yards, with 2 interceptions and 1 touchdown, an 8-yard pass to Irving Fryar late in the game.

RANDY GROSSMAN

Pittsburgh Steelers, tight end, 6 feet 1, 215, Temple. Grossman started for the Steelers at tight end in Super Bowl XIII, and played as a reserve in Super Bowls IX, X, and XIV. Grossman, who did not record any individual statistics in SB IX, caught only a single pass in SB X, but it was for a touchdown. With the Dallas Cowboys leading, 7–0, Pittsburgh drove to the Dallas 7-yard line, where the situation was third-and-1. Figuring the Cowboys would be lined up to stop the run, quarterback Terry Bradshaw threw to Grossman, who had lined up inside, in the end zone for the touchdown.

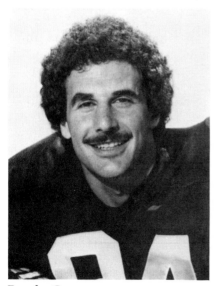

Randy Grossman

Grossman was the object of some of the verbal abuse Dallas Cowboy linebacker Thomas (Hollywood) Henderson threw at the Steelers before SB XIII. "Look at their tight end Randy Grossman," Henderson said. "He's a substitute . . . a backup tight end. How much respect can you have for a backup tight end? I mean, he's the guy that comes in when everybody else is dead." Grossman finished with 3 receptions for 29 yards, including a 10-yarder on an important third down that helped the Steelers continue a drive, which ended with a touchdown and a 28–17 Pittsburgh lead.

RAY GUY

Oakland and Los Angeles Raiders, punter, 6 feet 3, 195, Southern Mississippi. Guy handled the punting duties for the Raiders in three Super Bowls—SB XI, SB XV, and SB XVIII—and finished with the second best punting average over a career in the game's history, with an average of 41.9 yards per kick. In all, Guy had 14 punts for 587 yards, with the longest 51 yards. Guy had his first punt ever blocked in 4 NFL seasons in SB XI, against the Minnesota Vikings, as he kicked the ball squarely into linebacker Fred McNeill, who recovered the ball on the Oakland 2 in the 1st quarter. The Vikings, however, failed to capitalize, losing the ball themselves on a fumble.

DALE HACKBART

Minnesota Vikings, safety, 6 feet 3, 205, Wisconsin. Hackbart played as a reserve in Super Bowl IV.

ROGER HAGBERG

Oakland Raiders, running back, 6 feet 1, 215, Minnesota. Hagberg played as a reserve in Super Bowl II, but did not record any individual statistics.

CARL HAIRSTON

Philadelphia Eagles, defensive end, 6 feet 3, 260, Maryland State. The starting defensive right end for the Eagles in Super Bowl XV.

WILLIE HALL

Oakland Raiders, linebacker, 6 feet 2, 225, USC. Hall, starting right inside linebacker, took part in several key plays in Super Bowl XI and was named the game's top defensive player. He recovered a fumble late in the first quarter on his own 2, when Minnesota Vikings' running back Brent McClanahan dropped the ball. Hall stopped another Vikings' drive in the 4th quarter. After Minnesota had moved from its own 22 to the Oakland 37, Hall picked off a pass from Fran Tarkenton and returned it 16 yards to his own 46.

WINDLAN HALL

Minnesota Vikings, safety, 5 feet 11, 175, Arizona State. Hall played as a substitute for the Vikings in Super Bowl XI.

JACK HAM

Pittsburgh Steelers, linebacker, 6 feet 1, 225, Penn State. Starting linebacker for the Steelers in

Super Bowls IX, X, and XIII. Although on the roster, he was not able to play in SB XIV because of an ankle injury. Of Ham, author Lou Sahadi said, "Ham is like a matador. Nobody can drop or come up quicker than he. He is extremely quick and intelligent. . . . Ham and [Jack] Lambert influence opposing offenses more than any two players around."

DAN HAMPTON

Chicago Bears, defensive tackle and defensive end, 6 feet 5, 267, Arkansas. The starting left end for the Bears' formidable defense in Super Bowl XX. He was credited with 2 tackles, 1 assist, and 1 sack, along with a fumble recovery. The recovery came on the New England Patriots' third possession. On second down, Patriots' quarterback Tony Eason was sacked, the ball popped loose, and Hampton recovered at the New England 13. The Bears ended up with a 24-yard field goal to take a 6–3 lead.

CHRIS HANBURGER

Washington Redskins, linebacker, 6 feet 2, 218, North Carolina. Starting right linebacker for the Redskins in Super Bowl VII.

CHARLEY HANNAH

Los Angeles Raiders, guard, 6 feet 5, 260, Alabama. The starting left guard for the Raiders in Super Bowl XVIII, Hannah recovered a fumble by his own team in the game.

JOHN HANNAH

New England Patriots, 6 feet 3, 265, Alabama. Starting left guard for the Patriots in Super Bowl XX.

TERRY HANRATTY

Pittsburgh Steelers, quarterback, 6 feet 1, 210, Notre Dame. Hanratty did not play in Super Bowl IX, but was called on in SB X when starter Terry Bradshaw went down on his 64-yard touchdown pass to Lynn Swann. When the Dallas Cowboys scored on their next possession, to pull to within 4 points, at 21–17, Hanratty came in, but was unable to sustain a drive, and on fourth-and-9, the Steelers tried a run that came up short. "We were afraid a blocked punt would put them in too good a field position," Hanratty said. As it turned out, the Steelers intercepted a pass from Roger Staubach to end the game. Hanratty did not end up with any personal statistics in the game.

CEDRICK HARDMAN

Oakland Raiders, defensive end, 6 feet 4, 245, North Texas State. Played as a reserve for the Raiders in Super Bowl XV.

BRUCE HARDY

Miami Dolphins, tight end and kick returner, 6 feet 5, 232, Arizona State. Starting tight end for the Dolphins in Super Bowls XVII and XIX. He ended up with 2 kickoff returns for 31 yards in SB XIX.

JIM HARGROVE

Minnesota Vikings, linebacker, 6 feet 3, 233, Howard Payne. Hargrove played as a reserve for the Vikings in Super Bowl IV.

JIM HARGROVE

Cincinnati Bengals, running back, 6 feet 2, 228, Wake Forest. Hargrove played as a reserve in Super Bowl XVI.

CLARENCE HARMON

Washington Redskins, running back, 5 feet 11, 209, Mississippi State. Harmon, though not a starter, still was the Redskins' second-leading rusher in Super Bowl XVII with 9 carries for 40 yards, including a long run of 12 yards.

DERRICK HARMON

San Francisco 49ers, running back and kick returner, 5 feet 10, 202, Cornell. Harmon returned 2 kickoffs for 24 yards in SB XIX, with a long return of 23 yards. His 1-yard return was on the game's opening kickoff, when he caught the ball too near the sideline and stepped out of bounds at his own 6-yard line.

WILLIE HARPER

San Francisco 49ers, linebacker, 6 feet 2, 215, Nebraska. Starting left outside linebacker for the 49ers in Super Bowl XVI. He was credited with a fumble recovery late in the game as teammate Eric Wright intercepted a Ken Anderson pass, then fumbled when trying to lateral the ball to a teammate. Harper recovered the ball for the 49ers.

DENNIS HARRAH

Los Angeles Rams, guard, 6 feet 5, 251, Miami. Starting right guard for the Rams in Super Bowl XIV.

CHARLEY HARRAWAY

Washington Redskins, running back, 6 feet 2, 215, San Jose State. Starting running back for the Redskins in Super Bowl VII, he carried the ball 10 times for 37 yards, with a long run of 8 yards. He also caught 1 pass, for a loss of 3 yards.

PERRY HARRINGTON

Philadelphia Eagles, running back and kick returner, 5 feet 11, 210, Jackson State. Harrington carried the ball once for 4 yards and returned 1 kickoff for no gain in Super Bowl XV.

BILL HARRIS

Minnesota Vikings, running back, 6 feet, 204, Colorado. Harris played as a reserve in Super Bowl IV, but did not record any individual statistics.

BO HARRIS

Cincinnati Bengals, linebacker, 6 feet 3, 226, Louisiana State. Starting left outside linebacker for the Bengals in Super Bowl XVI.

CLIFF HARRIS

Dallas Cowboys, safety and kick returner, 6 feet, 184, Ouachita. Harris is one of seven players who have a share of the Super Bowl record of 5 games service. He played as a reserve in the defensive backfield in SB V, then started at right safety in SB VI, SB X, SB XII, and SB XIII. In SB V, he recovered a fumble by the Baltimore Colts in the 1st quarter that led to the game's first scoring, a 14-yard field goal by Mike Clark. He also returned 1 kickoff for 18 yards.

In SB VI, he signaled for a fair catch on a pair of punt returns. In SB X, it was Harris' blow on the helmet that felled Pittsburgh Steelers' quarterback Terry Bradshaw late in the game—but not before Bradshaw got off his 64-yard scoring pass to Lynn Swann. After the game, Harris said, "On that play, you've either got to sack the quarterback or make him get rid of it in a hurry. He managed to elude us and had time to hit Swann."

DURIEL HARRIS

Miami Dolphins, wide receiver, 5 feet 11, 176, New Mexico State. Starting wide receiver for the Dolphins in Super Bowl XVII, he carried the ball once for 1 yard and caught 2 passes for 15 yards, with a long reception of 8 yards.

FRANCO HARRIS

Pittsburgh Steelers, running back, 6 feet 2, 230, Penn State. Harris' name is all over the Super Bowl record book, but the game he is probably remembered for most is the first of his four Super Bowl appearances, SB IX, after which he was named the MVP.

Harris came into the game suffering from a severe head cold, but came out with an SB rushing record. With the Steelers leading, 2–0, in the 3rd quarter, the Vikings' Bill Brown fumbled and the

Franco Harris

Steelers' Marv Kellum recovered on the Minnesota 30. Harris ran around left end for 24, then lost 3, then went in from the 9 for the touchdown.

Ironically, a fumble by Harris in the 4th quarter almost let Minnesota into the game. The Vikings recovered at the Pittsburgh 47, advanced to the Pittsburgh 5 before losing the ball themselves on Chuck Foreman's fumble.

After Minnesota tightened the game at 9–6, the Steelers drove 66 yards, with Harris carrying 6 times in the drive. He finished the game carrying 34 times for 158 yards, which broke the previous SB mark of 145 set by Larry Csonka of the Dolphins the previous year.

Harris had a hard time believing his total: "One hundred fifty-eight yards? You have to be kid-ding me. I can't believe it. I never thought it could have been that high."

He again led the Steelers in rushing in SB X against the Dallas Cowboys with 27 carries for 82 yards. He also had 1 reception for 26 yards. He helped the Steelers break open SB XIII early in the 4th quarter. On a third-and-9 with the ball on the Cowboys' 22, Steeler quarterback Terry Bradshaw—figuring Dallas would blitz—called a trap play; Harris ran over the left side and into the end zone to give his team a 28–17 lead with 7:10 left. He finished with 20 carries for 68 yards, along with 1 reception for 22 yards.

Harris picked up only 46 yards on 20 carries in his final SB appearance, SB XIV, but he was still the Steelers rushing leader, and he scored a pair of touchdowns. Harris scored both touchdowns on runs of 1 yard, the first early in the 2nd quarter to give the Steelers a 10–7 lead and the second with 1:49 remaining to help make the final score 31–19.

Harris' final SB statistics included 101 carries for 354 yards and 24 points, all SB records for a career. He also caught 5 passes for 114 yards.

JOE HARRIS

Los Angeles Rams, linebacker, 6 feet 1, 225, Georgia Tech. Harris played as a reserve for the Rams in Super Bowl XIV.

LEROY HARRIS

Philadelphia Eagles, running back, 5 feet 9, 230, Arkansas State. Harris started in the backfield for the Eagles in Super Bowl XV and finished with 7 carries for 14 yards, with a long run of 5 yards, and 1 reception for 1 yard.

M. L. HARRIS

Cincinnati Bengals, tight end, 6 feet 5, 238, Kansas State. Harris played as a reserve for the Bengals in Super Bowl XVI.

DENNIS HARRISON

Philadephia Eagles, defensive end, 6 feet 8, 275, Vanderbilt. Starting left defensive end for the Eagles in Super Bowl XV.

REGGIE HARRISON

Pittsburgh Steelers, running back and kick returner, 5 feet 11, 215, Cincinnati. In Super Bowl IX, Harrison returned 2 kickoffs for a total of 17 yards. In SB X, he was credited with a blocked punt that went for a safety and helped change the momentum in the game. With the Cowboys ahead, 10–7, minutes into the final quarter, Dallas' Mitch Hoopes attempted to punt from his own 16. Harris, however, blocked the ball, and it rolled through the end zone for a safety, as the Steelers pulled to within 1 point, at 10–9.

DOUG HART

Green Bay Packers, defensive back, 6 feet, 190, Texas/Arlington. Hart played as a reserve for the Packers in both Super Bowls I and II.

MIKE HARTENSTINE

Chicago Bears, defensive end, 6 feet 3, 254, Penn State. Played as a reserve for the Bears in Super Bowl XX.

JOHN HARTY

San Francisco 49ers, nose tackle, 6 feet 4, 253, Iowa. A reserve in Super Bowl XVI, Harty had a hand in the key defensive stand by the 49ers in the 3rd quarter in SB XVI. With the ball on the 49ers' 3, and first down, the Cincinnati Bengals picked up 2 yards on Pete Johnson's run. On the next play, Harty stopped Johnson, who again attempted to run, and the 49ers held on the next 2 plays to retain a 20–7 lead.

JIM HARVEY

Oakland Raiders, guard, 6 feet 5, 245, Mississippi. Harvey played as a reserve in Super Bowl II.

DON HASSELBECK

Los Angeles Raiders, tight end, 6 feet 7, 240, Colorado. Hasselbeck, playing as a reserve in Super Bowl XVIII, blocked a point-after attempt by the Washington Redskins' Mark Moseley in the 3rd quarter.

DAVE HATHCOCK

Green Bay Packers, defensive back, 6 feet, 190, Memphis State. Hathcock played as a reserve for the Packers in Super Bowl I.

LEN HAUSS

Washington Redskins, center, 6 feet 2, 235, Georgia. Starting center for the Redskins in Super Bowl VII.

SAM HAVRILAK

Baltimore Colts, running back, 6 feet 2, 195, Bucknell. Look closely in the statistics for Super Bowl V, and you'll see Havrilak under the "passing" category. That's because he was involved in one of the numerous plays that resulted in the game being called the Stupor Bowl by many writers. With the Dallas Cowboys ahead, 13–6, with 9 minutes remaining, the Colts' quarterback Earl Morrall called for a flea flicker, and handed the ball off to Havrilak, who was supposed to lateral back to Morrall. However, Morrall was nowhere in sight, and Havrilak, a former quarterback, threw the ball downfield, and it was caught by Eddie Hinton, who ran for the end zone. But he was hit before he reached the goal line, and fumbled, and the ball went through the end zone for a touchback. Havrilak also carried the ball once for 3 yards and caught 2 passes for 27 yards.

ALEX HAWKINS

Baltimore Colts, flanker, 6 feet 1, 186, South Carolina. Hawkins played as a substitute in Super Bowl III.

FRANK HAWKINS

Los Angeles Raiders, running back, 5 feet 9, 210, Nevada–Reno. Hawkins played as a substitute in SB XVIII and carried the ball 3 times for 6 yards and caught 2 passes for 20 yards.

WAYNE HAWKINS

Oakland Raiders, guard, 6 feet, 240, Pacific. The starting right guard for the Raiders in Super Bowl II.

GREG HAWTHORNE

Pittsburgh Steelers and New England Patriots, wide receiver and halfback, 6 feet 2, 225, Baylor. Hawthorne played as a reserve for the Steelers in Super

Bowl XIV, then, after a trade in 1984, as a reserve for the Patriots in SB XX. He carried the ball 1 time for a loss of 4 yards.

BOB HAYES

Dallas Cowboys, wide receiver and kick returner, 5 feet 11, 185, Florida A&M. Hayes, billed as the World's Fastest Human, won a pair of gold medals in the 1964 Olympics in Tokyo, winning the 100 meters and anchoring the winning 4 × 100-meter relay. He started in both Super Bowl V—coming back after being benched by Coach Tom Landry earlier in the season—and SB VI at wide receiver and also returned punts in both games.

He caught 1 pass for 41 yards, which gave the Cowboys excellent field position in the 1st quarter of SB V, but the team could not score. He also returned 3 punts for 9 yards. In SB VI, he caught 2 passes for 23 yards and returned 1 punt for a loss of 1 yard.

JEFF HAYES

Washington Redskins, punter, 5 feet 11, 175, North Carolina. Hayes handled the Redskins' punting duties in Super Bowls XVII and XVIII. He had kicked 80 times without a block in the previous 18 games, until SB XVIII. Then, his first punt of the game, from his own 30, was blocked by the Los Angeles Raiders' Derrick

Jensen, who chased the ball into the end zone for a touchdown. Hayes finished the game with 7 punts for an average of 37 yards, with a long punt of 48 yards. In SB XVII, Hayes punted 4 times for an average of 42 yards, with a long punt of 54 yards.

LESTER HAYES

Oakland and Los Angeles Raiders, corner back, 6 feet, 195, Texas A&M. Hayes was the starting left corner back for the Raiders in Super Bowls XV and XVIII, part of their defense, which gave up only 19 points in 2 games.

WENDELL HAYES

Kansas City Chiefs, running back, 6 feet 1, 220, Humboldt State. Hayes played as a reserve and on special teams for the

Wendell Hayes

83

Chiefs in Super Bowl IV, carrying the ball 8 times for 31 yards, catching 1 pass for 3 yards and returning 2 kickoffs for 36 yards.

ALVIN HAYMOND

Washington Redskins, safety and kick returner, 6 feet, 194, Southern University. Returned 4 punts for a total of 9 yards in Super Bowl VII.

MIKE HAYNES

Los Angeles Raiders, corner back, 6 feet 2, 190, Arizona State. The starting right corner back for the Raiders in SB XVIII, Haynes' 4th-quarter interception against the Washington Redskins completed the Raiders' 38–9 romp. With Washington driving, Haynes picked off Joe Theismann's pass at the Raiders' 42-yard line. Los Angeles capitalized on the turnover, with a field goal, to complete the game's scoring.

SHERRILL HEADRICK

Kansas City Chiefs, linebacker, 6 feet 2, 240, Texas Christian. The starting middle linebacker for the Chiefs in Super Bowl I.

VINCE HEFLIN

Miami Dolphins, wide receiver, 6 feet, 185, Central State

(Ohio). Played as a reserve in Super Bowls XVII and XIX. He recovered a fumble on a punt in the 4th quarter in SB XIX, when the San Francisco 49ers' Dana McLemore signaled a fair catch, then fumbled the ball. But the Dolphins then turned the ball over themselves on an interception.

MIKE HEGMAN

Dallas Cowboys, linebacker, 6 feet 1, 225, Tennessee State. Hegman played as a reserve in both Super Bowls XII and XIII, scoring a touchdown in his second game on a fumble recovery return. Hegman and teammate Thomas Henderson rushed Pittsburgh quarterback Terry Bradshaw, and the ball was stripped out of Bradshaw's arms. Hegman picked it up and ran 37 yards for the touchdown, giving Dallas its only lead of the game, at 13–7, in the 2nd quarter.

BOB HEINZ

Miami Dolphins, defensive tackle, 6 feet 6, 280, Pacific. The starting defensive right tackle for the Dolphins in Super Bowls VI, VII, and VIII.

JOHN HENDERSON

Minnesota Vikings, wide receiver, 6 feet 3, 190, Michigan. A starting wide receiver for the Vikings in Super Bowl IV, he caught 7 passes for 111 yards to lead Minnesota in that category. He also lost the ball once on a fumble.

THOMAS (HOLLYWOOD) HENDERSON

Dallas Cowboys, linebacker, 6 feet 2, 220, Langston. A reserve in Super Bowl X, Henderson started at left linebacker for the Cowboys in SB XII and SB XIII.

He was the star of the pre-game hype for SB XIII, taunting opposing quarterback Terry Bradshaw in particular. Henderson said that Bradshaw couldn't spell cat if spotted "the C and A."

For a while in that game, it appeared as if Henderson was going to play a big role on the field,

too. With less than 3 minutes elapsed in the 2nd quarter, he and teammate Mike Hegman stripped Terry Bradshaw of the ball, and Hegman picked it up and ran 37 yards for a touchdown and a 13–7 Dallas lead. But Pittsburgh quickly came back to tie the score and went on to win the game.

Afterward, Henderson was again the focus of reporters, and he said: "I'm a little sad now. . . . Losing hurts. . . . But what a show, right? They ain't forgetting this one for a while."

ZAC HENDERSON

Philadelphia Eagles, safety, 6 feet 1, 190, Oklahoma. Henderson played as a substitute in Super Bowl XV.

TED (THE MAD STORK) HENDRICKS

Baltimore Colts, Oakland and Los Angeles Raiders, linebacker, 6 feet 7, 215, Miami. The Mad Stork started in four Super Bowls, SB V for the Colts, and SB XI, SB XV, SB XVIII for the Raiders. Hendricks blocked a field-goal attempt by the Philadelphia Eagles' Tony Franklin in the first half of SB XV.

WALLY HENRY

Philadelphia Eagles, wide receiver and kick returner, 5 feet 8,

Thomas Henderson

170, UCLA. Henry returned 1 punt for 2 yards in Super Bowl XV.

DAVE HERMAN

New York Jets, guard, 6 feet 1, 255, Michigan State. Starting right tackle for the Jets in Super Bowl III.

TERRY HERMELING

Washington Redskins, tackle, 6 feet 5, 255, Nevada/Reno. Starting left tackle for the Redskins in Super Bowl VII.

KEN HEROCK

Oakland Raiders, end, 6 feet 2, 230, West Virginia. Played as a substitute for the Raiders in Super Bowl II.

EFREN HERRERA

Dallas Cowboys, kicker, 5 feet 9, 190, UCLA. Herrera helped the Cowboys jump out to a 13–0 lead over the Denver Broncos early in the 2nd quarter of Super Bowl XII, as he kicked a point-after-touchdown and added 2 field goals, from 35 and 43 yards. Yet Herrera missed 3 field goals in the remainder of the 2nd quarter, from 43, 32, and 44 yards. He added 2 more point-after-touch-

downs in the second half to finish with 9 points.

ROB HERTEL

Philadelphia Eagles, quarterback, 6 feet 2, 198, USC. On the Eagles' roster, but did not play in Super Bowl XV.

RON HESTER

Miami Dolphins, linebacker, 6 feet 1, 218, Florida State. Played as a substitute for the Dolphins in Super Bowl XVII.

BRYAN HICKS

Cincinnati Bengals, safety, 6 feet, 192, McNeese State. Starting free safety for the Bengals in Super Bowl XVI.

DWIGHT HICKS

San Francisco 49ers, safety and kick returner, 6 feet 1, 189, Michigan. Starting free safety for the 49ers in Super Bowl XVI—but he is not related to the starting free safety for the opponent Cincinnati Bengals, Bryan Hicks. He also started at the position for the 49ers in SB XIX.

Hicks came up with a key interception early in SB XVI, picking off Ken Anderson's pass intended for Isaac Curtis at the SF 5 and returning it 27 yards. He also returned 1 punt for 6 yards and 1 kickoff for 23 yards. In SB XIX, he helped keep the Miami Dolphins' receiving duo, the Marks Brothers, Duper and Clayton, to a total of 7 receptions.

JAY HILGENBERG

Chicago Bears, center, 6 feet 3, 258, Iowa. Starting center for the Bears in Super Bowl XX. He is the nephew of Wally Hilgenberg, who played in 4 Super Bowls for the Minnesota Vikings in the 1970s.

WALLY HILGENBERG

Minnesota Vikings, linebacker, 6 feet 3, 231, Iowa. Starting right linebacker for the Vikings in Super Bowls IV, VIII, IX, and XI.

CALVIN HILL

Dallas Cowboys, running back, 6 feet 4, 227, Yale. The rookie of the year in the NFL in 1969, Hill went into both Super Bowls V and VI with injury problems. He returned 1 kickoff for 14 yards in SB V. He missed six weeks of the next season with a knee injury, and played in SB VI as a substitute, but still was able to carry 7 times for 25 yards and catch 1 pass for 12 yards. He

fumbled in the final minutes of the game, at the Miami Dolphins' 4-yard line, and the Dolphins recovered, but they were unable to score as time ran out.

DAVE HILL

Kansas City Chiefs, tackle, 6 feet 5, 260, Auburn. Started at right tackle for the Chiefs in Super Bowls I and IV. Hill was among the Chiefs' offensive linemen credited with holding off the Minnesota Vikings' famed front four, allowing quarterback Len Dawson enough time to operate, on the way to a 23–7 victory. After the game, Chiefs' guard Ed Budde said, "Dave Hill did an outstanding job. . . ."

DREW HILL

Los Angeles Rams, wide receiver and kick returner, 5 feet 9, 170, Georgia Tech. As a substitute, Hill caught 1 pass for 28 yards in Super Bowl XIV.

EDDIE HILL

Los Angeles Rams and Miami Dolphins, running back and kick returner, 6 feet 2, 197, Memphis State. With the Rams, he returned 3 kickoffs for a total of 47 yards in Super Bowl XIV. Utilized almost exclusively as a special teams player for the Dolphins after a trade in 1981, Hill did not record any individual statistics in SB XVII, but had 1 kickoff return for 16 yards in SB XIX.

JERRY HILL

Baltimore Colts, running back and kick returner, 5 feet 11, 215, Wyoming. Hill scored the Colts' only touchdown in Super Bowl III, on a 1-yard run with 3:19 left in the game. He finished with 9 carries for 29 yards and 2 receptions for 1 yard. In SB V, he returned 1 kickoff for 14 yards.

KENNY HILL

Los Angeles Raiders, safety, 6 feet, 195, Yale. Played as a reserve for the Raiders in Super Bowl XVIII.

KENT HILL

Los Angeles Rams, guard, 6 feet 5, 260, Georgia Tech. Starting left guard for the Rams in Super Bowl XIV.

TONY HILL

Dallas Cowboys, wide receiver, 6 feet 2, 196, Stanford. As a special-teams player in Super Bowl XII, he contributed one of 6 Dallas fumbles. Early in the game, Hill fumbled on a punt return at his own 1-yard line. But he quick-ly recovered his own fumble and did not record any other statistics in the game.

In SB XIII, he helped Dallas tie the game at 7–7 when he pulled in a pass at the Pittsburgh Steeler 26-yard line and ran in to complete a 39-yard play—the last of the 1st quarter. He finished with 2 receptions for 49 yards.

WINSTON HILL

New York Jets, tackle, 6 feet 4, 280, Texas Southern. Starting left tackle for the Jets in Super Bowl III.

ROY HILTON

Baltimore Colts, defensive end, 6 feet 6, 240, Jackson State. A reserve in Super Bowl III, Hilton started at defensive right end in SB V.

EDDIE HINTON

Baltimore Colts, wide receiver, 6 feet, 200, Oklahoma. Hinton had a hand—literally—in the Colts' first touchdown in Super Bowl V. After the Dallas Cowboys had taken a 6–0 lead early in the second quarter, the Colts came back. Quarterback Johnny Unitas threw a pass to Hinton, who tipped the ball. Cowboys' defensive back Mel Renfro also tipped the ball, and Colts' tight end John

Mackey pulled in the pass at the Dallas 45 and ran into the end zone, to complete a 75-yard play. Hinton's involvement in unusual plays didn't end there.

With the Cowboys ahead, 13–6, and 9 minutes remaining in the game, the Colts went to a trick play, the flea flicker. Quarterback Earl Morrall pitched back to halfback Sam Havrilak, who was to return the ball to Morrall, who was to pass to Hinton. But Havrilak could not find Morrall and instead threw a completion to Hinton. "I could see the end zone," Hinton said. "I knew I was going to score and tie the game." He didn't. At the 5-yard line, he was hit by Dallas' Cornell Green, the ball popped loose and into the end zone. Hinton was unable to go after it, as the Cowboys' Mel Renfro sat on him, and it was a touchback.

Hinton finished the game with 2 receptions for 51 yards.

JOHN HOLLAND

Minnesota Vikings, wide receiver, 6 feet, 190, Tennessee State. On the Vikings' roster for Super Bowl IX, but did not play.

BRIAN HOLLOWAY

New England Patriots, tackle, 6 feet 7, 288, Stanford. Starting left tackle for the Patriots in Super Bowl XX.

BOB HOLLY

Washington Redskins, quarterback, 6 feet 2, 205, Princeton. On the Redskins' roster for both Super Bowls XVII and XVIII, Holly did not play in either game.

ERNIE HOLMES

Pittsburgh Steelers, defensive tackle, 6 feet 3, 260, Texas Southern. Starting defensive right tackle in Super Bowls IX and X and part of the Steelers' famed front four, which held the Minnesota Vikings and Dallas Cowboys to 6 and 17 points, respectively. In SB IX, Holmes was particularly effective in hampering quarterback Fran Tarkenton, either lining up over center Mick Tingelhoff and attacking him directly or by looping around tackle Joe Greene and participating in a double team.

Ernie Holmes

ROBERT HOLMES

Kansas City Chiefs, running back, 5 feet 9, 220, Southern University. A starting running back in Super Bowl IV, he carried the ball 5 times for 7 yards.

TOM HOLMOE

San Francisco 49ers, safety, 6 feet 2, 180, Brigham Young. Played as a substitute in Super Bowl XIX, seeing considerable action and recording 5 tackles.

E. J. HOLUB

Kansas City Chiefs, linebacker and center, 6 feet 4, 236, Texas Tech. Holub started in both Super Bowl appearances for the Chiefs— once on defense, and once on offense. In SB I he started at the right linebacker position, then, in SB IV, started at offensive center.

DENNIS HOMAN

Dallas Cowboys, wide receiver, 6 feet 1, 181, Alabama. Played as a substitute in Super Bowl V, but did not record any individual statistics.

MITCH HOOPES

Dallas Cowboys, punter, 6 feet 1, 210, Arizona. Hoopes handled the punting duties for the Cowboys in Super Bowl X and punted 7 times. But a blocked punt figured as one of the keys in the scoring. With Dallas leading, 10–7, entering the 4th quarter, Hoopes stood on his goal line to punt. But the kick was blocked by Pittsburgh's Reggie Harrison, the ball rolled out of the end zone for a safety, and Dallas' lead was cut to 2 points. Pittsburgh also took advantage of good field position on the ensuing free kick and went into the lead for good with a 36-yard field goal by Roy Gerela. In all, Hoopes punted 7 times for an average of 35 yards, with a long punt of 48 yards.

DON HORN

Green Bay Packers, quarterback, 6 feet 2, 195, San Diego State. On the Packers' roster for Super Bowl II, Horn did not play.

ROD HORN

Cincinnati Bengals, nose tackle, 6 feet 4, 268, Nebraska. Horn played as a substitute in Super Bowl XVI.

PAUL HORNUNG

Green Bay Packers, running back, 6 feet 2, 215, Notre Dame. One of the most colorful players in the NFL's history, Hornung, a Hall of Fame selection, was injured and did not play in the first Super Bowl.

Paul Hornung

ard complained: "When I saw the pass coming, I knew it was mine. But I never got to touch the ball because this guy [Mel Blount] hit me, and he didn't have a chance to go for the ball. I was expecting a flag to be thrown, and so was he because he got up, looking around everywhere for it."

RON HOWARD

Dallas Cowboys, tight end, 6 feet 4, 225, Seattle. Played as a substitute in Super Bowl X, but did not record any individual statistics.

PAUL HOWARD

Denver Broncos, guard, 6 feet 3, 260, Brigham Young. Starting right guard for the Broncos in Super Bowl XII.

PERCY HOWARD

Dallas Cowboys, wide receiver, 6 feet 4, 210, Austin Peay. Howard, a reserve, recorded his first pro reception in Super Bowl X—for a 34-yard touchdown. Howard's reception, with 1:48 remaining, pulled the Cowboys to within 4 points of the Pittsburgh Steelers, at 21–17. Howard almost got another chance to become a hero on the Cowboys' last possession. But Roger Staubach's pass fell incomplete, after which How-

CHUCK HOWLEY

Dallas Cowboys, linebacker, 6 feet 2, 225, West Virginia. Only one losing player has ever been named the game's MVP—and it was a defensive player, Chuck Howley, at that. Howley was named the game's top player after Super Bowl V, which became known as the Stupor Bowl for its 6 interceptions and 6 fumbles.

Howley came up with 2 interceptions, stopping a pair of Baltimore Colts drives. Howley's first interception came on the Colts' second possession of the game, with Baltimore on its own 47. Quarterback Johnny Unitas attempted a short pass on first down, but Howley picked off the ball. Howley's next interception came in his own end zone on the first play of the 4th quarter, when he pulled down a pass from Earl Morrall.

When notified of his MVP award, Howley said, "The award is tremendous, but I wish it were the world championship. They go hand in hand."

Howley's key contributions to an SB game weren't over, though. In SB VI, he recovered a fumble by Larry Csonka on the Miami Dolphins' first possession, leading to the game's first scoring, a 9-yard field goal by Mike Clark. He also helped the Cowboys finish the game's scoring, picking off a Bob Griese pass in the opening minutes of the final quarter and returning it 41 yards to the Dolphins' 9-yard line, a turnover that helped set up the Cowboys' final touchdown and gave the team a 24–3 lead.

JIM HUDSON

New York Jets, defensive back, 6 feet 2, 210, Texas. Hudson, the Jets' starting left safety, came up with a key interception at the end of the 1st half of Super Bowl III. The Colts used their flea flicker play, with 25 seconds remaining and the ball on the Jets' 41. Earl Morrall handed off to Tom Matte, who returned the ball to Morrall. End Jimmy Orr was downfield, near the goal on the left side, waving for the ball, with no Jets in sight. Morrall seemed to look that way, then threw a floater over the middle toward fullback Jerry Hill. But Hudson intercepted the ball.

KEN HUFF

Washington Redskins, guard, 6 feet 4, 265, North Carolina. A substitute in Super Bowl XVIII.

RANDY HUGHES

Dallas Cowboys, safety, 6 feet 4, Oklahoma. Hughes, a reserve in Super Bowls X, XII, and XIII, came up with an interception and 2 fumble recoveries in SB XII. Midway through the 1st quarter, with the Broncos on their own 29, Hughes picked off a pass by Craig Morton on the 25. Five plays later, the Cowboys' Tony Dorsett scored. Hughes recovered both of his fumbles in the 1st half, one after a reception by Jack Dolbin, the other after a reception by Riley Odoms.

MIKE HULL

Washington Redskins, running back, 6 feet 3, 220, Southern California. Hull, a reserve, did not record any individual statistics in Super Bowl VII.

DAVID HUMM

Oakland and Los Angeles Raiders, quarterback, 6 feet 2, 184, Nebraska. Humm played as a substitute in both Super Bowls XI and XVIII, on special teams.

CLAUDE HUMPHREY

Philadelphia Eagles, defensive end, 6 feet 5, 258, Tennessee State. Humphrey, a 13-year veteran, played as a reserve in Super Bowl XV.

STEFAN HUMPHRIES

Chicago Bears, guard, 6 feet 3, 263, Michigan. A second-year player, Humphries played as a substitute in Super Bowl XX.

BOBBY HUNT

Kansas City Chiefs, defensive back, 6 feet 1, 193, Auburn. Hunt started at left safety for the Chiefs in Super Bowl I.

CHUCK HURSTON

Kansas City Chiefs, defensive end, 6 feet 6, 240, Auburn. The starting defensive right end for the Chiefs in Super Bowl I, Hurston played as a reserve in Super Bowl IV.

BRUCE HUTHER

Dallas Cowboys, linebacker, 6 feet 1, 217, New Hampshire. Huther, who played as a reserve in Super Bowls XII and XIII, was credited with a fumble recovery in SB XII when he caught a Dallas punt that caromed off the helmet of the Denver Broncos' John Schultz.

GLENN HYDE

Denver Broncos, tackle, 6 feet 3, 255, Pittsburgh. Hyde played as a substitute in Super Bowl XII.

BOB HYLAND

Green Bay Packers, center and guard, 6 feet 5, 250, Boston College. Hyland, a rookie, played as a substitute in Super Bowl II.

☆ ☆ ☆

BRIAN INGRAM

New England Patriots, linebacker, 6 feet 4, 235, Tennessee. Played as a reserve for the Patriots in Super Bowl XX.

BERNARD JACKSON

Denver Broncos, safety, 6 feet, 181, Washington State. The starting free safety for the Broncos in Super Bowl XII, his defensive positioning was targeted by the Dallas Cowboys, resulting in a touchdown that gave the Cowboys a 20–3 lead.

On second-and-10, midway through the 3rd quarter, Roger Staubach threw a pass to Butch Johnson, who split Jackson and right corner back Steve Foley and made a diving catch, hitting the end zone, then fumbling the ball. The officials ruled, however, that Johnson had made the catch and been in possession of the ball when he crossed the goal line.

Staubach said, "Jackson likes to make big plays, and sometimes he doesn't go back far enough. So I told Butch if Jackson didn't go deep, to run the post, instead of the in route. I knew I had to throw it ahead of Butch, but I thought it got too far to the right."

MONTE JACKSON

Oakland Raiders, corner back, 5 feet 11, 200, San Diego State. Played as a substitute for the Raiders in Super Bowl XV.

TOM JACKSON

Denver Broncos, linebacker, 5 feet 11, 224, Louisville. Starting right outside linebacker for the Broncos in Super Bowl XII. Jackson recovered a fumble by the Dallas Cowboys' Billy Joe DuPree on the Broncos' 12 in the 1st half, preventing the Cowboys from building a lead larger than their

13–0 margin at the end of the period.

WILBUR JACKSON

Washington Redskins, running back, 6 feet 1, 219, Alabama. Jackson played as a substitute for the Redskins in Super Bowl XVII.

JOE JACOBY

Washington Redskins, tackle, 6 feet 7, 295, Louisville. Starting left tackle for the Redskins in Super Bowls XVII and XVIII.

CRAIG JAMES

New England Patriots, fullback, 6 feet, 215, Southern Methodist. The Patriots' starting fullback and All-Pro selection had as frustrating a Super Bowl XX as his teammates, finishing with 5 carries for only 1 yard, 1 reception for 6 yards, and a fumble. Late in the 1st quarter, James was hit by the game's MVP, Richard Dent, and dropped the ball, and the Bears' Mike Singletary recovered at the New England 13. Two plays later, Matt Suhey scored on a 2-yard run, putting Chicago ahead, 13–3.

ROLAND JAMES

New England Patriots, safety, 6 feet 2, 191, Tennessee. Starting

strong safety for the Patriots in Super Bowl XX. He was credited with 5 tackles and 1 assist in the unofficial defensive statistics.

JON JAQUA

Washington Redskins, safety, 6 feet, 190, Lewis and Clark. Played as a substitute for the Redskins in Super Bowl VII.

RON JAWORSKI

Philadelphia Eagles, quarterback, 6 feet 2, 196, Youngstown State. Jaworski, the starting quarterback for the Eagles in Super Bowl XV, got off to a rough start—and it went downhill from there. On the third play of the game, the Oakland Raiders' Rod Martin

Ron Jaworski

picked off Jaworski's first pass attempt to set up an early Raider touchdown.

On the Eagles' only sustained drive of the 1st half, Philadelphia was able to get only a 30-yard field goal from Tony Franklin to trail, 14–3, at halftime. Jaworski finished the 1st half with only 9 completions in 22 attempts for 131 yards, while the Eagles' running game gained only 33 yards.

After Oakland scored again to start the 2nd half, Jaworski took the Eagles to the Raider 34-yard line, but on third-and-3, Martin again picked off a pass. Jaworski drove the Eagles to their only touchdown in the 4th quarter, finishing the drive with an 8-yard pass to Keith Krepfle. But 2 more drives ended when Jaworski fumbled the ball away, and Martin picked off his third pass.

Jaworski's final statistics: 18 completions in 38 attempts—then a Super Bowl record—for 291 yards, with 1 touchdown and 3 interceptions. He also carried the ball once for no gain.

ROY JEFFERSON

Baltimore Colts and Washington Redskins, wide receiver, 6 feet 2, 195, Utah. Jefferson started at wide receiver for the Colts in Super Bowl V and the Redskins in Super Bowl VII.

He was his team's leading receiver in both games. For the Colts, he recorded 3 receptions for 52 yards, with a long catch of 23

yards, and for the Redskins he caught 5 passes for 50 yards, with a long catch of 15.

ED JENKINS

Miami Dolphins, running back, 6 feet 2, 210, Holy Cross. Jenkins played as a substitute for the Dolphins in Super Bowl VII.

DERRICK JENSEN

Oakland and Los Angeles Raiders, running back, 6 feet 1, 225, Texas/Arlington. Played as a reserve for the Raiders in Super Bowls XV and XVIII. In SB XV, he carried the ball 3 times for 12 yards. In SB XVIII, he scored the game's first touchdown as he blocked a punt by the Washington Redskins' Jeff Hayes with the ball on the Washington 30. Jensen chased the ball into the end zone, where he fell on it for a touchdown, 4:52 in the game.

JIM JENSEN

Denver Broncos, running back and kick returner, 6 feet 3, 240, Iowa. Jensen carried once for 16 yards and returned 1 kickoff for 17 yards in Super Bowl XII.

JIM JENSEN

Miami Dolphins, quarterback, 6 feet 4, 212, Boston Univer-

sity. Jensen, who has played quarterback, wide receiver, tight end, punt snapper, and on special teams during his career, played in both Super Bowls XVII and XIX for the Dolphins. He recovered a fumble with less than a minute left in the 1st half of SB XIX, leading to a field goal. After the San Francisco 49ers' Guy McIntyre, a guard, picked up the ball on a kickoff and attempted to run, he was hit by the Dolphins' Joe Carter and dropped the ball. Jensen recovered at the 49ers' 12. Uwe von Schamann's 30-yard field goal cut the San Francisco lead to 28–16 at halftime.

BOB JETER

Green Bay Packers, defensive back, 6 feet 1, 205, Iowa. Started in the defensive backfield for the Packers in both Super Bowls I and II.

JIM JODAT

Los Angeles Rams, running back and kick returner, 5 feet 11, 207, Carthage. Jodat returned 2 kickoffs for 32 yards in Super Bowl XIV.

BUTCH JOHNSON

Dallas Cowboys, wide receiver and kick returner, 6 feet 1, 191, California/Riverside. Johnson started at wide receiver for the Cowboys in Super Bowl XII, scoring a touchdown, then played in SB XIII as a reserve, but again scoring.

Johnson's first touchdown catch was of the spectacular variety. On third-and-10, the Cowboys' Roger Staubach threw 45 yards to Johnson, who made a diving catch, crossed the goal line, then fumbled the ball. The officials, however, ruled it a touchdown.

Of the catch, Johnson later said: "I told Roger to get it out in front of me, and I could stretch for it." When it was suggested that the play looked spectacular, Johnson answered, "It *is* spectacular."

Johnson finished the game with 2 catches for 53 yards, 1 carry for minus-9 yards, and 2 kick returns for 29 yards. He also twice recovered his own fumbles.

In SB XIII, during Dallas' furious late rally, he scored on a 4-yard pass from Staubach with 22 seconds remaining in the game. But an onsides kick attempt failed, and the Cowboys lost to the Pittsburgh Steelers. Johnson finished the game with 2 receptions for 30 yards, 2 punt returns for 33 yards, and 3 kickoff returns for 63 yards.

CHARLIE JOHNSON

Philadelphia Eagles, nose tackle, 6 feet 3, 262, Colorado. Started in the defensive front line for the Eagles in Super Bowl XV.

97

CORNELIUS JOHNSON

Baltimore Colts, guard, 6 feet 2, 245, Virginia Union. Played as a substitute for the Colts in both Super Bowls III and V.

CURLEY JOHNSON

New York Jets, punter and tight end, 6 feet, 215, Houston. Johnson punted 4 times for an average of 38.8 yards and a long punt of 39 yards in Super Bowl III.

CURTIS JOHNSON

Miami Dolphins, corner back, 6 feet 1, 196, Toledo. Johnson started at the right corner back position for the Dolphins in Super Bowls VI, VII, and VIII. He intercepted a pass late in the final quarter of SB VIII, picking off a ball thrown by Fran Tarkenton at the goal line.

DAN JOHNSON

Miami Dolphins, tight end, 6 feet 3, 240, Iowa State. The starting tight end for the Dolphins in Super Bowl XIX, he scored the team's only touchdown in the game. In the 1st quarter, after a 21-yard reception gave the Dolphins the ball at the SF 2, Johnson pulled in a pass from Dan Marino in the end zone for the score. Johnson finished the game with 3 receptions for 28 yards.

GARY JOHNSON

San Francisco 49ers, defensive end, 6 feet 2, 261, Grambling. Played as a reserve in Super Bowl XIX.

MONTE JOHNSON

Oakland Raiders, linebacker, 6 feet 5, 240, Nebraska. The starting left inside linebacker for the Raiders in Super Bowl XI.

PETE JOHNSON

Cincinnati Bengals and Miami Dolphins, running back, 6 feet, 249, Ohio State. Johnson started in the backfield for the Bengals in Super Bowl XVI, but did not play for the Dolphins in SB XIX, after being obtained in a trade during the 1984 season.

In SB XVI Johnson was involved in one of the most memorable defensive stands in SB history. In the 3rd quarter, the Bengals were attempting to pull back into the game with the 49ers. A 2-yard plunge by Johnson gave the Bengals the ball with a first-and-goal at the Cincinnati 3, but thereafter the Bengals were stopped on 4 plays. First, Johnson ran for 2 yards, then was stopped cold by John Harty for no gain. On fourth down, Johnson was again given the ball, but he was met by the 49er front line and stopped short of the goal line.

Afterward, Bengal Coach Forrest Gregg said, "Nobody has stopped us on that play all year. In a situation like that you give it to the strongest guy. They did a good job. They jammed things up a little bit and we didn't get movement on the defensive backs and linebackers."

Johnson finished the game as the Bengals' leading rusher with 14 carries for 36 yards. He also caught 2 passes for 8 yards.

RON JOHNSON

Pittsburgh Steelers, corner back, 5 feet 10, 200, Eastern Michigan. Starting left corner back for the Steelers in Super Bowls XIII and XIV.

SAMMY JOHNSON

Minnesota Vikings, running back, 6 feet 1, 226, North Carolina. Johnson carried 2 times for 9 yards and caught 3 passes for 26 yards in Super Bowl XI as a reserve.

CEDRIC JONES

New England Patriots, wide receiver, 6 feet 1, 184, Duke. Played as a reserve for the Patriots in Super Bowl XX.

CLINT JONES

Minnesota Vikings, running back and kick returner, 6 feet, **200, Michigan State.** A substitute in Super Bowl IV, Jones returned 1 kickoff for 33 yards.

ED (TOO TALL) JONES

Dallas Cowboys, defensive end, 6 feet 9, 260, Tennessee State. Jones started at left end for the Cowboys in 3 Super Bowls—SB X, SB XII, and SB XIII. He played a key part of Dallas' Doomsday Defense, which was particularly effective in SB XII against the Denver Broncos. In that game, midway through the 3rd quarter, Jones nearly picked off a pass from Broncos' quarterback Craig Morton. But, having thrown 4 interceptions already, Morton was pulled from the game.

In SB XIII, against the Pittsburgh Steelers, Too Tall Jones recovered a fumble that led to a

Ed Jones

99

Dallas touchdown. Late in the first quarter, Harvey Martin sacked the Steelers' Terry Bradshaw, who dropped the ball. Jones recovered on the Pittsburgh 41, and 2 plays later, Roger Staubach hit Tony Hill with a 39-yard touchdown pass to tie the score at 7–7.

WILLIE JONES

Oakland Raiders, defensive end, 6 feet 4, 245, Florida State. Playing as a reserve in Super Bowl XV, Jones recovered a Philadelphia fumble late in the game to help hold an Eagles' rally.

On the Eagles' second-to-last possession, in Oakland territory, quarterback Ron Jaworski fumbled, and Jones recovered at the Oakland 42-yard line.

CURTIS JORDAN

Washington Redskins, safety, 6 feet 2, 205, Texas Tech. Played as a substitute for the Redskins in Super Bowls XVII and XVIII.

HENRY JORDAN

Green Bay Packers, defensive tackle, 6 feet 3, 250, Virginia. The starting defensive right tackle for the Packers in Super Bowls I and II. Jordan helped the Packers break open SB I. With the Packers ahead, 14–10, at halftime, Jordan and teammate Willie Davis rushed KC Chiefs' quarterback Len Dawson on his first pass attempt of the 2nd half. Jordan hit Dawson's arm on the follow-through, and Willie Wood picked off the ball, returning it 50 yards to the Chiefs' 5. Elijah Pitts scored on the next play.

In SB II, he threw a key block, at the 10-yard line, as Herb Adderley ran back an interception 60 yards for a touchdown to give the Packers a 33–7 lead over the Oakland Raiders.

LEE ROY JORDAN

Dallas Cowboys, linebacker, 6 feet 1, 221, Alabama. Starting middle linebacker for the Cowboys in Super Bowls V, VI, and X. Jordan's hard tackle of Johnny Unitas forced a fumble, which Dallas recovered, and led to a touchdown and a 13–6 lead over the Baltimore Colts midway through the 2nd quarter of SB V.

SHELBY JORDAN

Los Angeles Raiders, tackle, 6 feet 7, 285, Washington (Missouri.) Jordan played as a substitute in Super Bowl XVIII.

WILLIAM JUDSON

Miami Dolphins, corner back, 6 feet 1, 181, South Carolina State. Judson played as a reserve in Super Bowl XVII, then started at the right corner back position for the Dolphins in SB XIX.

JOE KAPP

Minnesota Vikings, quarterback, 6 feet 3, 208, California. Kapp, the Vikings' starting quarterback, who had played a good deal of his career in Canada, signed with the Vikings as a free agent in 1967. He suffered a beating at the hands of the KC Chiefs in Super Bowl IV and eventually had to be pulled from the game.

Earlier, Kapp completed 16 passes in 25 attempts for 183 yards with 2 interceptions, carried the ball twice for 9 yards, and fumbled once. He was greatly hampered by an active Chiefs' front line, which kept him contained and cut off his rollouts. Finally a hard tackle by the Chiefs' defensive end Aaron Brown left Kapp's arm hanging limply at his side.

After the game, Coach Bud Grant told reporters, "Joe's in too much pain to talk."

KARL KASSULKE

Minnesota Vikings, safety, 6 feet, 195, Drake. Kassulke started in the defensive backfield for the Vikings in Super Bowl IV. Was the last defender to have a shot at the Kansas City Chiefs' Otis Taylor on the way to a 46-yard touchdown completion. With the ball on the Minnesota 46, Len Dawson hit Taylor six yards out in the flat. Taylor ran over Earsell Mackbee at the 40, then faked Kassulke, who fell down at the 10.

Afterward, Kassulke said, "We made more mistakes today than we made in 22 games."

MEL KAUFMAN

Washington Redskins, linebacker, 6 feet 2, 218, Cal Poly/San Luis Obispo. Starting left linebacker for the Redskins in Super Bowls XVII and XVIII.

JIM KEARNEY

Kansas City Chiefs, safety, 6 feet 2, 206, Prairie View. Starting left safety for the Chiefs in Super Bowl IV.

TOM KEATING

Oakland Raiders, defensive tackle, 6 feet 2, 247, Michigan. Starting right tackle for the Raiders in Super Bowl II. He played despite a swollen right ankle, which grew worse as the game went on. And his battle with Packer guard Gale Gillingham was described by writer Jerry Izenberg of the Newark *Star-Ledger* as "the only genuine Super Bowl played."

LOUIE KELCHER

San Francisco 49ers, nose tackle, 6 feet 5, 310, Southern Methodist. Played as a reserve for the 49ers in Super Bowl XIX.

MARV KELLUM

Pittsburgh Steelers, linebacker, 6 feet 2, 225, Wichita State. A substitute in both Super Bowls IX and X. In SB IX Kellum recovered a fumble by the Minnesota Vikings' Bill Brown on the opening kickoff of the 2nd half, and 3 plays later, the Steelers' Franco Harris scored from 9 yards out to increase the Pittsburgh lead to 9–0.

BOBBY KEMP

Cincinnati Bengals, safety, 6 feet, 186, Cal State/Fullerton. Starting strong safety for the Bengals in Super Bowl XVI.

ALLAN KENNEDY

San Francisco 49ers, tackle, 6 feet 7, 245, Washington State. Kennedy played as a reserve for the 49ers in both Super Bowls XVI and XIX.

STEVE KENNEY

Philadelphia Eagles, tackle, 6 feet 4, 262, Clemson. Played as a reserve for the Eagles in Super Bowl XV.

JON KEYWORTH

Denver Broncos, running back, 6 feet 3, 234, Colorado. A backfield starter, Keyworth carried 5 times for 9 yards in Super Bowl XII.

TYRONE KEYS

Chicago Bears, defensive end, 6 feet 7, 267, Mississippi State. Played as a reserve in Super Bowl XX.

JIM KIICK

Miami Dolphins, running back, 5 feet 11, 215, Wyoming.
Kiick started in the backfield for the Dolphins in Super Bowls VI and VII and played as a substitute in SB VIII. He and backfield teammate Larry Csonka earned the nicknames "Butch Cassidy and the Sundance Kid" for their resemblance to the famous outlaws.

In Miami's 24–3 beating at the hands of the Dallas Cowboys in SB VI, Kiick ran 10 times for 49 yards, with a long run of 9 yards, and caught 3 passes for 21 yards. In SB VII, Kiick scored what proved to be the game's winning touchdown with 18 seconds left in the 1st half, going over from the 1-yard line behind guard Larry Little. Kiick finished the game

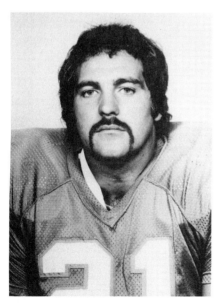

Jim Kiick

with 12 carries for 38 yards and also caught 2 passes for 6 yards.

Kiick scored again in SB VIII, again providing the winning points and again doing it from the 1-yard line, this time in the 1st quarter. He finished the game with 7 carries for 10 yards. His SB totals: 29 carries for 88 yards and 2 touchdowns and 5 receptions for 27 yards.

BILLY KILMER

Washington Redskins, quarterback, 6 feet, 204, UCLA. Kilmer's memorable NFL career included only 1 Super Bowl, but it may be a game he'd like to forget. The 11-year veteran threw 3 interceptions in SB VII and failed to lead the Washington offense to a single point. The Miami Dolphins scored twice in the 1st half on the way to their 14–7 victory, with the second touchdown set up by a Nick Buoniconti interception of a Kilmer pass.

The Redskins had started at their own 17-yard line, but on third down from the Miami 48, Kilmer threw a pass that was picked off by Buoniconti. Five plays later, Miami was ahead, 14–0.

Another Washington drive in the 4th quarter ended when a Kilmer pass was picked off in the end zone by Jake Scott. Washington was only able to climb back in because of Garo Yepremian's goof, when he attempted to throw a pass after a blocked field goal. The Redskins' Mike Bass ran the ball back for a touchdown.

The Redskins' final shot began with 1:14 left, from their own 30. But Kilmer's first 2 passes were incomplete, his third resulted in a 4-yard loss, and on fourth down he was sacked for a loss of 9 yards.

Kilmer, whose final statistics included 14 completions in 28 attempts for 104 yards, said, "I just didn't throw very well and 2 of my 3 interceptions had a lot to do with the outcome. One set up a Dolphins' touchdown, and the other took one away from us."

BRUCE KIMBALL

Washington Redskins, guard, 6 feet 2, 260, Massachusetts. A free agent in his first season with the Redskins, Kimball played mainly on special teams, including time in Super Bowl XVIII.

HOWARD KINDIG

Miami Dolphins, tackle and center, 6 feet 6, 260, Cal State/Los Angeles. Kindig's low snap to placekicker Garo Yepremian in Super Bowl VII led to one of the SB's most remembered incidents—Yepremian's attempted pass, which was picked up by Mike Bass and run back 49 yards for the Washington Redskins' only touchdown.

STEVE KINER

Dallas Cowboys, linebacker, 6 feet, 218, Tennessee. Played as a substitute for the Cowboys in Super Bowl V.

KENNY KING

Oakland and Los Angeles Raiders, running back, 5 feet 11, 205, Oklahoma. King started in the backfield for the Raiders in Super Bowls XV and XVIII. In SB XV King and quarterback Jim Plunkett combined for the longest completion in SB history, 80 yards. On a third-and-4, with the Raiders at their own 20, Plunkett scrambled out of the pocket and threw toward King, who came out of the backfield. Philadelphia corner back Herm Edwards scrambled to pick him up, but still had his back to King along the left sideline as Plunkett's pass floated into King's hands directly in front of the Oakland bench. King grabbed it and took off.

"When I turned and started running, I didn't see anybody," King said. "That's when I knew I was gone." The play gave the Raiders their winning points, and King finished with a total of 2 receptions for 93 yards and 6 carries for 18 yards. In SB XVIII, he carried 3 times for 12 yards and caught 2 passes for 8 yards.

DOUG KINGSRITER

Minnesota Vikings, tight end, 6 feet 2, 222, Minnesota. With his only reception of the game, a 9-yarder from Fran Tarkenton, Kingsriter recorded the Vikings' initial first down of Super Bowl VIII on the final play of the first quarter. He also played in SB IX, but did not record any individual statistics.

REGGIE KINLAW

Oakland and Los Angeles Raiders, nose tackle, 6 feet 2, 240, Oklahoma. The starting nose tackle for the Raiders in Super Bowls XV and XVIII.

CURT KNIGHT

Washington Redskins, kicker, 6 feet 2, 190, Coast Guard. Knight, who had kicked 7 consecutive field goals in the playoffs, missed his only attempt in Super Bowl VII, from 32 yards. The Redskins, down 14–0 at the half to the Miami Dolphins, entered Miami territory for the first time on their opening possession of the 2nd half, but then were halted. Knight came on, but missed wide to the right. Knight later kicked a successful point-after-touchdown, following Mike Bass's 49-yard fumble return.

DAVE KOCOUREK

Oakland Raiders, tight end, 6 feet 5, 240, Wisconsin. Kocourek, a reserve, was credited with one kickoff return, which he lateraled to teammate Dave Grayson after no gain, in Super Bowl II.

JON KOLB

Pittsburgh Steelers, tackle, 6 feet 3, 262, Oklahoma State. Starting left tackle for the Steelers in 4 Super Bowls—SB IX, SB X, SB XIII, and SB XIV.

MIKE KOLEN

Miami Dolphins, linebacker, 6 feet 2, 220, Auburn. Starting right linebacker for the Dolphins in Super Bowls VI, VII, and VIII.

RON KOSTELNIK

Green Bay Packers, defensive tackle, 6 feet 4, 260, Cincinnati. Starting defensive left tackle for the Packers in Super Bowls I and II. In the second game, Kostelnik threw one of 2 key blocks as Herb Adderley ran back an interception 60 yards for a touchdown in the final quarter.

MIKE KOZLOWSKI

Miami Dolphins, safety, 6 feet, 198, Colorado. A college running back, Kozlowski made the transition to pro defensive back and played mainly as a nickel back, including time in both Super Bowls XVII and XIX.

JERRY KRAMER

Green Bay Packers, guard, 6 feet 3, 245, Idaho. Kramer, who started at right guard for the Packers in Super Bowls I and II, went on to write several best-selling books about his days with the Packers. As a blocker in the Packers' famed sweep, he helped lead the way for a 14-yard touchdown run by Jim Taylor that gave the Packers a 14–7 lead in the first half in Super Bowl I.

KENT KRAMER

Minnesota Vikings, tight end, 6 feet 4, 235, Minnesota. Played as a substitute for the Vikings in Super Bowl IV.

PAUL KRAUSE

Minnesota Vikings, safety, 6 feet 3, 188, Iowa. The starting right safety for the Vikings in 4 Super Bowls—SB IV, SB VIII, SB IX and SB XI. Krause came up with an interception in SB IV and a fumble recovery in SB IX. The recovery, in the 4th quarter, at the Pittsburgh 47 gave the Vikings good field position as they trailed, 9–0. The Vikings fumbled the ball away, but after the Steelers couldn't move the ball, Minnesota's Matt Blair blocked the punt, and Terry Brown recovered it in the end zone for Minnesota's only touchdown.

STEVE KREIDER

Cincinnati Bengals, wide receiver, 6 feet 3, 192, Lehigh. Kreider had a key 19-yard reception in the Bengals' opening drive of the 2nd half of Super Bowl XVI. On third-and-4 from the Bengals' 41, Kreider caught a Ken Anderson pass and was tackled on the San Francisco 40. The drive ended with Anderson's 5-yard touchdown run, which brought the Bengals to within 13 points, at 20–7. Kreider finished with 2 receptions for 36 yards.

KEITH KREPFLE

Philadelphia Eagles, tight end, 6 feet 3, 230, Iowa State. The Eagles' starting tight end in Super Bowl XV, Krepfle scored Philadelphia's only touchdown of the game. Early in the 4th quarter, the Eagles' Ron Jaworski capped a 12-play, 88-yard drive with an 8-yard pass to Krepfle.

MIKE KRUCZEK

Pittsburgh Steelers, quarterback, 6 feet 1, 205, Boston College. One of the Steelers' backup quarterbacks, he was listed on the team's roster but did not play in either Super Bowls XIII or XIV.

BOB KRUSE

Oakland Raiders, guard, 6 feet 2, 250, Wayne State. Kruse played as a substitute for the Raiders in Super Bowl II.

LARRY KUBIN

Washington Redskins, linebacker, 6 feet 2, 238, Penn State. A special-teams standout, Kubin played as a substitute in both Super Bowls XVII and XVIII.

BOB KUECHENBERG

Miami Dolphins, guard, 6 feet 2, 247, Notre Dame. In the Super Bowl's amazing stories, Kuechenberg's has to be considered one of the standouts. As a second-year player, Kuechenberg started on the Dolphins' line at left guard in SB VI. Before his career was over in 1985, he would start in three more SBs—SB VII, SB VIII, and SB XVII. He was the last remaining player from the Dolphins' 1972 team, which finished its season with a 17–0 record. And he set a team record for games played, with 209, including playoffs.

He is best remembered in SB play for his matchup with the Minnesota Vikings' defensive tackle Alan Page in SB VIII. In that game, the Dolphins' running attack gained 196 yards and so dominated that quarterback Bob Griese needed to throw only 7 passes. As the Dolphins' press guide stated at the time of Kuechenberg's retirement, "His finest moment as a player probably occurred on January 13, 1974, when his total domination of Minnesota All-Pro Alan Page helped Miami to a 24–7 win over the Vikings in Super Bowl VIII."

Afterward, Kuechenberg was quoted as saying, "Alan was a bit annoyed."

Bob Kuechenberg

AARON KYLE

Dallas Cowboys, corner back, 5 feet 10, 185, Wyoming. The starting right corner back for the Cowboys in Super Bowls XII and XIII, he was one of the defensive stars for the Cowboys in the victory over the Denver Broncos in SB XII.

He accounted for one of 4 interceptions in the 1st half that helped the Cowboys jump off to a 13–0 lead over the Broncos. With the Cowboys ahead, 7–0, courtesy of an interception, the Broncos' Craig Morton attempted another pass. But the ball was tipped by linebacker Bob Breunig, and Kyle pulled it* in and ran it back 19 yards to the Denver 35-yard line. Six plays later, the Cowboys kicked a field goal.

Kyle wasn't finished though. In the final quarter, with Norris Weese in at quarterback for the Broncos, Kyle recovered the ball after a Weese fumble, and the Cowboys finished off the game's scoring, when Robert Newhouse hit Golden Richards with a 29-yard pass.

In SB XIII, he was one of the defenders John Stallworth eluded on his 75-yard touchdown pass from Terry Bradshaw in the 2nd quarter.

☆ ☆ ☆

ERIC LAAKSO

Miami Dolphins, tackle, 6 feet 4, 265, Tulane. Starting right tackle for the Dolphins in Super Bowl XVII.

PAUL LAAVEG

Washington Redskins, guard, 6 feet 4, 250, Iowa. Starting left guard for the Redskins in Super Bowl VII.

SCOTT LAIDLAW

Dallas Cowboys, running back, 6 feet, 205, Stanford. Played as a substitute in Super Bowls XII and XIII, carrying once for 1 yard in the first game and 3 times for 12 yards, including a long run of 7, in the second.

JACK LAMBERT

Pittsburgh Steelers, linebacker, 6 feet 4, 220, Kent State. Four times a starter for the Steelers at middle linebacker—in Super Bowls IX, X, XIII, and XIV. Lambert is credited with providing several sparks to the Steeler defense in their SB XIV victory over the LA Rams. His teammates said that in the middle of a defensive huddle near the end of the 1st half, Lambert had delivered an ear-splitting speech to the group.

"Our locker-room was kind of quiet at halftime," Lambert said later. "We knew that our defense hadn't been playing with the intensity we needed, but we are champions. We knew we would come back."

Later in the game, Lambert made sure the Rams didn't come back. Trailing, 24–19, the Rams drove to the Steeler 32, and Vince Ferragamo passed into a crowd at the 14, but Lambert picked off the ball. In all, unofficial statistics showed that Lambert was involved in 13 tackles in the game.

PETE LAMMONS

New York Jets, tight end, 6 feet 3, 233, Texas. The starting right end for the Jets in Super Bowl III, he caught 2 passes for 13 yards.

DARYLE LAMONICA

Oakland Raiders, quarterback, 6 feet 3, 215, Notre Dame. Lamonica, a Green Bay Packers draft choice who ended up signing with the American Football League, was obtained by the Raid-

ers in a trade before the season and ended up being voted the AFL's top player in the 1967 season. But his string of successes ended in Super Bowl II as he finished completing only 15 of 34 pass attempts for 208 yards, with 2 touchdowns and 1 interception. The interception, early in the 4th quarter, was run back 60 yards by Herb Adderley for a touchdown.

After the Packers had jumped to a 13–0 lead, Lamonica pulled the Raiders back into the game, driving the team 78 yards in 9 plays in the 2nd quarter. The drive ended with Lamonica's 23-yard scoring pass to Bill Miller.

The Packers went ahead after the 3rd quarter, 26–7, and sewed it up with Adderley's interception. Lamonica again hit Miller late in the game with a 23-yard touchdown pass to end the scoring.

JIM LANGER

Miami Dolphins, guard, 6 feet 2, 250, South Dakota. A substitute in Super Bowl VI, Langer started at center for the Dolphins in SB VII and SB VIII, and in SB VIII he was part of Miami's outstanding front line, which helped Larry Csonka to 33 carries and 145 yards.

WILLIE LANIER

Kansas City Chiefs, linebacker, 6 feet 1, 245, Morgan State.

Daryle LaMonica

Willie Lanier

The starting middle linebacker for the Chiefs in Super Bowl IV, he had one interception in the game. The Minnesota Vikings, down 23–7 entering the final quarter, had the ball 3 times in the period. Each time, though, the Chiefs intercepted, with Lanier pulling down the first one, a Joe Kapp pass, at the Kansas City 34.

PAUL LANKFORD

Miami Dolphins, corner back, 6 feet 1, 178, Penn State. Lankford played as a substitute for the Dolphins in Super Bowls XVII and XIX.

DAVE LAPHAM

Cincinnati Bengals, guard, 6 feet 4, 262, Syracuse. Starting left guard for the Bengals in Super Bowl XVI.

GARY LARSEN

Minnesota Vikings, defensive tackle, 6 feet 5, 255, Concordia (Minnesota). Starting defensive left tackle for the Vikings in Super Bowls IV and VIII and a substitute in SB IX.

JIM LASH

Minnesota Vikings, wide receiver, 6 feet 2, 199, Northwestern. A substitute in Super Bowl VIII, Lash was one of the Vikings' starters in SB IX. He caught 1 pass for 9 yards in the first game, but did not catch another in the second.

BILL LASKEY

Oakland Raiders, linebacker, 6 feet 3, 235, Michigan. Starting left linebacker for the Raiders in Super Bowl II.

ISAAC (IKE) LASSITER

Oakland Raiders, defensive end, 6 feet 5, 270, St. Augustine's. Starting left defensive end for the Raiders in Super Bowl II.

DONALD LASTER

Washington Redskins, tackle, 6 feet 5, 285, Tennessee State.

Played as a substitute for the Redskins in Super Bowl XVII.

BABE LAUFENBERG

Washington Redskins, quarterback, 6 feet 2, 195, Indiana. The Redskins' third-string quarterback, he did not play in Super Bowl XVIII.

JOE LAVENDER

Washington Redskins, corner back, 6 feet 4, 188, San Diego State. Played as a substitute in Super Bowl XVII.

BURTON LAWLESS

Dallas Cowboys, guard, 6 feet 4, 250, Florida. Starting left guard for the Cowboys in Super Bowl X, and a substitute for the Cowboys in SB XII and SB XIII.

AMOS LAWRENCE

San Francisco 49ers, running back and kick returner, 5 feet 10, 179, North Carolina. Lawrence took the opening kickoff of Super Bowl XVI, ran it back 17 yards, then fumbled, with the Cincinnati Bengals recovering on the 49ers' 26. The Bengals, however, themselves turned the ball over a short time later with an interception.

HENRY LAWRENCE

Oakland and Los Angeles Raiders, tackle, 6 feet 4, 273, Florida A&M. Played as a reserve in Super Bowl XI, then started at right tackle for the Raiders in SB XV and SB XVIII.

STEVE LAWSON

Minnesota Vikings, guard, 6 feet 3, 265, Kansas. Lawson, who was on the Vikings' roster but did not play in Super Bowl VIII, played as a substitute in Super Bowl IX.

JIM LeCLAIR

Cincinnati Bengals, linebacker, 6 feet 3, 234, North Dakota. Starting left inside linebacker for the Bengals in Super Bowl XVI.

BOB LEE

Minnesota Vikings and Los Angeles Rams, quarterback and punter, 6 feet 3, 195, Pacific. Lee handled the Vikings' punting duties in Super Bowl IV, his first. He punted 3 times for an average of 37 yards, with a long kick of 50 yards. Lee relieved starter Fran Tarkenton late in SB XI, with the Vikings behind, 32–7, to the Oakland Raiders. He closed out the game's scoring with a 13-yard touchdown pass to Stu Voigt and completed 7 of 9 passes for 81 yards. He also ran once for 4 yards. On the Rams' roster for SB XIV, he did not play in the game.

DAVID LEE

Baltimore Colts, punter, 6 feet 4, 215, Louisiana Tech. Handled the Colts' punting duties for Super Bowls III and V. In the first game, he punted 3 times for an average of 44.3 yards, with a long punt of 51 yards. In the second, he punted 4 times for an average of 41.5 with a long of 56.

RONNIE LEE

Miami Dolphins, tight end and tackle, 6 feet 3, 236, Baylor. Primarily a blocking tight end early in his career, Lee played that position as a substitute in Super Bowl XVII. Switched to tackle, he played as a backup in SB XIX.

CHARLES LEIGH

Miami Dolphins, running back, 5 feet 11, 206, no college. Leigh played as a substitute in Super Bowl VII.

FRANK LeMASTER

Philadelphia Eagles, linebacker, 6 feet 2, 238, Kentucky. A starting inside linebacker for the Eagles in Super Bowl XV.

BOBBY LEOPOLD

San Francisco 49ers, linebacker, 6 feet 1, 215, Notre Dame. A starting inside linebacker for the 49ers in Super Bowl XVI.

D. D. LEWIS

Dallas Cowboys, linebacker, 6 feet 1, 225, Mississippi State. A substitute in Super Bowls V and VI, he started at a linebacker position for the Cowboys in SB X, SB XII, and SB XIII, sharing with six other players the SB record for most games played.

In SB X, Lewis was involved in the unforgettable touchdown pass play in which Terry Bradshaw of the Pittsburgh Steelers completed a 64-yarder to Lynn Swann, but was knocked unconscious. At the snap, Lewis came across the line, but Bradshaw ducked under him and delivered, only to be hit by safety Cliff Harris.

Lewis again plagued Bradshaw in SB XIII, picking off a pass in the 1st quarter and running it back 21 yards.

FRANK LEWIS

Pittsburgh Steelers, wide receiver, 6 feet 1, 196, Grambling. Lewis started at a wide receiver position for the Steelers in Super Bowl IX, and caught 1 pass for 12 yards. He played as a substitute in SB X, but did not record any individual statistics.

TODD LIEBENSTEIN

Washington Redskins, defensive end, 6 feet 6, 245, Nevada/ Las Vegas. A substitute in Super Bowl XVII, Liebenstein started at defensive left end in SB XVIII.

BOB LILLY

Dallas Cowboys, defensive tackle, 6 feet 5, 260, Texas Christian. Starting defensive right tackle for the Cowboys in Super Bowls V and VI. Lilly was the object of a lot of the pregame concerns of the Miami Dolphins for SB VI. Jim Kiick of the Dolphins said before the game, "Even though they play great defense as a team, the name Lilly comes up when we talk about Dallas. His name just stands out." Kiick's words were prophetic. The Cowboys won the game, 24–3, shutting off Kiick and teammate Larry Csonka at 40 yards each.

JIM LINDSEY

Minnesota Vikings, running back, 6 feet 2, 210, Arkansas. Lindsey played as a substitute for the Vikings in Super Bowl IV.

RONNIE LIPPETT

New England Patriots, corner back, 5 feet 11, 180, Miami (Florida). Starting left corner back for the Patriots in Super Bowl XX.

Lippett was credited in unofficial statistics with 5 tackles and 2 defensed passes.

TONY LISCIO

Dallas Cowboys, tackle, 6 feet 5, 255, Tulsa. Liscio, who was on the Cowboys' roster but did not play in Super Bowl V, started at left tackle in SB VI.

LARRY LITTLE

Miami Dolphins, guard, 6 feet 1, 265, Bethune-Cookman. Starting right guard for the Dolphins in three straight Super Bowls—SB VI, SB VII, and SB VIII. Dolphins' line coach Monte Clark, quoted by writer Lou Sahadi, said of him, "Little's been outstanding for us. He's the kind of guy you're glad is on your side because he does everything well. He has an attitude when he leads a sweep that there's 'no way I can lose,' and that's just about what happens."

MIKE LIVINGSTON

Kansas City Chiefs, quarterback, 6 feet 3, 205, Southern Methodist. Livingston, who filled in for starter Len Dawson during the regular season, played as a substitute in Super Bowl IV, but did not record any individual statistics.

JERRY LOGAN

Baltimore Colts, defensive back, 6 feet 1, 190, West Texas State. Starting left safety for the Colts in Super Bowls III and V. In SB V he had 1 interception and also shared credit for forcing a fumble by tackling the Dallas Cowboys' Duane Thomas at the 1-yard line in the 3rd quarter. Teammate Jim Duncan recovered the ball.

RANDY LOGAN

Philadelphia Eagles, safety, 6 feet 1, 195, Michigan. Starting strong safety for the Eagles in Super Bowl XV.

BOB LONG

Green Bay Packers, flanker, 6 feet 3, 190, Wichita State. Long played as a reserve for the Packers in both Super Bowls I and II.

HOWIE LONG

Los Angeles Raiders, defensive end, 6 feet 5, 270, Villanova. Starting defensive left end for the Raiders in Super Bowl XVIII, he was credited with 5 tackles in the game.

CLINT LONGLEY

Dallas Cowboys, quarterback, 6 feet 1, 193, Abilene Chris- tian. Longley, a backup on the Cowboys' roster, did not play in Super Bowl X.

ED LOTHAMER

Kansas City Chiefs, defensive tackle, 6 feet 5, 270, Michigan State. Lothamer played as a substitute for the Chiefs in Super Bowl IV.

RONNIE LOTT

San Francisco 49ers, corner back, 6 feet, 199, Southern California. Lott started at left corner back for the 49ers in Super Bowls XVI and XIX, helping make up one of the strongest secondaries in pro football in the 1980s. Lott's second SB came after an injury-plagued season in which his ailments included a twisted ankle, sprained knee, jammed toe, and separated shoulder.

QUENTIN LOWRY

Washington Redskins, linebacker, 6 feet 2, 225, Youngstown State. Played as a substitute for the Redskins in Super Bowl XVII.

BOB LURTSEMA

Minnesota Vikings, defensive tackle and defensive end, 6 feet 6, 250, Western Michigan. Lurtsema played as a substitute for the Vikings in Super Bowls VIII and IX.

LENNY LYLES

Baltimore Colts, defensive back, 6 feet 2, 204, Louisville. Starting defensive right halfback and one of the captains for the Colts in Super Bowl III. Was credited with a hit that forced a fumble—the New York Jets' only turnover in the game.

JIM LYNCH

Kansas City Chiefs, linebacker, 6 feet 1, 235, Notre Dame. Starting right linebacker for the Chiefs in Super Bowl IV.

ROB LYTLE

Denver Broncos, running back, 6 feet 1, 198, Michigan. Though a reserve, Lytle ended up leading the Broncos in rushing in Super Bowl XII, carrying 10 times for 35 yards with a long run of 16 yards. He also scored once, on a 1-yard run. That touchdown, in the 3rd quarter, cut the Dallas Cowboys' lead to 20–10.

BILL (RED) MACK

Green Bay Packers, flanker, 5 feet 10, 185, Notre Dame. Mack played as a reserve for the Packers in Super Bowl I.

EARSELL MACKBEE

Minnesota Vikings, corner back, 6 feet, 195, Utah State. The starting left corner back for the Vikings in Super Bowl IV. Mackbee was involved in what turned out to be the final scoring play in the Kansas City Chiefs' victory. Chiefs' quarterback Len Dawson threw a short pass to receiver Otis Taylor on the Minnesota 41. Taylor broke tackles by Mackbee and Karl Kassulke on the way to a 46-yard score. Mackbee said later, "After that play, my arm went numb, and I didn't feel it any more."

JOHN MACKEY

Baltimore Colts, tight end, 6 feet 2, 224, Syracuse. A starter for the Colts in Super Bowls III and V, Mackey was involved in a 75-yard scoring play in SB V—a record for the longest pass play that was not broken for 12 years. With the Colts trailing the Dallas Cowboys, 6–0, quarterback Johnny Unitas threw a medium deep pass to Eddie Hinton. Hinton tipped the ball, defensive back Mel Renfro also touched it, and Mackey pulled it in at the Dallas 45 and ran untouched into the end zone. Renfro claimed he did not touch the ball, which would have made the reception illegal. The officials did not agree. Mackey finished the game with 2 receptions for 80 yards. In SB III, he finished with 3 receptions for 35 yards.

JACK MAITLAND

Baltimore Colts, running back, 6 feet 1, 210, Williams. Maitland played as a substitute for the Colts in Super Bowl V.

DAVE MANDERS

Dallas Cowboys, center, 6 feet 2, 250, Michigan State. Starting center for the Cowboys in Super Bowls V and VI. Credited along with teammate John Niland as having done such a good job that Miami Dolphin linebacker Nick Buoniconti left SB VI in a foggy daze.

JIM MANDICH

Miami Dolphins and Pittsburgh Steelers, tight end, 6 feet 2, 224, Michigan. Mandich played as a reserve for the Dolphins in Super Bowls VI and VII and started in SB VIII. After being obtained by the Steelers for the 1978 season, he played in SB XIII as a substitute.

Caught 1 pass for 9 yards in SB VI. Also had 1 reception in SB VII, but it was a key 19-yarder that gave the Dolphins the ball at the Washington Redskins' 2-yard line with 28 seconds remaining in the 1st half. Two plays later, Jim Kiick ran in for what proved to be the winning touchdown. In SB VIII, Mandich caught 2 passes for 21 yards. He did not record any individual statistics in SB XIII.

DEXTER MANLEY

Washington Redskins, defensive end, 6 feet 3, 240, Oklahoma State. Starting defensive right end for the Redskins in Super Bowls XVII and XVIII. He was credited with a key defensive play in SB XVII, when he forced a fumble in the 1st quarter. With the Miami Dolphins leading, 7–0, quarterback David Woodley pulled back from the line of scrimmage at the Washington 37, prepared to pass. But Manley charged in and hit him, forcing the ball loose. Teammate Dave Butz recovered the ball, the drive was blunted, and the Redskins went on to score a field goal.

CHARLES MANN

Washington Redskins, defensive end, 6 feet 6, 250, Nevada/ Reno. A top special teams player, Mann played as a substitute for the Redskins in Super Bowl XVIII.

ERROL MANN

Oakland Raiders, placekicker, 6 feet, 205, North Dakota. Mann had an up-and-down Super Bowl XI, making 2 of 3 field goal attempts and 2 of 4 point-after-touchdowns. Mann's first miss came on the first possession of the game, as the Raiders drove to the Minnesota Vikings' 11. Mann's attempted 29-yarder hit the left upright. The next two times he got a

118

chance, Mann didn't miss, hitting from 24 yards, to put his team ahead, 3–0, and again from 40, to put his team ahead, 16–0, at halftime.

BRISON MANOR

Denver Broncos, defensive end, 6 feet 4, 247, Arkansas. Manor, a rookie, played as a substitute for the Broncos in Super Bowl XII.

RAY MANSFIELD

Pittsburgh Steelers, center, 6 feet 3, 260, Washington. The starting center for the Steelers in Super Bowls IX and X.

BOBBY MAPLES

Denver Broncos, center, 6 feet 3, 250, Baylor. Played as a substitute for the Broncos in Super Bowl XII.

KEN MARGERUM

Chicago Bears, wide receiver, 6 feet, 180, Stanford. Margerum, a substitute in Super Bowl XX, caught 2 passes for 36 yards, including a long pass of 29 yards. That completion came during a Bears' 1st-half drive. The drive ended with a 24-yard field goal and a 23–3 Bears' lead at halftime.

ED MARINARO

Minnesota Vikings, running back, 6 feet 2, 212, Cornell. Marinaro's name first gained fame as a record-setting collegiate football player, then as a member of the Minnesota Vikings. A decade later, he would become even better known for his role in the highly rated TV series *Hill Street Blues.* Marinaro's Super Bowl ap-

Ed Marinaro

pearances were limited to backup roles. In SB VIII, he gained 3 yards on 1 carry and caught 2 passes for 39 yards, including a long pass of 27 yards. In SB IX, he did not record any individual statistics.

DAN MARINO

Miami Dolphins, quarterback, 6 feet 4, 214, Pittsburgh.

Dan Marino

What a season Marino had in 1984! It was only his second season in the pros, but he set several league passing records, was named the NFL's most valuable player by several news organizations, and was even picked as the most popular professional football player in America by a CBS/*New York Times* poll. That luck, however, did not continue in Super Bowl XIX, as the Dolphins were soundly beaten, 38–16.

San Francisco quarterback Joe Montana ended up being named the game's MVP—remember the Marino/Montana soda pop commercials filmed after the game?—but it was the 49er defense that really ruled, holding the Dolphins scoreless the final 2 quarters.

Marino helped the Dolphins score the first time they had the ball, on a 37-yard field goal by Uwe von Schamann, with the key play a 25-yard completion from Marino to Tony Nathan. San Francisco then came back to take a 7–3 lead. The Dolphins then scored their only touchdown of the game on the next series, as Marino hit Mark Clayton twice, for 18 and 13 yards, and Dan Johnson once, for 21 yards, to set up a 2-yard scoring pass to Johnson. But the 49ers scored 3 times, to go up, 28–10, before Miami finished the half with a pair of field goals by Von Schamann.

But the 49ers' front line began to wear the Dolphins down. And Miami's fine receivers, Clayton and Duper, were troubled constantly by the 49er defense. Marino ended up sacked 4 times, a career high. And though he finished with 29 completions in 50 attempts—both SB records—and 318 yards, most of the yardage came in the 4th quarter. He also was intercepted twice.

Marino finished the game with 1 carry for no yardage and 1 fumble, which he recovered.

It was a disgusted Marino, who stormed into the locker-room and raged at reporters. Later, more composed, he said, "Sometimes I didn't throw the ball well, sometimes I didn't have time, and sometimes guys didn't get open. . . . We knew what we had to do—we had to throw the ball against a 4-man line—and we didn't."

FRED MARION

New England Patriots, free safety, 6 feet 2, 191, Miami (Florida). Starting free safety for the Patriots in Super Bowl XX. He was credited with 6 tackles and 1 assist in the unofficial statistics.

JIM MARSALIS

Kansas City Chiefs, defensive back, 5 feet 11, 194, Tennessee State. Starting left corner back for the Chiefs in Super Bowl IV.

JIM MARSHALL

Minnesota Vikings, defensive end, 6 feet 3, 247, Ohio State. Marshall, a rugged member of the Vikings' celebrated front four, started at right end in 4 Super Bowls—SB IV, SB VIII, SB IX, and SB XI.

WILBER MARSHALL

Chicago Bears, linebacker, 6 feet 1, 225, Florida. Starting right linebacker for the Bears' overwhelming defense in Super Bowl XX, Marshall was credited with 4 tackles and 1 shared sack, and also recovered 1 fumble. He and teammate Richard Dent sacked New England quarterback Tony

Eason on third-and-10 with the ball on the Patriots' 41 midway through the 1st quarter, forcing a punt. In the 2nd half, with the Bears ahead, 37–3, New England quarterback Steve Grogan hit wide receiver Stanley Morgan, but he fumbled on the New England 37, and Marshall recovered.

AMOS MARTIN

Minnesota Vikings, linebacker, 6 feet 3, 228, Louisville. Played as a substitute for the Vikings in Super Bowls VIII, IX, and XI.

HARVEY MARTIN

Dallas Cowboys, defensive end, 6 feet 5, 250, East Texas State. Martin was one of only four defensive players to win the MVP award in a Super Bowl—sharing the honor with defensive teammate Randy White the only time the award has been shared. The two were honored after the Cowboys' 27–10 victory over the Denver Broncos in SB XII.

In the game, the Dallas defense rattled Denver quarterbacks Craig Morton and Norris Weese, who completed a total of only 8 of 25 passes, with 4 interceptions. In fact, the Broncos finished with only one first down passing and 35 net yards gained in the air.

The two co-MVPs helped set up Dallas' first touchdown as they pressured Morton into throwing a pass that was intercepted by safe-

Harvey Martin

ty Randy Hughes on the 25-yard line. Five plays later, Tony Dorsett scored to give Dallas a 7–0 lead.

Martin helped set up Dallas' final touchdown in the 4th quarter when he sacked Morton's replacement, Norris Weese, who fumbled. Aaron Kyle recovered for Dallas, which scored on the next play.

For Martin, the NFC victory, which broke a 5-game AFC streak, was important: "That was very personal to me. . . . No one wants to see his league degraded. The NFC is not a bush league."

Martin also forced a turnover in SB XIII against the Pittsburgh Steelers when he sacked quarterback Terry Bradshaw on a third-down play near the end of the 1st quarter. Ed (Too Tall) Jones recovered on the Steeler 41, but the Cowboys failed to capitalize on the break. He also played in SB X.

ROD MARTIN

Oakland and Los Angeles Raiders, linebacker, 6 feet 2, 210, Southern California. Martin went into Super Bowl XV an unheralded starting linebacker. He came out with a record 3 interceptions off the Philadelphia Eagles' Ron Jaworski and a newfound fame.

Martin's first interception came early—on the third play of the game. He picked the ball off at the Philadelphia 47 and ran it to the 30. Seven plays later, the Raiders scored to go ahead, 7–0. Martin's second interception, in the 3rd quarter, led to a field goal and a 24–3 Oakland lead. His final interception cut off Philadelphia's final drive at the Raider 37.

Martin was no less a hero in SB XVIII, finishing the game with 6 tackles, 1 sack for a loss of 7

Rod Martin

122

yards, and 1 fumble recovery. One of the tackles came in a key fourth-and-1 in the 3rd quarter, as Martin stopped the Washington Redskins' running back John Riggins.

SALADIN MARTIN

San Francisco 49ers, corner back, 6 feet 1, 180, San Diego State. On the 49ers' roster for Super Bowl XVI, Martin did not play.

RICH MARTINI

Oakland Raiders, wide receiver, 6 feet 2, 185, California/ Davis. Martini played as a substitute in Super Bowl XV but did not record any individual statistics.

MICKEY MARVIN

Oakland and Los Angeles Raiders, guard, 6 feet 4, 270, Tennessee. Starting right guard for the Raiders in Super Bowls XV and XVIII. The Raiders' offensive line gave up only 5 sacks in 3 playoff games in 1983–84 season.

LINDSEY MASON

Oakland Raiders, tackle and guard, 6 feet 5, 265, Kansas. Played as a substitute for the Raiders in Super Bowl XV.

BOB MATHESON

Miami Dolphins, linebacker, 6 feet 4, 240, Duke. Played as a substitute for the Dolphins in three Super Bowls—SB VI, SB VII, and SB VIII.

BILL MATHIS

New York Jets, running back, 6 feet 1, 220, Clemson. A member of the original New York Titans, Mathis made the transition to the Jets, and in Super Bowl III, he carried 3 times for 2 yards and caught 3 passes for 20 yards.

TOM MATTE

Baltimore Colts, running back, 6 feet, 214, Ohio State. The Colts' starting halfback set a Super Bowl record in SB III with a 58-yard run in the 1st half against the New York Jets. But after putting his team on the New York 16, Matte saw the drive end with an interception. Matte was also involved in a bizarre play at the end of the half, as he took a handoff from quarterback Earl Morrall, then passed back to Morrall, who failed to see his end, Jimmy Orr, wide open near the goal line. Instead, Morrall passed toward fullback Jerry Hill. But the ball was intercepted.

Matte fumbled away the ball on the first play from scrimmage of the 2nd half, the Jets recovered and used the turnover to kick a field goal, to take a 10–0 lead. Matte finished with 11 carries for 116 yards and 2 receptions for 30 yards.

IRA MATTHEWS

Oakland Raiders, kick returner, wide receiver, and running back, 5 feet 8, 175, Wisconsin. Matthews, primarily a special-teams player, returned 2 punts for a total of 1 yard and 2 kickoffs for a total of 29 yards.

JOHN MATUSZAK

Oakland Raiders, defensive end, 6 feet 8, 280, Tampa. Matuszak, a colorful character who has carved out a side career as an actor on television and movies, started at defensive left end for the Raiders in Super Bowls XI and

John Matuszak

XV. Before SB XV, Matuszak had proclaimed himself the Raiders' "Enforcer" for curfew purposes. But several nights before the game, he was seen partying in New Orleans, the site of the game, until 4 A.M. He ended up being fined $1,000. In the game, Matuszak was credited with keeping the pressure on Eagles quarterback Ron Jaworski. And responding to the pregame talk, which compared Philadelphia's regimented style to the more open Oakland approach, Matuszak said afterward, "We played an intelligent, aggressive game. Philadelphia didn't."

ANDY MAURER

Minnesota Vikings and Denver Broncos, guard, 6 feet 3, 247, Oregon. Started at left guard for the Vikings in Super Bowl IX, then, after being released by several teams, joined the Denver Broncos, for which he started at left tackle in SB XII.

TOM MAXWELL

Baltimore Colts, corner back, 6 feet 2, 195, Texas A&M. Played as a substitute for the Colts in Super Bowl V.

MARK MAY

Washington Redskins, guard, 6 feet 6, 288, Pittsburgh. Starting right guard for the Redskins in Super Bowls XVII and XVIII. One of the original members of the Redskins' Hogs front line, May led the way to many of running back John Riggins' strong performances.

RAY MAY

Baltimore Colts, linebacker, 6 feet 1, 230, Southern California. Starting left linebacker for the Colts in Super Bowl V. May was one of several Colts players given credit for forcing a fumble on their own goal line early in the 3rd quarter. Trailing 13–3, the Colts' backs were to the goal line. Running back Duane Thomas made a second-effort dive, but was hit on the 1, the ball was jarred loose, and the Colts recovered. Credit for the hit was shared by safety Jerry Logan, lineman Billy Ray Smith, and May.

DON MAYNARD

New York Jets, flanker, 6 feet 1, 179, Texas/El Paso. A holdover from the New York Titans, Maynard started for the Jets in Super Bowl III.

JERRY MAYS

Kansas City Chiefs, defensive end, 6 feet 4, 252, Southern Methodist. Starting left end for the Chiefs in both Super Bowls I and IV. In SB IV, he was part of Chiefs' defensive line that frustrated Minnesota quarterbacks Joe Kapp and Gary Cuozzo.

CARL McADAMS

New York Jets, defensive tackle and linebacker, 6 feet 3, 245, Oklahoma. Played as a substitute for the Jets in Super Bowl III.

BRENT McCLANAHAN

Minnesota Vikings, running back and kick returner, 5 feet 10, 202, Arizona State. McClanahan returned 1 kickoff for 22 yards in Super Bowl IX, then carried 3 times for 3 yards in SB XI, when he started in the backfield. McClanahan fumbled in the 1st quarter, as his team failed to capitalize on a blocked punt that gave them the ball on the Oakland Raider 3. Two plays later, McClanahan lost the ball, and the Raiders recovered it, then went 90 yards to put the first points on the board with a field goal.

RANDY McCLANAHAN

Oakland Raiders, linebacker, 6 feet 5, 255, Southwestern Louisiana. Played as a substitute for the Raiders in Super Bowl XV.

CURTIS McCLINTON

Kansas City Chiefs, running back and tight end, 6 feet 3, 227, Kansas. A backfield starter for the Chiefs in Super Bowl I, he played as a tight end in SB IV. McClinton scored the Chiefs' first touchdown in SB I, as the team capped a drive with a 7-yard pass from Len Dawson to McClinton in the 2nd quarter. McClinton finished with 6 carries for 16 yards and 2 receptions for 34 yards. He also fumbled once, but recovered the ball.

KENT McCLOUGHAN

Oakland Raiders, defensive back, 6 feet 1, 190, Nebraska. Starting defensive left halfback for the Raiders in Super Bowl II. McCloughan was one of two Raider defenders—neither of whom, according to reports, was assigned— to have a shot at Green Bay Packer receiver Boyd Dowler on the way to a 62-yard scoring play, a pass from Bart Starr. Starr hit Dowler in the middle and ran the rest of the way untouched. Dowler was quoted as saying, "I just bulled by McCloughan. He was playing me tight and he bumped me and I ran through him. . . . When I got by him, there was no one left to stop me."

MILT McCOLL

San Francisco 49ers, linebacker, 6 feet 6, 220, Stanford. Played as a substitute for the 49ers in Super Bowls XVI and XIX. In SB XVI McColl recovered a fumble with 5 seconds left in the 1st half, to allow the 49ers to score 2 field goals within 13 seconds. Later, with the 49ers leading 17–0, the Cincinnati Bengals' Archie Griffin bobbled the kickoff, and McColl grabbed the ball on the 4-yard line. After a 49er penalty, Ray Wersching delivered from 26 yards.

SAM McCULLUM

Minnesota Vikings, wide receiver and kick returner, 6 feet 2, 203, Montana State. McCullum returned 3 punts for 11 yards and 1 kickoff for 26 yards in Super Bowl IX.

LAWRENCE McCUTCHEON

Los Angeles Rams, running back, 6 feet 1, 205, Colorado State. McCutcheon put the Rams ahead, 19–17, in Super Bowl XIV by throwing for a touchdown in the 3rd quarter. With the ball on Pittsburgh Steelers' 24, quarterback Vince Ferragamo handed off to McCutcheon, who swept right, stopped, and then threw a 24-yard pass to Ron Smith for a touchdown. In his more traditional role, McCutcheon ran 5 times for 10 yards and caught 1 pass for 16 yards.

LeCHARLS McDANIEL

Washington Redskins, corner back, 5 feet 9, 169, Cal Poly/San Luis Obispo. McDaniel played as a substitute in Super Bowl XVII.

RON McDOLE

Washington Redskins, defensive end, 6 feet 4, 265, Nebraska. Starting defensive left end for the Redskins in Super Bowl VII. At 32, and a veteran of 12 seasons, McDole was typical of Coach George Allen's Over-the-Hill Gang.

VANN McELROY

Los Angeles Raiders, safety, 6 feet 2, 190, Baylor. Starting free safety for the Raiders in Super Bowl XVIII.

MAX McGEE

Green Bay Packers, end, 6 feet 3, 205, Tulane. McGee started neither Super Bowls I nor II, but became one of the first game's heroes.

McGee came in after the second play of SB I, when teammate Boyd Dowler reinjured a troublesome shoulder. At 34, McGee had spent the night before the game with teammate Paul Hornung, expressing doubt he would even get in.

On the Packers' second possession, quarterback Bart Starr threw from the KC 37, a pass that seemed to be behind McGee and covered well by the Chiefs' Willie Mitchell. But at the KC 20, McGee reached back with his right hand and brought the ball forward and under his arm without breaking stride. Mitchell was left behind, and the Packers scored first.

McGee scored another touchdown in the 3rd quarter, as he waited in the end zone for a 13-yard pass from Starr. In all, McGee caught 7 passes for 138 yards.

In SB II, history repeated itself faithfully. McGee again did not expect to play, but again replaced Dowler, who again came out with an injury. And once more McGee caught a key pass, this time for 35 yards on third down from the Packer 40, to set up a Packer touchdown. Donny Anderson's 2-yard touchdown run put the Packers ahead, 23–7.

After the second game, McGee said, "I was kidding Dowler before the game, telling him to get hurt so I could catch one more pass. Damned if he didn't. Damned if I didn't."

McGee's 138 yards receiving in the first game held up as an SB record until 1976, when broken by Lynn Swann.

TONY McGEE

Washington Redskins, defensive end, 6 feet 4, 250, Bishop. McGee played as a substitute for the Redskins in both Super Bowls XVII and XVIII.

127

MIKE McGILL

Minnesota Vikings, linebacker, 6 feet 2, 235, Notre Dame. McGill played as a substitute for the Vikings in Super Bowl IV.

MARK McGRATH

Washington Redskins, wide receiver, 5 feet 11, 175, Montana State. A free-agent signee, McGrath was on the Redskins' roster but did not play in Super Bowl XVIII.

LARRY McGREW

New England Patriots, linebacker, 6 feet 5, 233, Southern California. Starting right inside linebacker for the Patriots in Super Bowl XX. McGrew was credited with 3 tackles and 3 assists in the unofficial statistics, and also recovered 1 fumble. The fumble was one of the few bright spots in the Patriots' game. It occurred on the second play from scrimmage, as Chicago Bears' running back Walter Payton was hit and dropped the ball. McGrew recovered it on the Chicago 19, and the Patriots seemed ready to shock the Bears. But New England was held to a field goal, the Bears quickly came back, and the advantage was lost.

PAT McINALLY

Cincinnati Bengals, punter and wide receiver, 6 feet 6, 212, Harvard. McInally handled the Bengals' punting duties for Super Bowl XVI and punted 3 times for an average of 43.7 yards, with a long punt of 53 yards.

GUY McINTYRE

San Francisco 49ers, guard, 6 feet 3, 271, Georgia. A rookie backup in SB XIX, McIntyre picked up a squib kick at the end of the 1st half and fumbled when tackled, allowing the Miami Dolphins to gain possession. The Dolphins then kicked a field goal as time expired, to cut the 49ers' lead to 28–16 at the intermission.

ODIS McKINNEY

Oakland and Los Angeles Raiders, corner back, 6 feet 2, 190, Colorado. McKinney played as a substitute in both Super Bowls XV and XVIII, recording two tackles in SB XVIII.
G

DENNIS McKINNON

Chicago Bears, wide receiver, 6 feet 1, 185, Florida State. A starting wide receiver for the Bears in Super Bowl XX, he did not record any individual statistics.

DANA McLEMORE

San Francisco 49ers, corner back and kick returner, 5 feet 10,

183, Hawaii. McLemore handled punt-returning duties for the 49ers in Super Bowl XIX and twice gave the team good field position from which it scored. He finished with 5 returns for a total of 51 yards and a long return of 28 yards. He also fumbled once.

HAROLD McLINTON

Washington Redskins, linebacker, 6 feet 2, 235, Southern University. Played as a substitute for the Redskins in Super Bowl VII.

JIM McMAHON

Chicago Bears, quarterback, 6 feet 1, 190, Brigham Young. Brash, outspoken and slightly wacky at times, McMahon was one of the pregame stars of Super Bowl XX. And like the Jets' Joe Namath, he didn't disappoint when play began.

McMahon spent the pre-SB weeks fending off reports he had called the women of New Orleans (the game's site) "sluts," getting stuck by an acupuncturist to relieve a sore rear end, and keeping the press guessing as to what he would spell out on the headband he wore under his helmet during the game.

He spent the game completing 12 of 20 passes for 256 yards and rushing 5 times for 14 yards and 2 touchdowns—a record for a quarterback.

Jim McMahon

On the Bears' second possession—after Walter Payton's fumble led to a quick New England field goal—McMahon completed a 43-yard pass to Willie Gault to help set up a tying field goal.

In the 2nd quarter, he ran the ball in from the 2 as the Bears took a 20–3 lead. On the Bears' first possession of the 2nd half, he finished a drive with a 1-yard touchdown run to give his team a 30–3 lead, a drive he began with a 60-yard completion to Gault.

Naturally, McMahon was the object of much praise after the game. His coach, Mike Ditka, said, "McMahon put a lot of critics to rest. He is our trigger man, and I love him."

JOHN McMAKIN

Pittsburgh Steelers, tight end, 6 feet 3, 232, Clemson. Played as a substitute for the Steelers in Super Bowl IX.

HERB McMATH

Oakland Raiders, defensive end, 6 feet 4, 245, Morningside. Played as a substitute in Super Bowl XI.

STEVE McMICHAEL

Chicago Bears, defensive tackle, 6 feet 2, 260, Texas. Starting defensive left tackle for the Bears in Super Bowl XX. He was credited with 1 sack for a 5-yard loss, on New England's Steve Grogan in the 2nd half.

DON McNEAL

Miami Dolphins, corner back, 5 feet 11, 192, Alabama. Started at right corner back for the Dolphins in Super Bowl XVII, and at left corner back in SB XIX. A slip in SB XVII may have cost the Dolphins a touchdown and the game. Early in the 4th quarter, with the Washington Redskins facing fourth-and-1 at the Dolphins' 43, McNeal lined up, then went in motion, keeping pace with the Redskins' tight end, Clint Didier. Didier made a quick move, McNeal slipped, then regained his footing. It wasn't fast enough, though, as Redskins' back John Riggins headed to the open area. McNeal lunged, got a hold of Riggins' jersey, but was not able to stop him, as Riggins ran 43 yards for the touchdown and a 19–17 lead.

CLIFTON McNEIL

Washington Redskins, wide receiver, 6 feet 2, 187, Grambling. McNeil played as a substitute for the Redskins in Super Bowl VII.

FRED McNEILL

Minnesota Vikings, linebacker, 6 feet 2, 229, UCLA. McNeill, a substitute in both Super Bowls IX and XI, seemed to put the Vikings in good shape to open scoring in SB XI when he blocked Ray Guy's punt in the 1st quarter, and was tackled by Guy at the Oakland Raiders' 3. But the Vikings fumbled the ball away 2 plays later.

ROD McSWAIN

New England Patriots, corner back, 6 feet 1, 198, Clemson. Played as a substitute for the Patriots in Super Bowl XX. He was credited with a pair of tackles.

WARREN McVEA

Kansas City Chiefs, running back, 5 feet 10, 182, Houston.

McVea, a substitute, carried 12 times for 26 yards, with a long run of 9 yards, in Super Bowl IV.

DAN MEDLIN

Oakland Raiders, guard, 6 feet 4, 252, North Carolina State. Played as a substitute on defense for the Raiders in Super Bowl XI.

MAT MENDENHALL

Washington Redskins, defensive end, 6 feet 6, 255, Brigham Young. Starting defensive left end for the Redskins in Super Bowl XVII.

CHUCK MERCEIN

Green Bay Packers, running back, 6 feet 2, 225, Yale. The Packers picked up Mercein from the Washington Redskins' taxi squad midway through the 1967 season after a spate of injuries. He started several regular-season games, then played in Super Bowl II as a backup, carrying the ball once for no gain.

MIKE MERCER

Kansas City Chiefs, kicker, 6 feet, 210, Arizona State. Mercer handled the Chiefs' placekicking duties in Super Bowl I. He made 1 of 2 field-goal attempts, missing on a 40-yarder in the 1st quarter, then making a 31-yarder with less than a minute remaining in the 1st half to cut the Packers' lead to 14–10 at the intermission. He also made his only point-after-touchdown attempt.

CURT MERZ

Kansas City Chiefs, guard, 6 feet 4, 267, Iowa. Starting right guard for the Chiefs in Super Bowl I.

LOU MICHAELS

Baltimore Colts, defensive end and kicker, 6 feet 2, 250, Kentucky. Michaels handled the Colts' kicking duties in Super Bowl III, missing on field-goal attempts of 27 and 46 yards, but making his only point-after attempt. He pulled off a successful onsides kick in the final minutes, but the Colts did not score.

Before the game, he had made news by supposedly having a confrontation in a restaurant with the NY Jets' Joe Namath. But news service reports, Michaels said later, were exaggerated, and he actually got a ride back to his hotel from Namath. Michaels' older brother Walt was an assistant coach with the Jets.

MATT MILLEN

Oakland and Los Angeles Raiders, linebacker, 6 feet 2, 260,

Penn State. A starting linebacker for the Raiders in both Super Bowls XV and XVIII, he was considered one of the keys to the team's strong running defense. In SB XVIII, he was credited with 8 tackles and 1 quarterback sack for a minus 7 yards.

BILL MILLER

Oakland Raiders, end, 6 feet, 190, Miami. The starting left end for the Raiders in Super Bowl II, Miller caught a pair of 23-yard touchdown passes from Daryle Lamonica in the losing effort against the Green Bay Packers. His first scoring catch put the Raiders back in the game after the Packers had gone ahead, 13–0. Miller had slipped behind Packer defender Tom Brown in the end zone. Brown said later, "I played [Miller] too soft. . . . I should have taken him. But I didn't."

Miller's second touchdown was scored with the Raiders behind, 33–7. Again, he burned Brown on the play. Miller finished with 5 receptions for 84 yards.

FRED MILLER

Baltimore Colts, defensive tackle, 6 feet 3, 250, Louisiana State. Starting defensive right tackle for the Colts in Super Bowls III and V.

JIM MILLER

San Francisco 49ers, punter, 5 feet 11, 183, Mississippi. Miller handled the 49ers' punting duties in Super Bowl XVI, punting 4 times for an average of 46.3 yards and a long punt of 50 yards.

ROBERT MILLER

Minnesota Vikings, running back, 5 feet 11, 204, Kansas. Miller, a substitute in SB XI, carried the ball 2 times for 4 yards and caught 4 passes for 19 yards, including a long reception of 13 yards.

RICH MILOT

Washington Redskins, linebacker, 6 feet 4, 237, Penn State. Milot started on the right side for the Redskins in both Super Bowls XVII and XVIII.

CLAUDIE MINOR

Denver Broncos, tackle, 6 feet 4, 280, San Diego State. Starting right tackle for the Broncos in Super Bowl XII.

GEORGE MIRA

Miami Dolphins, quarterback, 5 feet 11, 192, Miami. Mira, on the Dolphins' roster for Super Bowl VI, did not play.

132

TOM MITCHELL

Baltimore Colts, tight end, 6 feet 2, 235, Bucknell. Mitchell played as a substitute for the Colts in both Super Bowls III and V.

In SB III, he was involved in several key plays. First, after a fumble recovery had given the Colts the ball deep in NY Jets' territory in the 1st quarter, Mitchell broke free from the defensive coverage and was free in the end zone. Quarterback Earl Morrall threw, but a leaping Al Atkinson grazed the ball, which then bounced off Mitchell's shoulder pads and was intercepted by Randy Beverly. Later, he was involved in a brief altercation with Jets' defensive back Johnny Sample, slapping Sample in the head with his empty helmet. Finally, Mitchell recovered Lou Michaels' onsides kick attempt in the final minutes, but the Colts could not score again. He finished the game with 1 catch for 15 yards. In SB V, he did not record any individual statistics.

WILLIE MITCHELL

Kansas City Chiefs, defensive back, 6 feet 1, 185, Tennessee State. The starting defensive right halfback for the Chiefs in Super Bowl I, he played as a reserve in SB IV. He was covering the Green Bay Packers' Max McGee when McGee made a spectacular catch for the first score of SB I. Mitchell, whose area the Packers picked on often during the game, later intercepted a pass off Starr in the 4th quarter.

ART MONK

Washington Redskins, wide receiver, 6 feet 3, 209, Syracuse. Monk, who missed Super Bowl XVII because of a stress fracture of the foot, started for the Redskins in SB XVIII. He caught only 1 pass for 26 yards as the LA Raiders shut down the Redskins.

CARL MONROE

San Francisco 49ers, running back and kick returner, 5 feet 8, 166, Utah. Monroe caught only one pass in Super Bowl XIX, but it was a big one, as it went for a 33-yard touchdown to open the 49ers' scoring in the game. Quarterback Joe Montana, seeing Monroe open on the right sideline, threw a pass over linebacker Mark Brown's head and past safety Lyle Blackwood. Monroe lost Blackwood and corner back Don McNeal to score. Monroe also returned 1 kickoff for 16 yards.

JOE MONTANA

San Francisco 49ers, quarterback, 6 feet 2, 200, Notre Dame. Montana went into Super Bowl XIX with a lot of impressive credentials under his belt—including the MVP award in SB XVI, when he led the 49ers over the Cincinnati Bengals, 26–21. But the pregame talk to XIX seemed to revolve more around Dan Marino, the young quarterback of the Miami Dolphins.

So who came out on top? Add a second MVP award to Montana's shelves, as he picked apart the Dolphin defense on the way to a 38–16 victory.

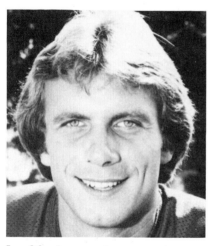

Joe Montana

For the record, Montana completed 14 of 22 passes for 157 yards and 1 touchdown in SB XVI, rushing 6 times for 18 yards and 1 touchdown. He scored the opening touchdown on a 1-yard run, then threw an 11-yard scoring pass to Earl Cooper to put San Francisco ahead, 14–0. When Cincinnati cut the 49ers' lead to 20–14 in the 4th quarter, he drove San Francisco 50 yards to a 40-yard field goal by Ray Wersching.

Montana's statistics were even more impressive in SB XIX, as he completed 24 of 35 attempts for 331 yards—an SB record for most yards gained in a game. He threw 3 touchdown passes, was not intercepted, and ran 5 times for 59 yards, a record for a quarterback.

After the second game, 49er Coach Bill Walsh said, "There was a lot of talk before the game about Marino . . . but I truly believe that Joe Montana is the finest quarterback in the game today."

Montana himself was modest in describing his own play: "When you have that much time to throw, you're going to be successful. I just can't say enough about the way our offensive line played."

BLANCHARD MONTGOMERY

San Francisco 49ers, line-backer, 6 feet 2, 236, UCLA. A special-teams standout, Montgomery played in Super Bowl XIX.

CLE MONTGOMERY

Los Angeles Raiders, wide receiver and kick returner, 5 feet 8, 180, Abilene Christian. Played as a substitute for the Raiders in Super Bowl XVIII. His older brother Wilbert also played in the SB (on following page).

WILBERT MONTGOMERY

Philadelphia Eagles, running back, 5 feet 10, 195, Abilene Christian. Started in the backfield for the Eagles in Super Bowl XV, carrying 16 times for 44 yards and catching 6 passes for 91 yards to lead the Eagles in both categories. One of his catches, for 25 yards, was a key in the Eagles' first scoring drive, which ended with a field goal. Brother of the Raiders' Cle (on preceding page).

MIKE MONTLER

Denver Broncos, center, 6 feet 4, 250, Colorado. Starting center for the Broncos in Super Bowl XII.

MAX MONTOYA

Cincinnati Bengals, guard, 6 feet 5, 275, UCLA. Starting right guard for the Bengals in Super Bowl XVI.

KEITH MOODY

Oakland Raiders, corner back and kick returner, 5 feet 11, 175, Syracuse. Moody returned 1 kickoff for 19 yards in SB XV.

BLAKE MOORE

Cincinnati Bengals, center and tackle, 6 feet 5, 267, Wooster. A free agent, Moore played as a substitute in Super Bowl XVI.

MANFRED MOORE

Oakland Raiders, running back, 6 feet, 200, Southern California. Moore played as a substitute for the Raiders in Super Bowl XI.

MAULTY MOORE

Miami Dolphins, defensive tackle, 6 feet 5, 265, Bethune-Cookman. Moore, a rookie, played as a substitute in Super Bowl VII, then again in SB VIII.

NAT MOORE

Miami Dolphins, wide receiver, 5 feet 9, 188, Florida. Moore played in Super Bowl XIX as an 11-year veteran and caught 2 passes for 17 yards. He also played as a substitute in SB XVII, but did not record any individual statistics.

STEVE MOORE

New England Patriots, guard and tackle, 6 feet 4, 285, Tennessee State. Starting right tackle for the Patriots in Super Bowl XX.

WAYNE MOORE

Miami Dolphins, tackle, 6 feet 6, 265, Lamar. A substitute in

Super Bowl VI, he started at left tackle in SB VII and SB VIII. He was an underrated (according to the coaches) member of the front line that blocked so successfully for Jim Kiick and Larry Csonka.

EMERY MOOREHEAD

Chicago Bears, tight end, 6 feet 2, 220, Colorado. The starting tight end for the Bears in Super Bowl XX, he caught 2 passes for 22 yards, with a long reception of 14 yards.

MO MOORMAN

Kansas City Chiefs, guard, 6 feet 5, 252, Texas A & M. Starting right guard for the Chiefs in Super Bowl IV. He was one of three blockers to help open a huge hole for running back Mike Garrett as he ran 5 yards for a touchdown to help put the Chiefs ahead, 16–0.

STANLEY MORGAN

New England Patriots, wide receiver, 5 feet 11, 181, Tennessee. A starting wide receiver for the Patriots in Super Bowl XX. He finished the team's leading receiver with 7 receptions for 70 yards and a long reception of 19 yards. He fumbled once in the 2nd half, following a reception, the Bears recovered and went on to score a touchdown that gave them a 44–3 lead.

EARL MORRALL

Baltimore Colts and Miami Dolphins, quarterback, 6 feet 2, 206, Michigan State. Before Super Bowl III, a brash Joe Namath said that Morrall wasn't much of a quarterback. Unfortunately for Morrall, SB III didn't do much to prove otherwise.

Morrall completed only 6 of 17 attempts for 71 yards and 3 interceptions and could not get the Colts into the end zone, as heavily favored Baltimore was upset by the NY Jets, 16–7.

One of Morrall's most-remembered miscues in the game came at the end of the 1st half, when he missed an open receiver and what may have been a sure touchdown.

With the Jets leading, 7–0, and 25 seconds left in the half, Baltimore had the ball at the NY 41. The Colts tried a flea flicker play, with Morrall handing off to

Earl Morrall

136

back Tom Matte, who ran to the right, pivoted, then passed back to Morrall. End Jimmy Orr was downfield, near the goal line, waving for the ball with no defenders in sight. Morrall appeared to see him, but passed over the middle toward back Jerry Hill. But Jets' safety Jim Hudson picked the ball off, and the Colts ended the half scoreless. Morrall later said, "The way I caught the ball from Matte, I was turned to the right and didn't see Orr."

Near the end of the 3rd quarter, Morrall was pulled in favor of Johnny Unitas.

In SB V, the error-ridden "Stupor Bowl," the situation was all but reversed, as Unitas started and Morrall relieved after the starter was injured. And this time the Colts won, on a time-running-out field goal. Morrall was 7 of 15 for 147 yards, with 1 interception.

Colts' Coach Don McCafferty said that Unitas could have returned to the game, but he decided to keep Morrall in. "I stuck with Earl because Earl was doing a fine job."

Morrall was also a member of the Miami Dolphins for SB VII and SB VIII, but played only on special teams.

EUGENE (MERCURY) MORRIS

Miami Dolphins, running back and kick returner, 5 feet 10, 190, West Texas State. In 1970 Eugene Morris gave the Dolphins

Mercury Morris

a three-pronged running attack, along with teammates Jim Kiick and Larry Csonka. After a loss in Super Bowl VI, the Dolphins went through the next season undefeated and became the first team in NFL history to have two running backs (Morris and Csonka) with over 1,000 yards. In all, Morris played in three SBs—SB VI, SB VII, and SB VIII.

His statistics: SB VI, 4 kickoff returns for 90 yards with a long return of 37 yards; SB VII, 10 carries for 34 yards with a long of 6 yards and 2 kickoff returns for 33 yards and a long of 17; and SB VIII, 11 carries for 34 yards with a long of 14.

Morris was later arrested and sentenced to 20 years in prison for cocaine trafficking and conspiracy. In 1986, however, the Florida Supreme Court ordered a new trial and though found guilty, Morris was given credit for the time he had spent in prison and released.

GUY MORRISS

Philadelphia Eagles and New England Patriots, center and guard, 6 feet 4, 255, Texas Christian. A starter for the Eagles at center in Super Bowl XV, Morriss was picked up as a free agent by the Patriots in 1984 and played as a substitute for the team in SB XX.

Craig Morton

JIM MORRISSEY

Chicago Bears, linebacker, 6 feet 3, 215, Michigan State. Morrissey, playing in a reserve role in Super Bowl XX, picked off a Steve Grogan pass midway through the 4th quarter and ran the ball back 47 yards to the New England 5-yard line, one of 2 interceptions made by the Bears' defense in the game.

CRAIG MORTON

Dallas Cowboys and Denver Broncos, quarterback, 6 feet 4, 214, California. Talk about irony. Here was Morton, a 13-year veteran at the age of 34, leading the young Denver Broncos into Super Bowl XII. And whom was he to face but his old team, the Dallas Cowboys, whom he had helped lead in SB V, and their quarter-back, Roger Staubach, who replaced him.

But Morton's Cinderella season turned into a pumpkin as the Cowboys' defense controlled the 1st half, forcing 4 interceptions and 3 fumbles, as they jumped out to a 13–0 lead. Finally, in the 3rd quarter, Morton, who had been sacked twice, was pulled with 6:42 left after Ed (Too Tall) Jones dropped what would have been Morton's fifth interception. Morton finished the game 4 of 15 for 39 yards.

Morton's first SB, game V, had been no more successful. He threw 12 completions in 26 attempts for 127 yards and 1 touchdown, but an interception—one of 3 in the game—with less than 2 minutes remaining set up the Baltimore Colts' game-winning touchdown. Morton was on the Cowboys' roster for SB VI, but did not play.

DON MOSEBAR

Los Angeles Raiders, guard, 6 feet 6, 265, Southern California. A substitute for the Raiders in Super Bowl XVIII.

MARK MOSELEY

Washington Redskins, kicker, 6 feet, 205, Stephen F. Austin. Handled the place kicking duties for the Redskins in Super Bowls XVII and XVIII. After being named player of the year in several polls for his 1982 season accomplishments, Moseley made both field-goal attempts, from 31 and 20 yards, as he helped the Redskins beat the Miami Dolphins in SB XVII. In SB XVIII, Moseley was 1 of 2 in field-goal attempts, missing his first attempt from 44 yards, then making his second, from 24.

RICK MOSER

Pittsburgh Steelers, running back and kick returner, 6 feet, 218, Rhode Island. A rookie, Moser played as a substitute in Super Bowl XIII and in the same role in SB XIV.

HAVEN MOSES

Denver Broncos, wide receiver, 6 feet 2, 200, San Diego State. A starting wide receiver for the Broncos in Super Bowl XII, Moses caught 1 pass for 21 yards.

CALVIN MUHAMMAD

Los Angeles Raiders, wide receiver, 5 feet 11, 190, Texas Southern. A top special teams player, Muhammad played in Super Bowl XVIII and was credited with a tackle.

HERB MUL-KEY

Washington Redskins, running back and kick returner, 6 feet, 190, no college. Mul-Key returned a single kickoff for 15 yards in Super Bowl VII.

MARK MULLANEY

Minnesota Vikings, defensive end, 6 feet 6, 242, Colorado State. Mullaney played as a substitute for the Vikings in Super Bowl XI.

GERRY MULLINS

Pittsburgh Steelers, guard and tackle, 6 feet 3, 244, Southern California. Four times, Mullins started at the right guard position for the Steelers—in Super Bowls IX, X, XIII, and XIV.

LLOYD MUMPHORD

Miami Dolphins, corner back, 5 feet 10, 180, Texas Southern. A substitute for the Dolphins in Super Bowl VI, he started at the left corner back position for the team in SB VII and SB VIII.

ANTHONY MUNOZ

Cincinnati Bengals, tackle, 6 feet 6, 278, Southern California. Starting left tackle for the Bengals in Super Bowl XVI.

MARK MURPHY

Washington Redskins, safety, 6 feet 4, 210, Colgate. A starter at free safety for the Redskins in Super Bowls XVII and XVIII, he had a key interception against the Miami Dolphins in his first appearance. In the 3rd quarter, with Miami leading, 17–13, and driving, Dolphins' quarterback David Woodley threw toward Jimmy Cefalo on the 5-yard line, but corner back Vernon Dean tipped the ball, and Murphy lunged and snared it.

ROB NAIRNE

Denver Broncos, linebacker, 6 feet 4, 220, Oregon State. Played as a substitute for the Broncos in Super Bowl XII.

JOE NAMATH

New York Jets, quarterback, 6 feet 2, 195, Alabama. It was probably one of the biggest sports upsets of the decade. After all, the Baltimore Colts were 18-point favorites to beat the upstart NY Jets in Super Bowl III.

It was probably the greatest sports boast of the decade, too, for Namath "guaranteed" the Jets would win.

And darn if Namath didn't deliver, helping the Jets become the first AFL team to win the title and taking the game's MVP award with him.

After a scoreless 1st quarter, Namath led the Jets on an 80-yard drive in the second period, helped by an interception of an Earl Morrall pass. The Jets' drive ended when Matt Snell went in from the 4-yard line.

The Jets also got 3 field goals from Jim Turner in the 2nd half, during which time Namath had to leave the game for a short time because of a jammed thumb.

If Namath provided a great deal to write about on the field, his pregame activities were even more colorful. First, there was his answer to the question of how good Morrall was: "I can think of five quarterbacks in the AFL better—myself, John Hadl, Bob Griese, Daryle Lamonica and either Babe Parilli or Len Dawson."

Then there was the celebrated restaurant "confrontation" with Colts player Lou Michaels—after which Namath gave Michaels a lift to his hotel. A few days later, Namath and several other Jets players missed the media picture day.

Colts players talked openly

Joe Namath

reception, of 25 yards, came in the Dolphins' first scoring drive, which ended with a field goal. He also carried 5 times for 18 yards, with a long run of 16 yards.

RALPH NEELY

Dallas Cowboys, guard, 6 feet 6, 255, Oklahoma. Starting left tackle for the Cowboys in three Super Bowls—SB V, SB X, and SB XII. He was one of the top Dallas players of all time.

RENALDO NEHEMIAH

San Francisco 49ers, wide receiver, 6 feet 1, 183, Maryland. A world-class sprinter, Nehemiah did not play football in college, but was encouraged to try the pro game and signed with the 49ers as a free agent. He played as a substitute in Super Bowl XIX, but did not record any individual statistics.

about showing Namath some "humility." But in the end, Namath showed them something else— championship form. Namath threw 17 completions in 28 attempts for 206 yards with no interceptions.

Don Shula, the Baltimore coach, summed up Namath's performance in ten telling words: "He was all we had heard—a fine football player."

JOHN NEIDERT

New York Jets, linebacker, 6 feet 2, 230, Louisville. Played as a substitute for the Jets in Super Bowl III.

TONY NATHAN

Miami Dolphins, running back, 6 feet, 206, Alabama. A backfield starter for the Dolphins in both Super Bowls XVII and XIX. In SB XVII, Nathan carried 7 times for 26 yards, with a long run of 12 yards. Two years later, he led the Dolphins with 10 receptions, finishing with 83 yards. His long

MIKE NELMS

Washington Redskins, safety and kick returner, 6 feet 1, 185, Baylor. Nelms, one of the top returners in the league in the 1980s, returned punts and kickoffs for the Redskins in Super Bowl XVII, but an injury in the 1983 season forced him to miss SB XVIII. In SB XVII, he returned 6 punts for a total of 52 yards, including a long return of 12 yards, which gave the Redskins excellent field position on the Miami Dolphins' 41 on the way to their final touchdown. He also returned 2 kickoffs for 44 yards, including a long return of 24.

BOB NELSON

Oakland and Los Angeles Raiders, linebacker, 6 feet 4, 230, Nebraska. Starting right inside linebacker for the Raiders in Super Bowls XV and XVIII. He recorded 6 tackles against the Washington Redskins in SB XVIII.

STEVE NELSON

New England Patriots, linebacker, 6 feet 2, 230, North Dakota State. A starter at left inside linebacker for the Patriots in Super Bowl XX, he was credited with 6 tackles and 3 assists. After the Patriots' embarrassing 46–10 defeat by the Chicago Bears, Nelson commented, "If I could crawl out of here, I would."

TERRY NELSON

Los Angeles Rams, tight end, 6 feet 2, 241, Arkansas/Pine Bluff.

The starting tight end for the Rams in Super Bowl XIV, Nelson caught 2 passes for 20 yards. His long reception, of 14 yards, came in a drive toward the end of the first half, which ended with a field goal and the Rams leading, 13–10, at halftime.

ROBERT NEWHOUSE

Dallas Cowboys, running back, 5 feet 10, 200, Houston. A backfield starter for the Cowboys in three Super Bowls—SB X, SB XII, and SB XIII. He led the team in rushing in SB X, with 16 carries for 56 yards, and also caught 2 passes for 12 yards, but perhaps is best remembered for throwing a touchdown pass in SB XII.

In that game, with the Cowboys' lead cut to 10 points, Dallas came up with a fumble recovery at

Robert Newhouse

143

the Denver Broncos' 29. On the next play, Newhouse went to the left side with the handoff, then pulled up and passed to Golden Richards, who was alone in the end zone.

Newhouse said later that he had not expected to use the play in the game and had coated his hands with stickum. Nevertheless, "I knew I could throw it," he said. "It was just a matter of getting my hip around. So I made sure I got my hip around."

Besides his touchdown pass, Newhouse's individual statistics in SB XII included 14 carries for 55 yards and 3 receptions for a loss of a yard. In SB XIII, he carried 8 times for 3 yards.

ED NEWMAN

Miami Dolphins, guard, 6 feet 2, 245, Duke. Newman joined the Dolphins in 1973, and played as a reserve in Super Bowl VIII and 11 years later, started at right guard in SB XIX. He missed SB XVII because of a knee injury.

BILLY NEWSOME

Baltimore Colts, defensive end, 6 feet 4, 240, Grambling. Played as a substitute for the Colts in Super Bowl V.

ROBBIE NICHOLS

Baltimore Colts, linebacker, 6 feet 3, 220, Tulsa. Played as a substitute for the Colts in Super Bowl V.

JOHN NILAND

Dallas Cowboys, guard, 6 feet 3, 245, Iowa. Starting left guard for the Cowboys in Super Bowls V and VI. Along with center Dave Manders, Niland was credited with negating Miami Dolphins' linebacker Nick Buoniconti on running plays in SB VI.

RAY NITSCHKE

Green Bay Packers, linebacker, 6 feet 3, 240, Illinois. One of the finest middle linebackers of all time, Nitschke is a member of the Pro Football Hall of Fame and one of the players chosen in 1969 for the all-time NFL team. He started in both Super Bowls I and II for the Packers.

KARL NOONAN

Miami Dolphins, wide receiver, 6 feet 2, 198, Iowa. Played as a substitute for the Dolphins in Super Bowl VI.

PETTIS NORMAN

Dallas Cowboys, tight end, 6 feet 3, 220, Johnson C. Smith. Starting tight end for the Cowboys in Super Bowl V.

DON NOTTINGHAM

Miami Dolphins, running back, 5 feet 10, 210, Kent State. Played as a substitute for the Dolphins in Super Bowl VIII, but did not record any individual statistics.

TOM NOWATZKE

Baltimore Colts, running back, 6 feet 3, 230, Indiana. Nowatzke, a backfield starter, went through a goat-to-hero Super Bowl V. He failed to block the Dallas Cowboys' Mark Washington on a point-after-touchdown attempt, and Washington blocked Jim O'Brien's kick, keeping the score tied, 6–6. But Nowatzke scored a touchdown on a 2-yard run in the 4th quarter—his second attempt—to help tie the game, at 13–13. Nowatzke finished with 10 carries for 33 yards and 1 reception for 45 yards.

BLAINE NYE

Dallas Cowboys, guard, 6 feet 4, 251, Stanford. Nye started at right guard for the Cowboys in three Super Bowls—SB V, SB VI, and SB X.

☆ ☆ ☆

CARLETON OATS

Oakland Raiders, defensive end, 6 feet 2, 235, Florida A&M. Played as a substitute for the Raiders in Super Bowl II.

JIM O'BRIEN

Baltimore Colts, kicker and wide receiver, 6 feet, 195, Cincinnati. A shaggy-haired visionary winning a Super Bowl game almost single-handedly? That's what happened in Super Bowl V, when O'Brien kicked his 32-yarder with 5 seconds left to give the Colts their 16–13 victory over the Dallas Cowboys. O'Brien's heroics came after he had missed a point-after-touchdown earlier in the game and another field-goal attempt in the 3rd quarter. It also came after he said he "dreamed" the ending.

"I had this dream all week," he said after the game. "I could see a field goal going over to win the game, but I couldn't tell who kicked it. It could have been Mike Clark of Dallas, or it could have been me. I never knew. I guess I kept waking up too soon."

The Colts' winning field goal was set up by an interception that gave the team the ball at the Dallas 28. Two running plays gained 3 yards and used 50 of the remaining 59 seconds.

O'Brien confessed later that his mother, a professional astrologer, had predicted something like his kick: "She told me there was no way we could lose. . . . She wouldn't tell me how it was going to happen, though. I guess she didn't want to make me nervous."

MIKE OBROVAC

Cincinnati Bengals, guard, 6 feet 6, 275, Bowling Green. Played as a substitute for the Bengals in Super Bowl XVI.

RILEY ODOMS

Denver Broncos, tight end, 6 feet 4, 232, Houston. The starting tight end for the Broncos in Super Bowl XII. Odoms caught 2 passes for 9 yards, but fumbled the ball away once after a 10-yard reception, one of 3 fumbles the Broncos lost in the 1st half.

RAY OLDHAM

Pittsburgh Steelers, safety, 5 feet 11, 192, Middle Tennessee State. Played as a substitute for the Steelers in Super Bowl XIII.

NEAL OLKEWICZ

Washington Redskins, linebacker, 6 feet, 230, Maryland. Starting middle linebacker for the Redskins in Super Bowls XVII and XVIII. His team won SB XVII on his 26th birthday.

TOM OROSZ

Miami Dolphins, punter, 6 feet 1, 204, Ohio State. Orosz handled the Dolphins' punting duties in Super Bowl XVII, kicking 6 times for an average of 37.8 yards and a long punt of 46 yards.

JIMMY ORR

Baltimore Colts, flanker, 5 feet 11, 185, Georgia. A starter at end in Super Bowl III, Orr did not play in SB V. Orr caught 3 passes for 42 yards, but a pass he did not get a chance to catch may be the most remembered. With 25 seconds left in the first half, and the NY Jets leading, 7–0, Baltimore pulled a flea flicker, with Earl Morrall handing off to Tom Matte, who passed it back to Morrall. Orr was downfield, near the goal on the left side, waving for the ball with no defenders near him. Morrall seemed to look that way, but instead passed toward fullback Jerry Hill. Jets' safety Jim Hudson picked the ball off. Morrall said later, "I never saw Jimmy. I saw Hill in the clear down the middle."

KEITH ORTEGO

Chicago Bears, wide receiver and kick returner, 6 feet, 180, McNeese State. The Bears' top punt returner, Ortego returned 2 punts for 20 yards in Super Bowl XX, with a long return of 12 yards.

DAVE OSBORN

Minnesota Vikings, running back, 6 feet, 205, North Dakota. A backfield starter for the Vikings in Super Bowls IV and IX, he played as a substitute in SB VIII. In SB IV, Osborn ran 7 times for 15 yards, including the Vikings' only touchdown, and caught 2 passes for 11 yards, as the Vikings' offense was shut down by the Kansas City Chiefs. His 4-yard touchdown run, in the 3rd quarter, culminated a 69-yard drive. Osborn did not record any individual statistics in SB VIII. In SB IX, Osborn carried 8 times for a loss of 1 yard and caught 2 passes for 7 yards. He was involved in one scoring play, albeit in the Pittsburgh Steelers' favor. With the game scoreless and the Vikings deep in their own territory, quarterback Fran Tarkenton attempted to pitch out to Osborn, but the ball never got to him, and Tarkenton chased it into the end zone, where he was touched for a safety. Tarkenton said later, "I thought it got back good enough to get it to him, but Ozzie said it never touched him."

DWAYNE O'STEEN

Los Angeles Rams and Oakland Raiders, corner back, 6 feet 1, 190, San Jose State. O'Steen played in two consecutive Super Bowls, for two different teams. He played in SB XIV as a reserve for the Rams, then, after a trade, started at right corner back for the Raiders in SB XV.

GUS OTTO

Oakland Raiders, linebacker, 6 feet 2, 220, Missouri. Starting linebacker for the Raiders in Super Bowl II.

JIM OTTO

Oakland Raiders, center, 6 feet 2, 249, Miami (Florida). A member of the original Raiders franchise, which began in 1960, Otto started for the Raiders in Super Bowl II. He wore number 00 and was inducted into the Pro Football Hall of Fame in 1980.

TOM OWEN

Washington Redskins, quarterback, 6 feet 1, 194, Wichita State. Owen, the backup for Joe Theismann, did not play in Super Bowl XVII.

BRIG OWENS

Washington Redskins, safety, 5 feet 11, 190, Cincinnati. The starting left safety for the Redskins in Super Bowl VII, Owens prevented the Miami Dolphins from breaking open the game by intercepting a Bob Griese pass in the end zone in the 3rd quarter. The Dolphins led, 14–0, at the time.

BURGESS OWENS

Oakland Raiders, safety, 6 feet 2, 200, Miami (Florida). Started at free safety for the Raiders in Super Bowl XV.

DENNIS OWENS

New England Patriots, nose tackle, 6 feet 1, 258, North Carolina State. Owens, a substitute for the Patriots in Super Bowl XX, finished with 4 tackles, 1 assist, and 2 sacks for a loss of 4 yards.

☆ ☆ ☆

ALAN PAGE

Minnesota Vikings, defensive tackle, 6 feet 4, 245, Notre Dame. A member of the Vikings' famous front four of the 1970s, Page still came up a loser in four Super Bowls—SB IV, SB VIII, SB IX, and SB XI.

JACK PARDEE

Washington Redskins, linebacker, 6 feet 2, 225, Texas A&M. Pardee, a starting linebacker for the Redskins in Super Bowl VII, later went on to coach the team, from 1978–80.

BABE PARILLI

New York Jets, quarterback, 6 feet, 190, Kentucky. Parilli replaced Jets' starter Joe Namath briefly in the second half of Super Bowl III after Namath jammed his thumb. Parilli threw 1 incomplete pass.

WILLIAM (BUBBA) PARIS

San Francisco 49ers, tackle, 6 feet 6, 295, Michigan. Paris started at left tackle for the 49ers in Super Bowl XIX. Paris was nicknamed "Bubba" in high

Alan Page

149

school by teammates who compared him to former great Bubba Smith.

RODNEY PARKER

Philadelphia Eagles, wide receiver, 6 feet 1, 190, Tennessee State. Parker caught 1 pass for 19 yards, playing as a substitute in Super Bowl XV, and another 40-yarder from Ron Jaworski that appeared to tie the game with the Oakland Raiders at 7–7. But the touchdown was nullified because of an illegal-motion penalty on veteran wide receiver Harold Carmichael.

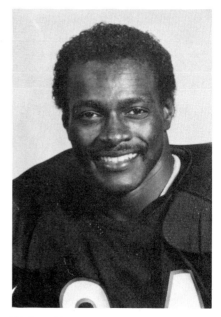

Walter Payton

RICKY PATTON

San Francisco 49ers, running back, 5 feet 11, 192, Jackson State. A backfield starter for the 49ers in Super Bowl XVI, Patton led the team in rushing with 17 carries for 55 yards and caught 1 pass for 6 yards.

WALTER PAYTON

Chicago Bears, running back, 5 feet 10, 202, Jackson State. It is said that some players deserve to play in the Super Bowl. One of those players was Payton, an 11-year pro who has rewritten the NFL's record book. But Payton's long-awaited SB, XX, seemed to end up bittersweet. For starters, after carrying for a 7-yard gain on

the first play of the game, Payton fumbled on the second, the New England Patriots recovered and went on to take a 3–0 lead with a field goal.

Payton did finish up as the Bears' leading rusher with 22 carries for 61 yards, but he was not called on again to carry the ball for a touchdown.

Afterward his teammates commented. "I think he should have been carrying the football," said quarterback Jim McMahon. Bears' tackle Jim Covert added, "Walter deserved [a touchdown], but when the game's going on, you don't realize what's happening."

Payton himself, when asked if he was upset by not scoring, said, "Que sera sera. Just get a lot of ticker tape ready—we're coming."

DAVE PEAR

Oakland Raiders, nose tackle, 6 feet 2, 250, Washington. Played as a substitute for the Raiders in Super Bowl XV.

DREW PEARSON

Dallas Cowboys, wide receiver, 6 feet, 180, Tulsa. Pearson started at a wide receiver position for the Cowboys in Super Bowls X, XII, and XIII, and scored the opening points in SB X with a 29-yard touchdown pass from Roger Staubach. Pearson's touchdown followed a Pittsburgh Steeler miscue in which punter Bobby Walden bobbled the snap and was tackled on the 29. He finished the game with 2 receptions for 59 yards.

In SB XII, Pearson had 1 catch for 13 yards. In SB XIII, he was involved in several key plays. His fumble on an attempted double reverse play in the 1st quarter gave the Pittsburgh Steelers the ball on the Pittsburgh 47. From there, the Steelers drove for a touchdown to take a 7–0 lead. Pearson had his longest reception of the day, 25 yards, in a Dallas drive that helped pull the Cowboys to within 4 points, at 35–31, with 22 seconds remaining. But the Steelers' Rocky Bleier fell on the onsides kick attempt. Pearson finished the game with 4 receptions for 73 yards.

PRESTON PEARSON

Baltimore Colts, Pittsburgh Steelers, and Dallas Cowboys, running back and kick returner, 6 feet 1, 190, Illinois. Pearson played in five Super Bowls—sharing the career service record with six other players—but did it with three teams. He played in SB III with the Colts, SB IX with the Steelers, and SB X, SB XII, and SB XIII with the Cowboys, who had picked him up as a free agent after he was released by the Steelers in 1975.

In SB III, he returned a pair of kickoffs for 59 yards, with a long return of 33 yards. After he was traded to the Steelers in 1970, he returned 1 kickoff for 15 yards in SB IX. SB X with the Cowboys was Pearson's first time as an SB

Preston Pearson

starter. He carried 5 times for 14 yards and caught 5 passes for 53 yards. He returned 4 kickoffs for 48 yards, with a long return of 24, and fumbled once, but recovered the ball.

In SB XII, as a reserve, Pearson carried 3 times for 11 yards and caught 5 passes for 37 yards. In SB XIII, Pearson again came in and contributed, with 1 carry for 6 yards and 2 receptions for 15 yards.

CRAIG PENROSE

Denver Broncos, quarterback, 6 feet 3, 205, San Diego State. Penrose was on the Broncos' roster for Super Bowl XII but did not play.

WOODY PEOPLES

Philadelphia Eagles, guard, 6 feet 2, 260, Grambling. Starting right guard for the Eagles in Super Bowl XV.

RAY PERKINS

Baltimore Colts, end, 6 feet, 183, Alabama. Perkins, who played as a substitute in Super Bowls III and V and did not record any individual statistics, later went on to become an assistant coach and head coach in the NFL.

EDWARD (PETEY) PEROT

Philadelphia Eagles, guard, 6 feet 2, 261, Northwestern Louisiana. Perot started at the left guard position for the Eagles in Super Bowl XV.

LONNIE PERRIN

Denver Broncos, running back, 6 feet 1, 224, Illinois. A substitute for the Broncos in Super Bowl XII, Perrin carried the ball 3 times for 8 yards and caught 1 pass for a loss of 7 yards.

ROD PERRY

Los Angeles Rams, corner back, 5 feet 9, 177, Colorado. Starting right corner back for the Rams in Super Bowl XIV. He picked off a Terry Bradshaw pass in the 3rd quarter to preserve the Rams' 19–17 lead over the Pittsburgh Steelers. He was involved in the Steelers' go-ahead play when John Stallworth got behind him and teammate Dave Elmendorf, and pulled in a 73-yard pass to score and go ahead 24–19 in the 4th period.

WILLIAM (THE REFRIGERATOR) PERRY

Chicago Bears, defensive tackle, 6 feet 2, 308, Clemson. He

William Perry

Given the ball, Perry headed to the right side, looking for his tight end in the end zone. When he didn't find him, he was tackled by the Patriots for a 1-yard loss—a sack on a defensive tackle.

Afterward, a gap-toothed Perry said, "I want to thank Coach Ditka for letting me score. . . . It's the end of my whole life. What I dreamed as a boy was to play in the Super Bowl. To score a touchdown in the twentieth Super Bowl—I'm overwhelmed."

started off the year the object of derision, so big that he was nicknamed The Refrigerator. It looked as though the Bears had wasted a draft choice on Perry. Who would have figured he'd end up a national hero, a Super Bowl champion, and an offensive threat?

In SB XX, in addition to his defensive statistics, Perry scored a touchdown rushing, threw a block, and ran an option play. The idea to use Perry in the offensive backfield was first sprung during the regular season in a game against the Green Bay Packers. In that game, Perry scored 1 touchdown running and threw blocks on 2 more touchdown plays.

In the SB, Perry scored his touchdown in the 2nd half, with the Bears well ahead. He capped a short drive with a 1-yard run, to help the Bears take a 44–3 lead. The option play came earlier.

TONY PETERS

Washington Redskins, safety, 6 feet 1, 190, Oklahoma. The starting strong safety for the Redskins in Super Bowl XVII, Peters was arrested in the team's training camp in 1983 and later pleaded guilty to two drug-related charges. He was given a four-year suspended sentence, and sat out the entire 1983 season, missing Super Bowl XVIII.

TED PETERSEN

Pittsburgh Steelers, center and tackle, 6 feet 5, 244, Eastern Illinois. Petersen played as a substitute for the Steelers in Super Bowls XIII and XIV.

CAL PETERSON

Dallas Cowboys, linebacker, 6 feet 3, 220, UCLA. Peterson

153

played as a substitute for the Cowboys in Super Bowl X.

BOB PETRELLA

Miami Dolphins, safety, 5 feet 11, 190, Tennessee. Petrella played as a substitute for the Dolphins in Super Bowl VI.

GERRY PHILBIN

New York Jets, defensive end, 6 feet 2, 245, Buffalo. In Super Bowl III, Philbin helped the Jets contain the heavily favored Baltimore Colts, particularly in the 3rd quarter. Afterward, Philbin was asked if he was surprised by the outcome of the game. He replied, "Yeah, I'm surprised that they scored on us."

CHARLES PHILLIPS

Oakland Raiders, safety, 6 feet 2, 215, Southern California. Played as a substitute for the Raiders in Super Bowl XI.

RAY PHILLIPS

Philadelphia Eagles, linebacker, 6 feet 4, 230, Nebraska. Phillips played as a substitute for the Eagles in Super Bowl XV.

REGGIE PHILLIPS

Chicago Bears, corner back, 5 feet 10, 170, Southern Methodist. Phillips replaced injured starter Leslie Frazier in the 2nd quarter and ended up running back an interception of a Steve Grogan pass 28 yards for a touchdown. He also had a team-high 7 tackles in the unofficial statistics and 2 passes defensed.

CHARLES PHILYAW

Oakland Raiders, defensive end, 6 feet 9, 270, Texas Southern. Philyaw played as a substitute for the Raiders in Super Bowl XI.

BILL PICKEL

Los Angeles Raiders, defensive end, 6 feet 5, 260, Rutgers. A rookie, Pickel played as a substitute in Super Bowl XVIII and recorded a tackle and a 9-yard sack.

LAWRENCE PILLERS

San Francisco 49ers, defensive end, 6 feet 4, 260, Alcorn State. A substitute for the 49ers in Super Bowl XVI, Pillers started at the defensive left end position for the team in SB XIX.

RAY PINNEY

Pittsburgh Steelers, tackle and center, 6 feet 4, 240, Washington. Starting right tackle for the Steelers in Super Bowl XIII.

JOE PISARCIK

Philadelphia Eagles, quarterback, 6 feet 4, 220, New Mexico State. A backup quarterback, Pisarcik did not see action in Super Bowl XV.

ELIJAH PITTS

Green Bay Packers, running back, 6 feet 1, 205, Philander Smith. Pitts started in the backfield for the Packers in Super Bowl I and scored twice. A 5-yard scoring run followed a 50-yard interception return by teammate Willie Wood and helped the Packers take a 21–10 lead in the 3rd quarter. He scored the game's final touchdown in the 4th quarter on a 1-yard run. Pitts finished with 11 carries for 45 yards and also caught 2 passes for 32 yards.

FRANK PITTS

Kansas City Chiefs, flanker and wide receiver, 6 feet 2, 190, Southern University. A substitute in Super Bowl I, Pitts started at a wide receiver position in SB IV. He played a key role in the Chiefs' opening scoring drive in SB IV, with a 20-yard reception. He also carried the ball on 3 end-around plays for a total of 37 yards. He finished with 3 receptions for 33 yards. He did not have any individual statistics in Super Bowl I.

ART PLUNKETT

New England Patriots, tackle, 6 feet 7, 260, Nevada/Las Vegas. Played as a substitute for the Patriots in Super Bowl XX.

JIM PLUNKETT

Oakland and Los Angeles Raiders, quarterback, 6 feet 2, 205, Stanford. He was a Heisman trophy winner in college, a rookie of the year when he joined the New England Patriots in the NFL in 1971. But when the 1980 season began, he was a bench warmer, having been picked up by the Raiders as a free agent in 1978.

But when Dan Pastorini went down during the 1980 season with a broken leg, Plunkett took

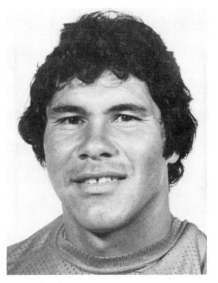

Jim Plunkett

155

over and led the Raiders to two Super Bowl victories.

In SB XV, Plunkett delivered early, taking advantage of an interception to throw a 2-yard touchdown pass to Cliff Branch for a 7–0 lead. Still in the 1st quarter, Plunkett went back to pass from his own 20 and, under a heavy rush, found Kenny King for an 80-yard touchdown and Super Bowl record.

Early in the 2nd half, Plunkett lofted a pass toward Branch. Just when it seemed as if the Philadelphia Eagles' Roynell Young would intercept, Branch reached around, grabbed the ball, and fell into the end zone.

Plunkett ended up with 261 yards passing, 3 touchdowns, and was named MVP for the game.

In SB XVIII, Plunkett helped the Raiders to what was then the most decisive victory in SB history, a 38–9 victory over the Washington Redskins. In the game, he completed 16 passes in 25 attempts for 172 yards, with 1 touchdown and no interceptions.

After being staked to a 7–0 lead by a blocked punt, Plunkett helped put the Redskins away with a quick drive. He hit Branch with a 50-yard completion, then came back a couple of plays later with a 12-yard scoring pass to Branch.

BOBBY PLY

Kansas City Chiefs, defensive back, 6 feet 1, 196, Baylor. Played as a substitute for the Chiefs in Super Bowl I.

ED PODOLAK

Kansas City Chiefs, running back, 6 feet 1, 204, Iowa. Podolak, a rookie, played as a substitute for the Chiefs in Super Bowl IV and did not record any individual statistics.

RANDY POTL

Minnesota Vikings and Denver Broncos, corner back, 6 feet 3, 190, Stanford. Played as a substitute for the Vikings in Super Bowl IX and Broncos in SB XII. He was credited with a fumble recovery in SB XII.

RON PORTER

Baltimore Colts and Minnesota Vikings, linebacker, 6 feet 3, 232, Idaho. Played as a substitute for the Colts in Super Bowl III and the Vikings in SB VIII. In SB III, he recovered a fumble early in the game at the NY Jets' 12. But the Colts did not take advantage of the turnover.

STEVE POTTER

Miami Dolphins, linebacker, 6 feet 3, 235, Virginia. Played as a substitute for the Dolphins in Super Bowl XVII.

MYRON POTTIOS

Washington Redskins, linebacker, 6 feet 2, 232, Notre Dame. Starting middle linebacker for the Redskins in Super Bowl VII.

JESSE POWELL

Miami Dolphins, linebacker, 6 feet 2, 215, West Texas State. Played as a substitute for the Dolphins in Super Bowls VI and VII.

WARREN POWERS

Oakland Raiders, defensive back, 6 feet, 190, Nebraska. Starting right safety for the Raiders in Super Bowl II.

REMI PRUDHOMME

Kansas City Chiefs, center, 6 feet 4, 250, Louisiana State. A substitute in Super Bowl IV, Prudhomme recovered a fumble on a kickoff to help set up a Chiefs' touchdown. After Jan Stenerud had kicked his third field goal, to give the Chiefs a 9–0 lead, the Minnesota Vikings' Charlie West fumbled the kickoff, and Prudhomme recovered on the Vikings' 19, to set up Mike Garrett's 5-yard touchdown run.

GREG PRUITT

Los Angeles Raiders, running back and kick returner, 5 feet 10, 190, Oklahoma. A substitute in the backfield, Pruitt handled the Raiders' punt and kick return duties for Super Bowl XVIII. He carried the ball 5 times for 17 yards, returned 1 punt for 8 yards, calling for fair catches on 3, and returned 1 kickoff 17 yards.

GARRY PUETZ

Washington Redskins, tackle, 6 feet 4, 265, Valparaiso. On the Redskins' roster for Super Bowl XVII, he did not play.

JETHRO PUGH

Dallas Cowboys, defensive tackle, 6 feet 6, 260, Elizabeth City State. A starter at left tackle for the Cowboys in four Super Bowls—SB V, SB VI, SB X, and SB XII—he was a member of the team's Doomsday Defense. Pugh was on the roster for SB XIII, but did not play. In SB V, Pugh recovered a fumble by the Baltimore Colts' Johnny Unitas late in the 1st half, which led to a Dallas touchdown and a 13–6 lead.

CRAIG PUKI

San Francisco 49ers, linebacker, 6 feet 1, 231, Tennessee. Starting right inside linebacker for the 49ers in Super Bowl XVI.

FRED QUILLAN

San Francisco 49ers, center, 6 feet 5, 260, Oregon. The starting center for the 49ers in both Super Bowls XVI and XIX. In SB XIX, he was termed the "focal point" for the 49ers' line, which helped the team set a game record with 537 total yards on offense.

☆ ☆ ☆

BILL RADEMACHER

New York Jets, split end, 6 feet 1, 190, Northern Michigan. Played as a substitute for the Jets in Super Bowl III.

MIKE RAE

Oakland Raiders, quarterback, 6 feet 1, 190, Southern California. Played as a reserve in Super Bowl XI.

TOM RAFFERTY

Dallas Cowboys, guard and center, 6 feet 3, 250, Penn State. Started at right guard for the Cowboys in Super Bowls XII and XIII.

DERRICK RAMSEY

Oakland Raiders and New England Patriots, tight end, 6 feet 4, 225, Kentucky. Played as a substitute for the Raiders in Super Bowl XV and the Patriots in SB XX. In his second appearance, he replaced the injured Lin Dawson and caught 2 passes for 16 yards, but also fumbled the ball away once.

TOM RAMSEY

New England Patriots, quarterback, 6 feet 1, 189, UCLA. The only member of the Patriots' roster who did not play in Super Bowl XX.

EASON RAMSON

San Francisco 49ers, tight end, 6 feet 2, 234, Washington State. Played as a substitute for the 49ers in Super Bowl XVI.

TOM RANDALL

Dallas Cowboys, guard, 6 feet 5, 245, Iowa State. Played as

a substitute for the Cowboys in Super Bowl XIII.

AHMAD RASHAD

Minnesota Vikings, wide receiver, 6 feet 2, 200, Oregon. Rashad (formerly Bobby Moore) started at wide receiver for the Vikings in Super Bowl XI and caught 3 passes for 53 yards, including a long reception of 25 yards. He later went on to a career in broadcasting.

RANDY RASMUSSEN

New York Jets, guard, 6 feet 2, 255, Kearney State. Starting right guard for the Jets in Super Bowl III, he was one of the mainstays of the New York front line.

RICK RAZZANO

Cincinnati Bengals, linebacker, 5 feet 11, 227, Virginia Tech. Played as a substitute for the Bengals in Super Bowl XVI.

DAVE REAVIS

Pittsburgh Steelers, tackle, 6 feet 5, 250, Arkansas. Played as a substitute for the Steelers in both Super Bowls IX and X.

OSCAR REED

Minnesota Vikings, running back, 6 feet, 220, Colorado State. Reed played as a substitute in Super Bowls IV and IX and started in the backfield for the Vikings in SB VIII. In SB IV, Reed carried 4 times for 17 yards, with a long run of 15 yards, and caught 2 passes for 16 yards, with a long reception of 12 yards. In SB VIII, Reed led the Vikings in rushing with 11 carries for 32 yards, but fumbled away the ball on a key play at the end of the first half. Trailing 17–0, the Vikings drove 74 yards to the Miami 6-yard line, where they faced fourth-and-1. Reed, however, fumbled on the play, and the Dolphins recovered. Reed also caught 1 pass for 1 yard in the game. In SB IX, Reed's only statistics were 1 pass reception for a loss of 2 yards.

ARCHIE REESE

San Francisco 49ers, nose tackle, 6 feet 3, 262, Clemson. Starting nose tackle for the 49ers in Super Bowl XVI.

DAN REEVES

Dallas Cowboys, running back, 6 feet 1, 220, South Carolina. Reeves played in both Super Bowls V and VI as a reserve, but led the team in receiving in SB V with 5 catches for 46 yards. One pass, however, got away. With the score tied, 13–13 in SB V, Reeves was the target for quarterback Craig Morton. The ball skipped off Reeves' fingers and was picked off by Mike Curtis of the Baltimore Colts, setting up his team's winning field goal.

MIKE REILLY

Minnesota Vikings, linebacker, 6 feet 2, 240, Iowa. Reilly was on the Vikings' roster, but did not play in Super Bowl IV.

JOHNNY REMBERT

New England Patriots, linebacker, 6 feet 3, 234, Clemson. Played as a substitute for the Patriots in Super Bowl XX.

MEL RENFRO

Dallas Cowboys, safety, 6 feet, 190, Oregon. Starting right corner back for the Cowboys in Super Bowls V, VI, and X and a substitute for the team in SB XII. In SB V, he was involved in one of the bizarre plays that marked the game as the Stupor Bowl. With the Cowboys leading, 6–0, Baltimore's Johnny Unitas threw a pass toward wide receiver Eddie Hinton. Hinton tipped the ball, Renfro also tipped it, and it was finally hauled in by the Colts' John Mackey, who carried it into the end zone for a 75-yard touchdown play. Renfro later intercepted a Unitas pass, the last the quarterback was to throw in that game, as he left the game holding his side. In SB VI, he was credited with

Mel Renfro

helping hold Miami wide receiver Paul Warfield in check.

GLENN RESSLER

Baltimore Colts, guard, 6 feet 3, 250, Penn State. Starting left guard for the Colts in Super Bowls III and V.

AL REYNOLDS

Kansas City Chiefs, guard, 6 feet 3, 250, Tarkio. A substitute for the Chiefs in Super Bowl I.

ED REYNOLDS

New England Patriots, linebacker, 6 feet 5, 230, Virginia. Reynolds played as a substitute in Super Bowl XX.

161

JACK REYNOLDS

Los Angeles Rams and San Francisco 49ers, linebacker, 6 feet 1, 231, Tennessee. Reynolds started for two teams in Super Bowl competition, playing at the middle linebacker position for the Rams in SB XIV and at left inside linebacker for the 49ers in SB XVI and SB XIX.

He was involved in the 49ers' key defensive stand in the 3rd quarter of SB XVI—considered the championship game's greatest goal-line stand. Starting from the 49ers' 3, the Bengals failed on 3 straight efforts. Then, on fourth down from the 1, Pete Johnson attempted to go over the left side but was met by Reynolds and Dan Bunz and was unable to get the ball over.

EARNIE RHONE

Miami Dolphins, linebacker, 6 feet 2, 224, Henderson State. Starting right inside linebacker for the Dolphins in Super Bowl XVII and a substitute in SB XIX. He led both the Dolphins and Washington Redskins in defensive statistics in SB XVII with 11 solo tackles and 3 assists.

ANDY RICE

Kansas City Chiefs, defensive tackle, 6 feet 2, 260, Texas Southern. Starting defensive left tackle for the Chiefs in Super Bowl I.

FLOYD RICE

Oakland Raiders, linebacker, 6 feet 3, 225, Alcorn State. Rice played as a substitute for the Raiders in Super Bowl XI.

RANDY RICH

Denver Broncos, safety, 5 feet 10, 181, New Mexico. A rookie, Rich played as a substitute in Super Bowl XII.

GOLDEN RICHARDS

Dallas Cowboys, wide receiver and kick returner, 6 feet, 183, Hawaii. Richards started at wide receiver in Super Bowl X, but did not catch a pass. He returned 1 punt for 5 yards, calling for fair catches on 3 others. In SB XII, though not a starter, he was involved in one of the more memorable plays, the Cowboys' final touchdown.

After a Dallas fumble recovery on the Denver Broncos' 29, Cowboy running back Robert Newhouse took a handoff and went left, then pulled up and fired a strike to Richards in the end zone. "They were supposed to think it was a run," Richards said. "But at the last [corner back] Steve Foley recognized it. . . . I had to go the opposite way I wanted to go. But the pass was right there." Richards finished the game with 2 receptions for 38 yards.

JIM RICHARDS

New York Jets, defensive back, 6 feet 1, 180, Virginia Tech. Richards played as a substitute for the Jets in Super Bowl III.

GLOSTER RICHARDSON

Kansas City Chiefs and Dallas Cowboys, wide receiver, 6 feet, 200, Jackson State. After playing as a substitute for the Chiefs in Super Bowl IV, Richardson was on the Cowboys' roster for SB VI but did not play. His brother Willie also played in the SB (below).

JEFF RICHARDSON

New York Jets, tackle and center, 6 feet 3, 250, Michigan State. Played as a substitute for the Jets in Super Bowl III.

JOHN RICHARDSON

Miami Dolphins, defensive tackle, 6 feet 2, 250, UCLA. On the Dolphins' roster, but did not play in Super Bowl VI.

MIKE RICHARDSON

Chicago Bears, corner back, 6 feet, 188, Arizona State. Starting left corner back for the Bears in Super Bowl XX. He finished with 1 tackle, 1 assist, and 3 passes defensed.

WILLIE RICHARDSON

Baltimore Colts, flanker, 6 feet 2, 198, Jackson State. The Colts' starting flanker in Super Bowl III, he led the team in receiving with 6 catches for 58 yards, with a long reception of 21 yards. Brother of the Chiefs' and Cowboys' Gloster (above).

JOHN RIGGINS

Washington Redskins, running back, 6 feet 2, 235, Kansas. Riggins played in two Super Bowls and made powerful impressions in each.

In SB XVII, he rushed for an SB record 166 yards, including a dramatic 43-yard run that put the Redskins in the lead to stay.

In SB XVIII, the Raiders shut down Riggins—holding him to 64

John Riggins

163

yards in a 38–9 defeat. But again, there were Riggins dramatics. Fourth and 1, 12 seconds left in the 3rd quarter, the Redskins trailing, and their chances slipping away. Riggins gets the call, but he's met by Raider linebacker Rod Martin for no gain.

That type of center stage has never been a place Riggins shirked. Eccentric, even flaky, he's remembered for things like wearing his hair in a mohawk and falling asleep at an awards dinner. But off-the-field antics never seem to get in the way of his play. His coach, Joe Gibbs, said, "For all the kidding around, John Riggins is a team man first."

In SB XVII, he carried the ball 4 straight times in Washington's first scoring drive and had a 15-yard reception in the second. But his play in the 4th quarter left its mark on SB history.

With a fourth-and-1 on the Miami 43, Riggins took the ball, found a spot open, bulled through, and passed a Miami defender for 43 yards, a touchdown, and a 20–17 lead.

Riggins credited the Hogs, the offensive line, for his success. However, it was the Raiders who took away the Hogs' effectiveness in SB XVIII, and Riggins' game suffered as well.

Riggins did score the Redskins' only touchdown, in the 3rd quarter, but his team trailed, 21–3, by that time.

And with the ball on the Raiders' 26, on fourth-and-1, Riggins was called on again. But the Raiders' Martin stopped him and stopped the Redskins' hope for consecutive victories.

JIM RILEY

Miami Dolphins, defensive end, 6 feet 4, 250, Oklahoma. Starting defensive left end for the Dolphins in Super Bowl VI.

KEN RILEY

Cincinnati Bengals, corner back, 6 feet, 183, Florida A&M. Riley, one of the NFL's top defensive backs for many a year, started at right corner back for the Bengals in Super Bowl XVI.

STEVE RILEY

Minnesota Vikings, tackle, 6 feet 6, 258, Southern California. Riley was on the Vikings' roster but did not play in Super Bowl IX, then started at left tackle for the team in SB XI.

BILL RING

San Francisco 49ers, running back and kick returner, 5 feet 10, 215, Brigham Young. Ring, a special teams captain for the 49ers, played as a substitute for the team in both Super Bowls XVI and XIX. He carried the ball 5 times for 17 yards with a long carry of 7 yards in SB XVI. He did not record any individual statistics in his second appearance.

RON RIVERA

Chicago Bears, linebacker, 6 feet 3, 239, California. Played as a substitute for the Bears in Super Bowl XX and finished with 2 tackles in unofficial statistics.

JOE RIZZO

Denver Broncos, linebacker, 6 feet 1, 223, Merchant Marine Academy. The fourth-year player started at left inside linebacker for the Broncos in Super Bowl XII.

DAVE ROBINSON

Green Bay Packers, linebacker, 6 feet 3, 245, Penn State. The starting left linebacker for the Packers in both Super Bowls I and II and part of a feared trio of Packer linebackers along with Ray Nitschke and Lee Roy Caffey. He recovered a fumble in SB II and returned it 16 yards, although the Packers did not capitalize on the turnover.

JERRY ROBINSON

Philadelphia Eagles, linebacker, 6 feet 2, 218, UCLA. Starting right outside linebacker for the Eagles in Super Bowl XV.

JOHNNY ROBINSON

Kansas City Chiefs, defensive back, 6 feet 1, 205, Louisiana State. A starter for the Chiefs in both Super Bowls I and IV. Despite playing with three broken ribs, Robinson recovered a fumble and intercepted a pass—in the 4th quarter—for the Chiefs in SB IV.

JOHNNY ROBINSON

Los Angeles Raiders, nose tackle, 6 feet 2, 260, Louisiana Tech. Played as a substitute for the Raiders in Super Bowl XVIII.

REGGIE ROBY

Miami Dolphins, punter, 6 feet 2, 243, Iowa. One of the NFL's top punters, Roby punted 6 times for an average of 39.3 in Super Bowl XIX.

PAUL ROCHESTER

New York Jets, defensive tackle, 6 feet 2, 250, Michigan State. Starting defensive left tackle for the Jets in Super Bowl III.

WALTER ROCK

Washington Redskins, tackle, 6 feet 5, 255, Maryland. Starting right tackle for the Redskins in Super Bowl VII.

JOE ROSE

Miami Dolphins, tight end, 6 feet 3, 230, California. Listed as a third-string tight end, Rose played for the Dolphins in both Super Bowls XVII and XIX. While not recording any individual statistics in his first appearance, he caught 6 passes for 73 yards in SB XIX. His longest reception, 30 yards, came in the Dolphins' last-minute spree of the 1st half, on the way to a field goal, which brought the team to within 15 points of the San Francisco 49ers at the time, at 28–13.

DAN ROSS

Cincinnati Bengals, tight end, 6 feet 4, 235, Northeastern. Ross, the starting tight end, led the Bengals in receiving in Super Bowl XVI, catching 11 passes for 104 yards with 2 touchdowns. Both of Ross's touchdown receptions came in the final quarter, as the Bengals frantically scrambled to get back into the game. His first, a 4-yarder, helped bring the Bengals to within 6 points, at 20–14, with 10:06 left. His second, of 3 yards, helped finish the game's scoring, as the Bengals trailed 26–21, with 16 seconds left in the game. The onsides kick attempt by the Bengals failed, though.

DAVE ROWE

Oakland Raiders, nose tackle, 6 feet 7, 271, Penn State. Start-ing nose tackle for the Raiders in Super Bowl XI, and part of the Raiders' defense which held the Minnesota Vikings to 14 points and 71 yards rushing.

JOHN ROWSER

Green Bay Packers, defensive back, 6 feet 1, 180, Michigan. Rowser, a rookie, played as a substitute for the Packers in Super Bowl II.

REGGIE RUCKER

Dallas Cowboys, wide receiver, 6 feet 2, 190, Boston University. A starter for the Cowboys, Rucker did not record any individual statistics, although he was overthrown in the end zone in the 1st quarter by quarterback Craig Morton in Super Bowl V.

MAX RUNAGER

Philadelphia Eagles, punter, 6 feet 1, 189, South Carolina. Runager handled punting duties for the Eagles in Super Bowl XV and the 49ers in SB XIX after he was cut by the Eagles in 1984 and picked up as a free agent by San Francisco.

In SB XV, Runager punted 3 times for an average of 36.7 yards with a long punt of 46 yards. In SB XIX, he punted 3 times for an average of 32.7 yards.

ANDY RUSSELL

Pittsburgh Steelers, linebacker, 6 feet 2, 225, Missouri. Starting right linebacker for the Steelers in both Super Bowls IX and X. In SB X Russell dropped Dallas running back Robert Newhouse for a loss on the Pittsburgh 20-yard line in the 1st half as the Cowboys threatened to increase a 10–7 lead. The Pittsburgh defense held, and the team went on to win.

JEFF RUTLEDGE

Los Angeles Rams, quarterback, 6 feet 2, 200, Alabama. Listed on the Rams' roster for Super Bowl XIV, Rutledge did not play in the game.

DAN RYCZEK

Los Angeles Rams, center and guard, 6 feet 3, 245, Virginia. Played as a substitute for the Rams in Super Bowl XIV.

☆ ☆ ☆

MIKE ST. CLAIR

Cincinnati Bengals, defensive end, 6 feet 5, 254, Grambling. Played as a substitute for the Bengals in Super Bowl XVI.

JOHNNY SAMPLE

New York Jets, defensive back, 6 feet 1, 204, Maryland/ Eastern Shore. The starting left halfback, Sample made his mark on Super Bowl III with an interception and several altercations with Baltimore Colt players. A former Colt, Sample picked off a pass thrown by Earl Morrall into a crowd near the Jets' end zone in the 1st half, ending a Baltimore drive.

Constantly chattering during the game, with Colt flanker Willie Richardson his main target, Sample finally was retaliated against by the Colts when—late in the game—he found himself following a play out of bounds into the Baltimore bench area. Before he could get back on the field safely, the Colts' Tom Mitchell swung his empty helmet at Sample, hitting him on the helmet. Several minutes later, after teammate Randy Beverly intercepted a Baltimore pass, Sample slapped the back of the helmet of the Colts' Tom Matte, who had to be restrained from going after Sample.

THOMAS SANDERS

Chicago Bears, running back, 5 feet 11, 203, Texas A&M. A substitute, Sanders carried 4 times for 15 yards in Super Bowl XX.

GEORGE SAUER, JR.

New York Jets, end, 6 feet 2, 195, Texas. The Jets' leading receiver in Super Bowl III with 8 receptions for 133 yards, including a long reception of 39 yards.

He was the son of the Jet's personnel director at the time of the game.

Sauer fumbled once, the Jets' only turnover of the game. The fumble gave the Baltimore Colts the ball on the Jets' 12 in the 1st quarter. But Baltimore failed to capitalize, when an Earl Morrall pass was intercepted by Randy Beverly. Sauer later caught passes of 14 and 11 yards in the Jets' first scoring drive.

RICH SAUL

Los Angeles Rams, center, 6 feet 3, 243, Michigan State. Starting center for the Rams in Super Bowl XIV.

JOHN SCHMITT

New York Jets, center, 6 feet 4, 245, Hofstra. Starting center for the Jets in Super Bowl III.

RAY SCHOENKE

Washington Redskins, tackle, 6 feet 4, 250, Southern Methodist. Listed on the Redskins' roster in Super Bowl VII but did not play.

TURK SCHONERT

Cincinnati Bengals, quarterback, 6 feet 1, 185, Stanford. Schonert, a backup quarterback,

was listed on the Bengals' roster but did not play in Super Bowl XVI.

HARRY SCHUH

Oakland Raiders, tackle, 6 feet 2, 260, Memphis State. Starting right tackle for the Raiders in Super Bowl II.

JOHN SCHULTZ

Denver Broncos, wide receiver and kick returner, 5 feet 10, 183, Maryland. Schultz handled some of the Broncos' punt and kickoff return duties in Super Bowl XII and fell victim to a string of miscues, when one punt hit him on the helmet and was recovered by the Dallas Cowboys. In all, Schultz returned 1 punt for no yardage, and returned 2 kickoffs for 62 yards, with a long return of 37 yards.

JOHN SCIARRA

Philadelphia Eagles, safety and kick returner, 5 feet 11, 185, UCLA. Sciarra was credited with 2 punt returns for a total of 18 yards with a long return of 12 yards in Super Bowl XV.

HERBERT SCOTT

Dallas Cowboys, guard, 6 feet 2, 250, Virginia Union. A substitute in Super Bowl X, Scott started at left guard in SB XII and SB XIII for the Cowboys.

JAKE SCOTT

Miami Dolphins, safety and kick returner, 6 feet, 188, Georgia. The starting right safety for the Dolphins in Super Bowls VI, VII, and VIII, Scott was named the MVP of SB VII.

In SB VII, Scott intercepted 2 passes in his team's 14–7 victory over the Washington Redskins. The first interception, in the 2nd quarter, stopped a Redskins' drive. The second was even more spectacular. A 79-yard Washington drive ended when Scott picked off a pass from Billy Kilmer intended for Charley Taylor in the

end zone and ran it back 55 yards to the Redskins' 48-yard line.

Afterward, Kilmer was to say, "On the Scott interception, Charley Taylor was open for a moment, but Jake just jumped in front of him."

Scott also handled some kick return duties, returning 1 punt for 21 yards in SB VI, 2 punts for 4 yards with 2 fair catches in SB VII, and 3 punts for 20 yards with 1 fair catch and 2 kickoffs for 47 yards in SB VIII. He also fumbled once and recovered a Minnesota Viking fumble in his last appearance.

VIRGIL SEAY

Washington Redskins, wide receiver, 5 feet 8, 175, Troy State. Played as a substitute for the Redskins in Super Bowl XVII, and while on the Redskins' roster for SB XVIII, was injured and did not play.

LARRY SEIPLE

Miami Dolphins, punter, 6 feet, 215, Kentucky. Seiple handled the Dolphins' punting in three Super Bowls—SB VI, SB VII, and SB VIII. In SB VI, he punted 5 times for an average of 40 yards with a long punt of 45 yards. In SB VII, he punted 7 times for a 43-yard average and a long punt of 50 yards. In SB VIII, he punted 3 times for a 39.7 average and a long punt of 57 yards. His 15 total

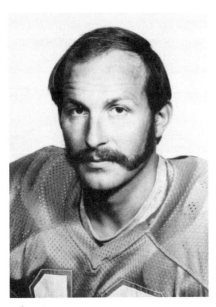

Jake Scott

punts ranks him second behind Mike Eischeid (Oakland and Minnesota) for most punts in a career in the SB.

GOLDIE SELLERS

Kansas City Chiefs, corner back, 6 feet 2, 198, Grambling. Mainly a special teams player, he was a substitute for the Chiefs in Super Bowl IV.

RON SELLERS

Miami Dolphins, wide receiver, 6 feet 4, 204, Florida State. Sellers was on the Dolphins' roster for Super Bowl VIII, but did not play.

RAFAEL SEPTIEN

Dallas Cowboys, place kicker, 5 feet 9, 171, Southwestern Louisiana. Septien was a key figure in the Cowboys' late but unsuccessful rally in Super Bowl XIII. After Dallas came back from a 35–17 deficit to pull to within 11, at 35–24, Septien's onside kick was dropped by the Steelers and recovered by Dallas, which went on to score again with 22 seconds left. Septien again tried an onside kick, but the Steelers' Rocky Bleier pulled it in. Earlier, Septien had made a 27-yard field goal and finished with 7 points with 4 point-after-touchdowns.

JEFF SEVERSON

Washington Redskins, defensive back, 6 feet 1, 180, Long Beach State. Played as a substitute for the Redskins in Super Bowl VII.

RON SHANKLIN

Pittsburgh Steelers, wide receiver, 6 feet 1, 190, North Texas State. Shanklin started at a wide receiver position for the Steelers in Super Bowl IX, but did not record any individual statistics.

ED SHAROCKMAN

Minnesota Vikings, corner back, 6 feet, 200, Pittsburgh. A starter on the right side of the defensive backfield for the Vikings in Super Bowl IV. After the game, the Kansas City Chiefs said Sharockman was one of the players who became "frustrated" by the Chiefs' successful end-around plays.

ART SHELL

Oakland Raiders, tackle, 6 feet 5, 265, Maryland/Eastern Shore. The starting left tackle for the Raiders in Super Bowls XI and XV. In SB XI he was one of the players credited with aiding the Raiders' powerful offense in their 32–14 victory over the Vikings. His team did much of its running over the left side, behind Shell and guard Gene Upshaw. After the game, Raiders quarterback Ken Stabler said of Shell and Upshaw: "We just line up and try to knock you out of there. Nobody's better at it than those two guys."

DONNIE SHELL

Pittsburgh Steelers, safety and corner back, 5 feet 11, 190, South Carolina State. As a rookie, Shell played as a substitute in Super Bowl IX, then played in the same capacity in SB X before starting at strong safety in two more games—SB XIII and SB XIV.

In the 3rd quarter, Shell had a key tackle to stop Dallas Cowboy running back Tony Dorsett on the Pittsburgh 10. The Cowboys ended up settling for a field goal, and Pittsburgh scored the next two touchdowns to break the game open.

TODD SHELL

San Francisco 49ers, linebacker, 6 feet 4, 225, Brigham Young. Shell, a rookie first-round draft choice, played as a substitute in Super Bowl XIX.

ROD SHERMAN

Oakland Raiders, flanker, 6 feet, 190, Southern California. Sherman was on the Oakland Raiders' roster but did not play in Super Bowl II.

BILLY SHIELDS

San Francisco 49ers, tackle, 6 feet 8, 279, Georgia Tech. A free-agent acquisition before the season, Shields played mainly on special teams and was a substitute in Super Bowl XIX.

DON SHINNICK

Baltimore Colts, linebacker, 6 feet, 228, UCLA. The starting right linebacker for the Colts in Super Bowl III.

JACKIE SHIPP

Miami Dolphins, linebacker, 6 feet 2, 236, Oklahoma. A rookie, Shipp played as a substitute in Super Bowl XIX.

SANDERS SHIVER

Miami Dolphins, linebacker, 6 feet 2, 235, Carson-Newman. Shiver, in his only year with the Dolphins, played as a substitute for the team in Super Bowl XIX.

STEVE SHULL

Miami Dolphins, linebacker, 6 feet 1, 220, William and Mary. Shull played as a substitute for the Dolphins in Super Bowl XVII.

172

MIKE SHUMANN

San Francisco 49ers, wide receiver, 6 feet, 175, Florida State. Shumann played as a substitute in Super Bowl XVI but did not record any individual statistics.

MIKE SIANI

Oakland Raiders, wide receiver, 6 feet 2, 195, Villanova. Siani played as a substitute for the Raiders in Super Bowl XI, but did not record any individual statistics.

JEFF SIEMON

Minnesota Vikings, linebacker, 6 feet 2, 230, Stanford. Starting middle linebacker for the Vikings in Super Bowls VIII, IX, and XI. He was involved in a scoring play in SB IX, when Larry Brown caught a 4-yard pass from Terry Bradshaw for the Steelers' final touchdown. Bradshaw said of Brown, "He stopped after running toward the corner of the end zone, then started again. That made the middle linebacker (Siemon) commit himself."

JOHN SIMMONS

Cincinnati Bengals, corner back, 5 feet 11, 192, Southern Methodist. Simmons, a rookie, played as a substitute in Super Bowl XVI and recovered a fumble on the opening kickoff. The SF 49ers' Amos Lawrence had returned the ball 17 yards before he fumbled on his own 26, where Simmons recovered. But the Bengals did not score after the turnover, as the 49ers regained control by an interception several plays later.

ROY SIMMONS

Washington Redskins, guard, 6 feet 3, 264, Georgia Tech. A free-agent acquisition before the season began, Simmons played as a substitute for the Redskins in Super Bowl XVIII.

MIKE SINGLETARY

Chicago Bears, linebacker, 6 feet, 228, Baylor. The 1985 NFL defensive player of the year, Singletary was considered one of the keys to the Bear defense, which helped the team into Super Bowl XX, then dominated the game against the New England Patriots.

The starting middle linebacker, he finished the game with 1 tackle, 1 assist, 1 pass defensed, and 2 fumble recoveries—the latter statistic tying an SB record shared by four others. His first recovery came in the opening quarter; after Richard Dent hit Patriot running back Craig James, Singletary recovered at the New England 13. Two plays later, the Bears scored a touchdown that put them ahead, 13–3. Singletary also recovered a fumble in the 4th quarter.

JERRY SISEMORE

Philadelphia Eagles, tackle, 6 feet 4, 265, Texas. Starting right tackle for the Eagles in Super Bowl XV.

MANNY SISTRUNK

Washington Redskins, defensive tackle, 6 feet 5, 265, Arkansas/Pine Bluff. Played as a substitute for the Redskins in Super Bowl VII. He was a first cousin of Otis Sistrunk, who also played in the SB (below).

OTIS SISTRUNK

Oakland Raiders, defensive end, 6 feet 3, 273, no college. Sistrunk, from Columbus, Georgia, began playing pro football with the West Allis (Wisconsin) Racers of the Central States League and was first signed as a free agent by the LA Rams in 1972, then was traded to the Raiders. He started Super Bowl XI as the defensive right end for the Raiders. First cousin of Redskins' Manny Sistrunk (above).

BOB SKORONSKI

Green Bay Packers, tackle, 6 feet 3, 250, Indiana. The starting left tackle for the Packers in Super Bowls I and II. A Packer cocaptain, Skoronski was charged—wrongly he said later—with a motion penalty that brought back a 64-yard scoring pass from Bart Starr to Carroll Dale. But the team recovered and scored 11 plays later to take a 14–7 lead. Following the game, Skoronski said, "I didn't even move before the snap. I was even late off the ball."

JACKIE SLATER

Los Angeles Rams, tackle, 6 feet 4, 269, Jackson State. Starting right tackle for the Rams in Super Bowl XIV.

MARK SLATER

Philadelphia Eagles, center, 6 feet 2, 257, Minnesota. Played as a substitute for the Eagles in Super Bowl XV.

RICHARD SLIGH

Oakland Raiders, defensive tackle and end, 7 feet, 300, North Carolina College. Sligh, who played with the Raiders one season, was a substitute with the team in Super Bowl II.

GERALD SMALL

Miami Dolphins, corner back, 5 feet 11, 192, San Jose

State. The starting left corner back for the Dolphins in Super Bowl XVII, Small had a pass caught over his head by Washington Redskin receiver Alvin Garrett for a 4-yard touchdown that tied the score at 10–10 in the first half.

BILLY RAY SMITH

Baltimore Colts, defensive tackle, 6 feet 4, 250, Arkansas. The starting defensive left tackle and defensive captain for the Colts in Super Bowls III and V. After SB III, he blamed his own defensive unit for the defeat: "It was us. We let down our teammates and the entire National Football League. My pride is bent."

In SB V, his last game as a pro, Smith was given credit by at least one teammate for causing a key fumble recovery. Smith and teammate Jerry Logan hit Cowboys' running back Duane Thomas on the Colt's goal line. He fumbled, and Colts' corner back Jim Duncan came up with the recovery. Smith agreed with his teammate, saying, "I take full credit for that there recovery." It was a play that Dallas Coach Tom Landry said was the key to the game.

CHARLES (BUBBA) SMITH

Baltimore Colts, defensive end, 6 feet 7, 295, Michigan State. Smith, highly touted coming out of college, was often greeted by cries of "Kill! Bubba, Kill!" but his first Super Bowl experience, in SB III, was anything but positive. So Smith was one of several Colts to feel a personal relief after victory in SB V.

CHARLES SMITH

Philadelphia Eagles, wide receiver, 6 feet 1, 185, Grambling. A substitute, Smith caught 2 passes for 59 yards in Super Bowl XV, including a 43-yarder in the Eagles' late scoring drive. The drive ended with Ron Jaworski's 8-yard touchdown pass to Keith Krepfle.

FLETCHER SMITH

Kansas City Chiefs, defensive back, 6 feet 2, 188, Tennessee State. A rookie, Smith played as a substitute for the Chiefs in Super Bowl I.

JACKIE SMITH

Dallas Cowboys, tight end, 6 feet 4, 230, Northwestern Louisiana. Smith, a 16-year veteran playing as a reserve, did not catch a single pass in Super Bowl XIII— but one that got away may qualify him among the SB's hard luck stories.

In the 3rd quarter, with the Pittsburgh Steelers leading, 21–

14, the Cowboys drove to the Steeler 10. On a third-and-3 play, Dallas quarterback Roger Staubach found Smith wide open in the end zone. But Smith dropped the ball.

Afterward, Staubach said, "If I'd thrown a better pass, he would have caught it."

The Cowboys ended up with a field goal, but Pittsburgh scored the next 2 touchdowns to win.

JERRY SMITH

Washington Redskins, tight end, 6 feet 3, 208, Arizona State. The starting tight end for the Redskins in Super Bowl VII, Smith ran 1 time for 6 yards and caught 1 pass for 11 yards.

JIM SMITH

Pittsburgh Steelers, wide receiver and kick returner, 6 feet 2, 205, Michigan. Smith played as a substitute in Super Bowls XIII and XIV, and returned 2 punts for 14 yards in the second game.

PAUL SMITH

Denver Broncos, nose tackle, 6 feet 3, 250, New Mexico. Played as a substitute in Super Bowl XII.

RON SMITH

Los Angeles Rams, wide receiver, 6 feet, 185, San Diego State.

Smith, a reserve, had a part in two key plays in Super Bowl XIV. In the 3rd quarter, he caught a 24-yard pass for a touchdown from Lawrence McCutcheon on a halfback option, to give the Rams a 19–17 lead over the Pittsburgh Steelers. But later, with the Steelers ahead, 24–19, a pass intended for Smith was stolen by Pittsburgh's Jack Lambert deep in Steeler territory. The interception capped a Pittsburgh victory.

STEVE SMITH

Minnesota Vikings, defensive end, 6 feet 5, 250, Michigan. Played as a substitute for the Vikings in Super Bowl IV.

TODY SMITH

Dallas Cowboys, defensive end, 6 feet 5, 245, Southern California. A rookie, Smith played as a substitute for the Cowboys in Super Bowl VI.

MARK SMOLINSKI

New York Jets, running back and tight end, 6 feet 1, 215, Wyoming. Smolinski played as a substitute in Super Bowl III, but did not record any individual statistics.

MATT SNELL

New York Jets, running back, 6 feet 2, 219, Ohio State. Snell set a rushing record that held for 8 years and scored the Jets' first touchdown in Super Bowl III.

After a scoreless 1st quarter, Snell capped an 80-yard drive by running off left tackle for 4 yards and a touchdown. He finished the game with 30 carries for 121 yards, with a long run of 12 yards. His 121 yards held as a single-game high until 1977. He also caught 4 passes for 40 yards.

Snell had also been involved in a collision early that knocked Colts' safety Rich Volk momentarily unconscious. And late in the game, he carried the ball 6 times in a Jets drive that ate up the final minutes on the clock.

FREDDIE SOLOMON

San Francisco 49ers, wide receiver and kick returner, 5 feet

Freddie Solomon

11, 185, Tampa. A college quarterback, Solomon provided the 49ers with a deep threat in two Super Bowls—SB XVI and SB XIX. He led the team in receiving in SB XVI with 4 receptions for 52 yards and caught 2 passes for 9 and 14 yards in a drive that led to the 49ers' first touchdown.

Solomon also had a 20-yard reception in a key situation in the 2nd quarter, helping keep alive a drive that ended with the 49ers' second touchdown.

In SB XIX, Solomon had 1 reception for 14 yards and rushed once for 5 yards.

ROBERT SOWELL

Miami Dolphins, corner back, 5 feet 11, 175, Howard. Sowell, labeled "the special teams spark plug" by the Dolphins, played as a substitute in Super Bowl XIX.

JOHN SPAGNOLA

Philadelphia Eagles, tight end, 6 feet 4, 240, Yale. The starting tight end for the Eagles in Super Bowl XV, Spagnola caught 1 pass for 22 yards in the game.

JACK SQUIREK

Los Angeles Raiders, linebacker, 6 feet 4, 225, Illinois. In Super Bowl XVIII, the second-year player, in as a substitute, intercepted a pass late in the 1st half and ran it back 5 yards for a stunning touchdown, to give the Raiders a 21–3 lead over the Washington Redskins at halftime.

The Redskins had taken over the ball on their own 12 with only 12 seconds left. Redskins Coach Joe Gibbs called for a screen. Squirek, in as part of the Raiders' prevent defense, got instructions from Charlie Sumner, the team's defensive coordinator, that the Redskins might try a screen, and was ready.

When Redskins quarterback Joe Theismann sent the pass in the direction of halfback Joe Washington, Squirek read the Splay, stepped in front of Washington, and returned it the 5 yards for a touchdown with 7 seconds left in the half.

Squirek said later, "Charlie sent me in there and said, 'Watch the screen to Washington.' I never expected a screen that late in the half with so little time left, but Charlie did. . . . When I came off the field, I went up to Charlie and said, 'Thanks, coach.'"

Squirek was also in on 3 tackles in the game.

Ken Stabler

KEN STABLER

Oakland Raiders, quarterback, 6 feet 3, 215, Alabama. While the Raider defense kept the Minnesota Vikings off balance, Stabler did the same to the Viking defense as he took his team to a decisive 32–14 victory in Super Bowl XI.

Mixing the rushing and passing game, Stabler's Raiders set an SB record with 429 yards gained, including 266 rushing and 163 passing. Stabler completed 12 of 19 passes for 180 yards and 1 touchdown.

The touchdown was a 1-yard toss to Dave Casper, which gave Oakland a 10–0 lead. Stabler then led the Raiders to another touchdown, and they led, 16–0, at halftime.

A 48-yard pass to Fred Biletnikoff—who was named the game's MVP—in the 2nd half was the key play in another scoring drive. Afterward, Stabler said, "When it comes to the Super Bowl, some teams have a problem of wanting to play conservative. People don't want to make the key mistake. But we don't play our best football that way. We do better when we come out wheeling and dealing and smoking and throwing. I have confidence in our running game. I knew we could run. The whole thing is play selection. That puts the monkey on my back."

DAVE STALLS

Dallas Cowboys and Los Angeles Raiders, defensive tackle, 6 feet 4, 236, North Colorado. Stalls played in three Super Bowls in a substitute role—in SB XII and SB XIII for the Cowboys and SB XVIII for the Raiders.

JOHN STALLWORTH

Pittsburgh Steelers, wide receiver, 6 feet 2, 183, Alabama A&M. Stallworth and teammate Lynn Swann made up one of the most dangerous pass-receiving

John Stallworth

pairs of all time, and both left their marks on the Super Bowl record book.

Stallworth's career ended with a share of the record for most touchdowns in a career, 3.

In SB XIII, he tied what was then a record with a 75-yarder in the 1st half of an exciting 35–31 victory over the Dallas Cowboys and tied the score at 14–14. Earlier, Stallworth had caught a 28-yard pass from Terry Bradshaw for the first scoring of the game. Stallworth finished the game with 3 receptions for 115 yards.

Stallworth and Bradshaw combined for more long-range magic in SB XIV. Stallworth caught a 73-yard scoring pass from Bradshaw to go ahead, 24–19. He then caught a 45-yard pass to help set up the game's final touchdown, finishing with 3 catches for 121 yards.

In his first SB, game IX, he caught 3 passes for 24 yards, then caught 2 passes for 8 yards in SB X.

Stallworth's SB totals include 11 receptions for 268 yards and 3 touchdowns. He has the highest average gain figure for a career with an average of 24.4 yards per gain and the highest for a game at 40.3.

BILL STANFILL

Miami Dolphins, defensive end, 6 feet 5, 250, Georgia. Stanfill started at defensive right end for the Dolphins in three consecutive Super Bowls—SB VI, SB VII, and SB VIII. In SB VII, Stanfill made sure the Washington Redskins were unable to come back from the final 14–7 deficit by sacking quarterback Billy Kilmer for a 9-yard loss on fourth down on the Redskins' final offensive play of the game. Going into SB VIII, he was considered one of the keys to containing Minnesota quarterback Fran Tarkenton.

Bart Starr

GEORGE STARKE

Washington Redskins, tackle, 6 feet 5, 260, Columbia. Starke, a 10-year veteran going into Super Bowl XVII, had earned the title of "Head Hog" because of his seniority among the Redskins' front line. He started at right tackle in both SB XVII and SB XVIII.

BART STARR

Green Bay Packers, quarterback, 6 feet 1, 200, Alabama. Starr, the model of cool and calm, led the Packers to victories in the first two Super Bowls—and was named the MVP following each.

In SB I, Starr marched the Packers to the Kansas City Chiefs' 37, then caught the Chiefs in a defensive coverage mistake and threw to end Max McGee. The pass was a bit behind McGee, but he made a spectacular save and went in for the touchdown.

After the Chiefs tied the game, Starr did what he seemed to do best—come back coolly from an adverse situation—as an apparent 64-yard touchdown pass to Carroll Dale was called back because of a penalty. But Starr put the Packer drive back on track, and it ended with a 14-yard touchdown run by Jim Taylor.

The Packer defense took over in the 3rd quarter, and Starr continued to drive the offense, finishing the game with 16 completions in 23 attempts for 250 yards and 2 touchdowns, as he threw another to McGee later in the game.

After the game, Norm Van Brocklin, the respected coach of the Minnesota Vikings, commented on the touchdown that was called back. "That's the way the Packers are. Starr . . . was the difference in there today."

In SB II, the Packers again turned it on in the 2nd half. The

Packers led, 16–7, at halftime, but had scored only 1 touchdown, on a 62-yard pass from Starr to Boyd Dowler.

Starr then led the team on a 82-yard drive in the 3rd quarter, hitting on key passes in two third-down situations. Donny Anderson finished the drive with a 2-yard scoring run.

Starr's final Super Bowl statistics included 29 completions in 47 attempts for 452 yards, 3 touchdowns, 1 interception, and 1 carry for 14 yards. He remains one of three players—along with Terry Bradshaw and Joe Montana—to win the MVP award twice.

Roger Staubach

STEPHEN STARRING

New England Patriots, wide receiver and kick returner, 5 feet 10, 172, McNeese State. Starring was a starting wide receiver and handled the Patriots' kick return duties in Super Bowl XX. He caught 2 passes for 39 yards, including a long reception of 24 yards. He also returned 7 kickoffs for 153 yards, with a long return of 36 yards.

ROGER STAUBACH

Dallas Cowboys, quarterback, 6 feet 3, 197, Navy. Battered and bruised, Staubach led the Dallas Cowboys to their first title ever, in Super Bowl VI, earning the game's MVP award in the process. In all, Staubach helped the

Cowboys to four SBs—SB VI, SB X, SB XII, and SB XIII—and finished 2–2, with both defeats coming at the hands of the Pittsburgh Steelers.

In SB VI, despite being sacked 3 times in the 1st quarter and despite sore ribs, he completed 12 of 19 passes for 119 yards and 2 touchdowns, throwing no interceptions. His touchdown passes were 7 yards to Lance Alworth in the 1st half and 7 yards to Mike Ditka in the 2nd, completing the game's scoring.

The Cowboys lost the first of two SBs to the Steelers in SB X, an exciting 21–17 match. Staubach went down throwing, though, as his final pass was intercepted by safety Glen Edwards deep in Steeler territory with just seconds left.

Staubach had thrown 2 touchdown passes in the game, finishing 15 of 24 for 204 yards. He also threw 3 interceptions and fumbled 3 times, recovering 2.

"We didn't have the timeouts, and they [Pittsburgh] knew it," Staubach said later of the game's final minutes. "I was just throwing them up for grabs and hoping one of our guys would get them."

Staubach, helped by a strong defensive showing, led the Cowboys past the Denver Broncos in SB XII. Playing most of the last quarter with a broken right index finger, Staubach threw a 45-yard touchdown pass to Butch Johnson in the 3rd quarter to put the Cowboys well ahead, 20–3.

In SB XIII, a game reminiscent of the Cowboys' earlier defeat by the Steelers, Staubach had the Cowboys in competition until the final seconds. After trailing, 35–17, the Cowboys began their rally. First, they drove 89 yards, with Staubach passing to Billy Joe DuPree to end the drive with a touchdown. Dallas recovered the onside kickoff, and 9 plays later, Staubach passed 4 yards to Butch Johnson for another touchdown with 22 seconds left. Staubach didn't get another chance, however, as Rocky Bleier pulled in the onside kick.

Staubach's SB totals include records for most passes attempted, 98, and most completed, 61. He finished with 734 yards, 8 touchdown passes, and 4 interceptions.

ROBERT STEELE

Dallas Cowboys, wide receiver, 6 feet 4, 196, North Alabama. Steele, a rookie, played as a substitute in Super Bowl XIII.

BOB STEIN

Kansas City Chiefs, linebacker, 6 feet 3, 235, Minnesota. Stein played as a substitute for the Chiefs in Super Bowl IV.

JAN STENERUD

Kansas City Chiefs, kicker, 6 feet 2, 187, Montana State. Stenerud, a native of Norway who came over to the United States on a skiing scholarship and ended up putting together a record-studded NFL career, made all three of his field-goal attempts to give the Chiefs a 9–0 lead and enough points to win Super Bowl IV against the Minnesota Vikings.

Stenerud, who also kicked 2 point-after-touchdowns, kicked a 48-yard field goal to end the Chiefs' first drive. The kick is still the longest in the game's history. Stenerud kicked field goals of 32 and 25 yards in the 2nd quarter and then, when the Vikings fumbled the kickoff following the third field goal, added a point-after-touchdown as the Chiefs capitalized on the turnover and led, 16–0, at halftime.

DWIGHT STEPHENSON

Miami Dolphins, center, 6 feet 2, 255, Alabama. One of the most honored offensive linemen in the game, Stephenson started at center for the Dolphins in Super Bowls XVII and XIX.

TOM STINCIC

Dallas Cowboys, linebacker, 6 feet 4, 230, Michigan. Stincic played as a substitute for the Cowboys in Super Bowls V and VI.

CLIFF STOUDT

Pittsburgh Steelers, quarterback, 6 feet 4, 210, Youngstown State. A backup to Terry Bradshaw, Stoudt did not play in either Super Bowl XIII or XIV.

JEFF STOVER

San Francisco 49ers, defensive end, 6 feet 5, 275, Oregon. Stover, who took six years off from football after high school only to return to the game, played as a substitute for the 49ers in Super Bowl XIX.

STEWART (SMOKEY) STOVER

Kansas City Chiefs, linebacker, 6 feet, 227, Northeast Louisi- ana. Stover, a member of the original 1960 Dallas Texans, played as a substitute for the Chiefs in Super Bowl I.

OTTO STOWE

Miami Dolphins, wide receiver, 6 feet 2, 188, Iowa State. Stowe played as a substitute in Super Bowl VI, then, although on the Dolphins' roster for SB VII, did not play.

DON STROCK

Miami Dolphins, quarterback, 6 feet 5, 220, Virginia Tech. Strock, a placement holder for kicks, served as a backup for David Woodley in Super Bowl XVII and Dan Marino in SB XIX. He played briefly late against the Washington Redskins in SB XVII, throwing incompletions on all 3 attempts, as he and Woodley combined for only 4 completions in 17 attempts, none in the 2nd half.

HENRY STUCKEY

Miami Dolphins, defensive back, 6 feet, 180, Missouri. Stuckey, a rookie, played as a substitute in Super Bowl VII, then played in the same capacity in SB VIII.

JIM STUCKEY

San Francisco 49ers, defensive end, 6 feet 4, 251, Clemson.

Studkey started at defensive left end for the 49ers in Super Bowl XVI, then played as a reserve in SB XIX. In the first game, Stuckey came up with a key tackle, dropping Cincinnati quarterback Ken Anderson for a 6-yard loss at the 49er 11. On the next play, the 49ers intercepted.

CHARLES STUKES

Baltimore Colts, defensive back, 6 feet 3, 212, Maryland State. Played as a substitute in Super Bowl III, then as a starter at left corner back in SB V.

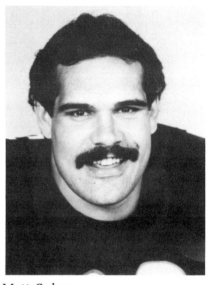

Matt Suhey

MATT SUHEY

Chicago Bears, fullback, 5 feet 11, 216, Penn State. Suhey, a backfield starter, scored the Bears' first touchdown in Super Bowl XX and had a key reception in another scoring drive as he overshadowed his more famous backfield running mate, Walter Payton.

Suhey finished with 11 carries for 52 yards, with his longest carry the 11-yard touchdown. That came near the end of the 1st quarter, as the Bears led by only 3 points, 6–3. Then, the Bear defensive unit came up with a fumble recovery on the New England 13. Suhey got the handoff on the next play and went 2 yards. The Bears went right back to Suhey, who carried the ball in the final 11 yards.

On the Bears' next possession, quarterback Jim McMahon connected on a 24-yard pass with Suhey to put the ball on the New England 15. Suhey carried the ball the next 3 plays, for gains of 7, 1, and 3 yards; Payton carried to the 2, and McMahon carried the ball in to help the Bears go ahead, 20–3.

DAN SULLIVAN

Baltimore Colts, guard and tackle, 6 feet 3, 250, Boston College. Sullivan started Super Bowl III at the right guard position, then started SB V at right tackle. Sullivan was involved in a famous pre-SB III "confrontation" between his teammate, Lou Michaels, and the Jets' Joe Namath and Jim Hudson at a restaurant in Fort Lauderdale. The four ended up sharing a table, and Namath is said to have driven Michaels and Sullivan back to their hotels.

IVORY SULLY

Los Angeles Rams, safety and corner back, 6 feet, 193, Delaware. Sully, a rookie, played as a substitute for the Rams in Super Bowl XIV.

MILT SUNDE

Minnesota Vikings, guard, 6 feet 2, 250, Minnesota. Sunde started at right guard for the Vikings in Super Bowl IV, then played as a substitute in SB IX. He did not play in SB VIII because of a knee injury.

DOUG SUTHERLAND

Minnesota Vikings, defensive tackle, 6 feet 3, 250, Wisconsin/ Superior. After playing in Super Bowl VIII as a substitute, Sutherland started at defensive left tackle for the Vikings in SB IX and SB XI, as part of a famous defensive front line.

BOB SVIHUS

Oakland Raiders, tackle, 6 feet 4, 245, Southern California. Starting left tackle for the Raiders in Super Bowl II.

LYNN SWANN

Pittsburgh Steelers, wide receiver, 5 feet 10, 178, Southern California. Of all the Super Bowl images that fans will remember, one of the most vivid has to be that of Swann's receiving acrobatics on the way to the MVP award in SB X.

Adding to the impact of the story was the fact that Swann had suffered a concussion only weeks before the game, had gone through workouts dizzy, was told he would be susceptible to another injury—and was baited by the Dallas Cowboys' safety Cliff Harris, who intimated he would send Swann to the sidelines again.

Swann played the game and had 4 receptions for 161 yards and 1 touchdown. He scored on a play that covered 64 yards with 3:02 left in the game as the Steelers

Lynn Swann

185

held a 15–10 lead. "Terry called the play in the huddle," Swann said later. "I got by my man, the ball was there, and it worked. It was the best catch I've ever made in professional football."

Swann's other catches included a 32-yarder that set up the Steelers' first touchdown and a tumbling, diving grab for 53 yards.

Earlier, in SB IX, Swann played as a substitute, did not catch any passes but returned 3 punts for 34 yards.

Swann again led his team in receiving in SB XIII, as he caught 7 passes for 124 yards and 1 touchdown—which gave the Steelers their winning points.

In the first half, he had 2 receptions—of 29 and 21 yards— in a scoring drive. He then played a part in the final 2 Pittsburgh drives. He helped set up Franco Harris' 22-yard run, drawing an interference penalty on corner back Benny Barnes. Then, when the Steelers recovered a fumble on the following kickoff, he caught an 18-yarder for a touchdown and a 35–17 lead.

Swann again led the Steelers in receiving in SB XIV, with 5 receptions for 79 yards and 1 touchdown. Swann caught a 47-yard touchdown pass from Bradshaw in the 2nd half to give the Steelers a brief 17–13 lead.

Swann's SB totals include 16 receptions for 364 yards and 3 touchdowns, all SB career records. His 161 yards in SB X was a game record.

BOB SWENSON

Denver Broncos, linebacker, 6 feet 3, 255, California. A starting linebacker for the Broncos in Super Bowl XII.

DOUG SWIFT

Miami Dolphins, linebacker, 6 feet 3, 228, Amherst. Starting left linebacker for the Dolphins in Super Bowls VI, VII, and VIII. In SB VII, Swift blitzed Washington quarterback Billy Kilmer and forced him to pass hurriedly, and Miami's Nick Buoniconti picked the ball off for one of 3 Dolphin interceptions.

STEVE SYLVESTER

Oakland Raiders, center, 6 feet 4, 262, Notre Dame. The Raiders' "handyman," Sylvester played in 3 Super Bowls as a substitute— SB XI, SB XV, and SB XVIII.

DICK SZYMANSKI

Baltimore Colts, center, 6 feet 3, 235, Notre Dame. Szymanski, a 13-year veteran, played as a substitute in Super Bowl III.

☆ ☆ ☆

BOB TALAMINI

New York Jets, guard, 6 feet 1, 255, Kentucky. The starting left guard for the Jets in Super Bowl III.

DIRON TALBERT

Washington Redskins, defensive tackle, 6 feet 5, 255, Texas. Talbert started at defensive right tackle for the Redskins in Super Bowl VII and was one of the veteran players Coach George Allen picked up for his Over the Hill Gang.

FRAN TARKENTON

Minnesota Vikings, quarterback, 6 feet, 190, Georgia. A Hall of Fame selection, considered one of the top quarterbacks of all time in the NFL, Tarkenton ended up among the bigger losers among Super Bowl quarterbacks, as the Vikings went 0–3 under Tarkenton, in SB VIII, SB IX, and SB XI.

In SB VIII, the Miami Dolphins went ahead early and controlled the game on the way to a 24–7 victory. Tarkenton scored the lone Minnesota touchdown on a 4-yard run, and also set a record with 18 completions, but the Viking running game was effectively shut down.

After the game, Bill Arnsparger, the Miami defensive coach, said the early Dolphin points also helped shut down Tarkenton. "When your offense can go out and put two touchdowns on the board in the first quarter," he said, "it takes away some of the things they can do. I know I wouldn't want to try to contain Tarkenton through four quarters of scoreless ball."

The Vikings not only caught the last of the Dolphins' 1970s dynasty, but they also experienced firsthand the start of another, losing 16–6 to the Pittsburgh Steelers in SB IX.

Fran Tarkenton

totally dominated us. We were up. We had the emotion, but you have to make the plays to keep it going. We made one play, the blocked punt, but we didn't make the others. The Raiders played extremely well. We played badly."

Tarkenton's Super Bowl totals were 46 completions in 89 attempts for 489 yards, 1 touchdown, and 6 interceptions. He also ran 5 times for 17 yards.

JACK TATUM

Oakland Raiders, safety, 5 feet 11, 206, Ohio State. Tatum started at right safety for the Raiders in Super Bowl XI.

The Vikings finished with 119 yards total offense including 17 net yards rushing. Tarkenton was 11 of 26, but had 3 passes intercepted, as the Minnesota offense did not score in the game.

The Vikings made their final SB appearance in SB XI, and suffered through their worst defeat of all, 32–14, by the Oakland Raiders.

Tarkenton completed 17 of 35 attempts for 205 yards and 1 touchdown—an 8-yard pass to Sammy White—but also had 2 passes intercepted.

The second interception ended Tarkenton's game, as he was pulled in favor of Bob Lee. Tarkenton reflected later, saying, "We played. We tried. We just weren't good enough. They just

MOSI TATUPU

New England Patriots, fullback, 6 feet, 227, Southern California. A native of American Samoa, Tatupu played as a substitute in Super Bowl XX.

CHARLEY TAYLOR

Washington Redskins, wide receiver, 6 feet 2, 210, Arizona State. Taylor, a member of the Pro Football Hall of Fame, started at one wide receiver position for the Redskins in Super Bowl VII and caught 2 passes for 20 yards. He also rushed once for a gain of 8 yards.

JIM TAYLOR

Green Bay Packers, running back, 6 feet, 215, Louisiana State. A member of the Pro Football Hall of Fame, playing his last game with the Packers, Taylor carried 16 times for 53 yards and scored a touchdown in Super Bowl I. His touchdown was fitting—a 14-yard sweep behind Fred (Fuzzy) Thurston and Jerry Kramer.

KEN TAYLOR

Chicago Bears, corner back, 6 feet 1, 185, Oregon State. Taylor, playing as a substitute, recorded one tackle in Super Bowl XX.

OTIS TAYLOR

Kansas City Chiefs, flanker and wide receiver, 6 feet 2, 211, Prairie View A&M. Taylor started

Otis Taylor

both Super Bowls I and IV, the first at flanker, the second at wide receiver. In SB I, he caught 4 passes for 57 yards, including a long reception of 31 yards that Green Bay defender Willie Wood admitted "stung him."

In SB IV, Taylor caught 6 passes for 81 yards, including a 46-yard touchdown pass that completed the game's scoring. The pass portion of the play, however, was only 6 yards, as Taylor broke from the grasp of one Minnesota Viking defender and bulled past another to score.

ROOSEVELT TAYLOR

Washington Redskins, safety, 5 feet 11, 186, Grambling. Taylor, a 12-year veteran, started at right safety for the Redskins in Super Bowl VII.

TOM THAYER

Chicago Bears, guard and center, 6 feet 4, 261, Notre Dame. Thayer, a rookie by NFL standards (although he played three seasons in the US Football League), started at right guard for the Bears in Super Bowl XX. It was the 46th consecutive game he had played within one year, including a USFL season.

JOE THEISMANN

Washington Redskins, quarterback, 6 feet, 198, Notre Dame.

189

Joe Theismann

Theismann, who finished second to Jim Plunkett in the Heisman voting, started his pro career in the Canadian Football League, where he played for three seasons after being drafted by the Miami Dolphins in 1971.

Theismann joined the Redskins in 1974, after the Dolphins traded his rights to Washington, and finally led his team to consecutive appearances in Super Bowls XVII and XVIII.

Theismann helped the Redskins rally to a victory in his first appearance, against the Miami Dolphins. Behind, 17–10, at halftime, the Redskins scored 17 points in the 2nd half, with Theismann throwing a 6-yard touchdown toss to Charlie Brown to finish the scoring.

Theismann ended up 15 of 23 for 143 yards with 2 touchdowns and 2 interceptions. He also carried 3 times for 20 yards.

The Redskins and Theismann took a 38–9 pasting in SB XVIII at the hands of Plunkett and the LA Raiders, with a Theismann interception playing a key role.

Trailing, 14–3, with just 12 seconds left in the half, the Redskins took over the ball at their own 12. Washington Coach Joe Gibbs disdained a safe play and called for a screen pass. The Raiders' Jack Squirek was waiting, however, and picked off the ball and carried it into the end zone to help LA to a 21–3 halftime lead.

Theismann's afternoon didn't get any better in the 2nd half. Once, on the Raiders' 8, he was blitzed and hit by LA's Mike Davis, and he fumbled the ball away. Later, he had a second pass intercepted.

He finished the game 16 of 35 for 243 yards with 2 interceptions and was sacked 6 times for a loss of 50 yards.

BEN THOMAS

New England Patriots, defensive end, 6 feet 4, 280, Auburn. The rookie played as a substitute in Super Bowl XX and recorded 2 tackles and 1 sack for 11 yards.

CALVIN THOMAS

Chicago Bears, fullback, 5 feet 11, 245, Illinois. Thomas played as a substitute in Super

Bowl XX and ran 2 times for 8 yards and caught 1 pass for 4 yards.

DUANE THOMAS

Dallas Cowboys, running back, 6 feet 1, 220, West Texas State. Super Bowl V, the famous Stupor Bowl, ended Thomas' rookie season, and Thomas made one of the game's key mistakes, fumbling the ball on the Baltimore Colt 1 as the Cowboys led, 13–6. Thomas had given the Cowboys that lead earlier when he had caught a 7-yard pass from Craig Morton. Ultimately the Cowboys lost 16–13.

Of the fumble, Dallas Coach Tom Landry said, "That was the turning point. If we'd scored there, they would have been 14 points back." Thomas, who ended the game with 18 carries for 35 yards and 4 receptions for 21 yards, left immediately afterward and was unavailable for interviews.

Thomas wasn't talking again a year later—before or after Super Bowl VI, which culminated a season in which he had fought with Cowboy management over his contract, been traded to the New England Patriots, then returned to the Cowboys as "uncooperative."

But once the game began, Thomas didn't need to talk to impress the Miami Dolphins. He led both teams in rushing, with 19 carries for 95 yards, scoring the Cowboys' second touchdown on a 3-yard run, early in the second half, to give the team a 17–3 lead. He also caught 3 passes for 17 yards. But again, he had nothing to say.

Duane Thomas

EMMITT THOMAS

Kansas City Chiefs, defensive back and kick returner, 6 feet 2, 189, Bishop. Thomas, who played as a substitute, returned 1 punt for 2 yards in Super Bowl I. He started SB IV at right corner back, and having led the AFL in interceptions that season, picked off a Minnesota Viking pass in the closing minutes.

GENE THOMAS

Kansas City Chiefs, running back, 6 feet 1, 210, Florida A&M.

Thomas played as a substitute in Super Bowl I, but did not record any individual statistics.

ISAAC (IKE) THOMAS

Dallas Cowboys, corner back and kick returner, 6 feet 2, 193, Bishop. Ike Thomas returned 1 kickoff for 23 yards in Super Bowl VI.

J. T. THOMAS

Pittsburgh Steelers, corner back, 6 feet 2, 196, Florida State. Starting left corner back for the Steelers in Super Bowls IX and X and free safety in SB XIV. He intercepted a Roger Staubach pass early in the 2nd half of SB X, but the Steelers did not capitalize on the turnover. He also recovered a Dallas fumble in the game.

LYNN THOMAS

San Francisco 49ers, corner back, 5 feet 11, 181, Pittsburgh. Thomas, playing in a reserve role, recovered a fumble deep in 49er territory in Super Bowl XVI. After the Cincinnati Bengals drove to the San Francisco 27, Cris Collinsworth caught a pass from Ken Anderson, then fumbled when hit by Eric Wright. Thomas recovered on the 8, and his team ended up scoring after the turnover, marching a record 92 yards for a touchdown.

PAT THOMAS

Los Angeles Rams, corner back, 5 feet 9, 184, Texas A&M. The starting left corner back for the Rams in Super Bowl XIV, Thomas received an interference call that gave the Pittsburgh Steelers the ball on the Rams' 1 and led to the final scoring of the game, Franco Harris' 1-yard run. After the game, Thomas said, "It was a sorry call." Earlier in the game, Thomas had prevented a Steeler touchdown by knocking down a pass from Terry Bradshaw intended for wide receiver Lynn Swann in the end zone. He also picked up 6 yards on an interception runback, as teammate Eddie Brown lateraled the ball to him after picking it off.

ALONZO (SKIP) THOMAS

Oakland Raiders, corner back, 6 feet 1, 205, Southern California. Skip Thomas started at left corner back for the Raiders in Super Bowl XI.

BILL THOMPSON

Denver Broncos, safety, 6 feet 1, 200, Maryland State. The starting strong safety for the Broncos in Super Bowl XII, Thompson had an apparent interception called back after it was ruled that Dallas quarterback Roger Staubach had stepped out of bounds before releasing the ball.

JACK THOMPSON

Cincinnati Bengals, quarterback, 6 feet 3, 217, Washington State. Thompson, a backup, did not play in Super Bowl XVI.

STEVE THOMPSON

New York Jets, defensive end, 6 feet 5, 240, Washington. Thompson played as a substitute for the Jets in Super Bowl III.

SIDNEY THORNTON

Pittsburgh Steelers, running back, 5 feet 11, 230, Northwestern Louisiana. Thornton played as a reserve for the Steelers in both Super Bowls XIII and XIV. In the second game, he ran 4 times for 4 yards and caught 1 pass for 22 yards.

CLIFF THRIFT

Chicago Bears, linebacker, 6 feet 1, 230, East Central Oklahoma. Thrift played as a substitute in Super Bowl XX.

DENNIS THURMAN

Dallas Cowboys, corner back, 5 feet 11, 170, Southern California. Playing as a substitute in Super Bowl XIII, Thurman recovered a fumble on an onside kick late in the game, helping keep alive a Cowboy rally against the Pittsburgh Steelers. After Dallas had scored to pull to within 11, at 35–24, Rafael Septien's kick was bobbled by the Steelers' Tony Dungy, and Thurman recovered. The Cowboys scored again, to pull to within 4 points, but Pittsburgh held on to win.

FRED (FUZZY) THURSTON

Green Bay Packers, guard, 6 feet 1, 245, Valparaiso. Fuzzy Thurston, one of the members of the Packers' famed sweep, started at left guard for the team in Super Bowl I, then played as a substitute in SB II. He and right guard Jerry Kramer led one of those sweeps in the first game, helping Jim Taylor to a 14-yard touchdown run and the Packers to a 14–7 lead.

RUSTY TILLMAN

Washington Redskins, linebacker, 6 feet 2, 230, Northern Arizona. Tillman played as a substitute for the Redskins in Super Bowl VII.

MICK TINGELHOFF

Minnesota Vikings, center, 6 feet 2, 237, Nebraska. Tingelhoff, who joined the team in 1962 as a free agent, started at center for the Vikings in four Super Bowls—SB IV, SB VIII, SB IX, and SB XI. He had been in the league 15 years at the time of his last SB.

returned 3 kicks for 63 yards, with a long return of 23 yards.

ANDRE TIPPETT

New England Patriots, linebacker, 6 feet 3, 241, Iowa. The starting left outside linebacker for the Patriots in Super Bowl XX,

Andre Tippett

Tippett finished with 5 tackles, 1 assist, and 1 pass defensed.

LARRY TODD

Oakland Raiders, running back and kick returner, 6 feet 1, 185, Arizona State. Todd played as a substitute in Super Bowl II and carried 2 times for 37 yards, with a long run of 32 yards, and

JEFF TOEWS

Miami Dolphins, guard and center, 6 feet 3, 255, Washington. A valuable backup, according to the Dolphins, Toews started Super Bowl XVII at right guard because of an injury, then played in SB XIX as a substitute. His brother Loren also played in the SB (below).

LOREN TOEWS

Pittsburgh Steelers, linebacker, 6 feet 3, 212, California. Toews played in four Super Bowls—as a substitute in SB IX, SB X and SB XIV, and as a starter at right linebacker in SB XIII. Brother of Miami's Jeff Toews (above).

MIKE TOMCZAK

Chicago Bears, quarterback, 6 feet 1, 195, Ohio State. Played at quarterback the final series of downs for the Bears in Super Bowl XX.

PAT TOOMAY

Dallas Cowboys, defensive end, 6 feet 5, 244, Vanderbilt. Toomay played as a substitute for the Cowboys in both Super Bowls V and VI.

BOB TORREY

Philadelphia Eagles, running back, 6 feet 2, 232, Penn State. Torrey was on the Eagles' roster for Super Bowl XV, but did not play.

GREG TOWNSEND

Los Angeles Raiders, defensive end, 6 feet 3, 240, Texas Christian. Townsend, a rookie playing as a substitute, recorded 1 sack for a 10-yard loss and 2 tackles in Super Bowl XVIII.

GENE TROSCH

Kansas City Chiefs, defensive end, 6 feet 7, 277, Miami. Trosch played as a substitute for the Chiefs in Super Bowl IV.

BILL TRUAX

Dallas Cowboys, tight end, 6 feet 5, 240, Louisiana State. Truax played as a substitute for the Cowboys in Super Bowl VI.

MANU TUIASOSOPO

San Francisco 49ers, nose tackle, 6 feet 3, 252, UCLA. Acquired in a trade with the Seattle Seahawks earlier in the season, Tuiasosopo (pronounced *TWO-ee-ah-so-so-po*) took over at a starting position and had a sack of Dan Marino of the Miami Dolphins in Super Bowl XIX.

GODWIN TURK

Denver Broncos, linebacker, 6 feet 2, 230, Southern University. Turk played as a substitute for the Broncos in Super Bowl XII.

BAKE TURNER

New York Jets, end, 6 feet 1, 179, Texas Tech. Turner played as a substitute in Super Bowl III, but did not record any individual statistics.

JIM TURNER

New York Jets, kicker and quarterback, 6 feet 2, 205, Utah State. Turner, a 5-year veteran, kicked 3 field goals and 1 point-after-touchdown to help the Jets beat the Baltimore Colts in Super Bowl III. Turner attempted 5 field goals, and made 3—from 32, 30, and 9 yards.

KEENA TURNER

San Francisco 49ers, linebacker, 6 feet 2, 219, Purdue. Turner, a second-year player, started at right outside linebacker for the 49ers in Super Bowls XVI and XIX. In his second appearance, he led his team with 6 tackles.

HOWARD TWILLEY

Miami Dolphins, wide receiver, 5 feet 10, 185, Tulsa. Twilley started at a wide receiver position for the Dolphins in Super Bowls VI and VII and played as a substitute in SB VIII. He scored the game's first touchdown in SB VII, capping a 63-yard drive with a 28-yard scoring pass from Bob Griese. On the play, Twilley ran a pattern that turned Washington defender Pat Fischer completely around. Later Twilley said, "I knew [Fischer] had looked at a lot of film on us. We thought we could sell Fischer an inside move, and it worked out." In SB VI, Twilley caught 1 pass for 20 yards. In SB VIII, he did not record any individual statistics.

WENDELL TYLER

Los Angeles Rams and San Francisco 49ers, running back, 5 feet 10, 188, UCLA. Tyler started in the backfield both for the Rams in Super Bowl XIV and, after a trade in 1983, for the 49ers in SB XIX and led both teams in rushing.

In SB XIV, he carried 17 times for 60 yards with a long run of 39 yards. He also caught 3 passes for 20 yards, with a long reception of 11 yards. His 39-yard run came in the Rams' first scoring drive.

In SB XIX, he carried 13 times for 65 yards, with a long run of 9 yards and also caught 4 passes for 70 yards, with a long catch of 40 yards. The 40-yarder helped key the 49ers' final scoring drive.

JIM TYRER

Kansas City Chiefs, tackle, 6 feet 6, 292, Ohio State. One of the Chiefs' mainstays in the front line, he started at left tackle in both Super Bowls I and IV.

JOHNNY UNITAS

Baltimore Colts, quarterback, 6 feet 1, 196, Louisville.
They called him the master, and he was no less than the choice for quarterback on the all-time all-pro team named in 1969 by the Hall of Fame Selection Committee.

But by the time Unitas got to the Super Bowl, his prime was past and injuries overshadowed his two appearances, in SB III and SB V.

In the first game, Unitas, his throwing arm injured, was only inserted after starter Earl Morrall proved ineffective against Joe Namath and the NY Jets. He did lead the Colts to their only touchdown, on a 80-yard drive ending with Jerry Hill's 1-yard touchdown run with 3:19 remaining in the game. But it was too little, too late.

Afterward, Unitas took the loss like the veteran he was, saying "I've been in football a long time. You always hate to lose. But a football player can't feel sorry for himself."

If Unitas was calm just after the defeat, he showed fire before his appearance in SB V against the Dallas Cowboys. "This is the thing we've played for all year long," he said. "We can't blow it. We were a

Johnny Unitas

197

little overconfident two years ago, but we don't have that now."

The Colts didn't "blow" SB V, but Unitas wasn't the one to lead the team to victory. Unitas did start, but was hit hard by Cowboys' lineman George Andrie in the 2nd quarter and left with bruised ribs. He was replaced by Morrall.

Before that, he had thrown a 75-yard touchdown pass, which touched a Colts' player and a Cowboys' defender before being caught by John Mackey, who took it in for the score. And he had fumbled the ball while running, a turnover that helped the Cowboys go ahead early, 13–6.

Unitas' SB totals: SB III, 11 completions in 24 attempts for 110 yards and 1 interception; and SB V, 3 of 9 for 88 yards, 2 interceptions, and 1 touchdown.

RICK UPCHURCH

Denver Broncos, wide receiver and kick returner, 5 feet 10, 180, Minnesota. Upchurch played the role of a workhorse for the Broncos in Super Bowl XII, with 1 reception for 9 yards, 3 punt returns for 22 yards and 3 kickoff returns for 94 yards, including a long return of 67 yards.

His 67-yard return, which set a record, put the ball on the Dallas 26 and led to the Broncos' only touchdown, as they cut the Cowboy lead to 20–10 in the 3rd quarter.

GENE UPSHAW

Oakland Raiders, guard, 6 feet 5, 255, Texas A&I. One of a handful of Raiders to play in both the team's earlier Super Bowl appearance, SB II, and their appearance in SB XI. He started at left guard in SB II, SB XI, and SB XV. After the Raiders demolished the Minnesota Vikings in SB XI and ran for 266 yards, quarterback Ken Stabler referred to Upshaw and left tackle Art Shell by saying, "When you've got the horses, you ride them."

TED VACTOR

Washington Redskins, corner back, 6 feet, 185, Nebraska. Vactor played as a substitute for the Redskins in Super Bowl VII.

ZACK VALENTINE

Pittsburgh Steelers, linebacker, 6 feet 2, 220, East Carolina. Valentine played as a substitute for the Steelers in Super Bowl XIV.

PHIL VANDERSEA

Green Bay Packers, running back, 6 feet 3, 225, Massachusetts. Vandersea, a rookie, played as a substitute in Super Bowl I, but did not record any individual statistics.

MARK VAN EEGHEN

Oakland Raiders, running back, 6 feet 2, 225, Colgate. A starting running back for the Raiders in Super Bowls XI and XV, he led his team in rushing in his second appearance. An integral part of the Raiders' strong ground attack, he gained 73 yards on 18 carries in SB XI. In SB XV, he carried 19 times for 80 yards and played a key role in Oakland's first scoring drive with several carries.

KEITH VAN HORNE

Chicago Bears, tackle, 6 feet 6, 280, Southern California. Starting right tackle for the Bears in Super Bowl XX. After the Bears' lopsided victory, he talked about the Bears' late founder, George Halas: "I'm sure he was watching. We did it for him. That's what we wanted."

JOHN VELLA

Oakland Raiders, tackle, 6 feet 4, 260, Southern California. The starting right tackle for the Raiders in Super Bowl XI.

JIM VELLONE

Minnesota Vikings, guard, 6 feet 3, 255, Southern California. The starting left guard for the Vikings in Super Bowl IV.

GARIN VERIS

New England Patriots, defensive end, 6 feet 4, 255, Stanford. A rookie, Veris started at left end for the Patriots in Super Bowl XX and recorded 3 tackles and 2 assists.

DAVID VERSER

Cincinnati Bengals, wide receiver and kick returner, 6 feet 1, 200, Kansas. Despite a fractured thumb, Verser handled the bulk of the Bengals' kickoff return duty in Super Bowl XVI, returning 5 kicks for 52 yards, including a long return of 16 yards.

TOM VIGORITO

Miami Dolphins, running back and kick returner, 5 feet 10, 197, Virginia. Vigorito ran 1 time for 4 yards and returned 2 punts for 22 yards with 1 fair catch in Super Bowl XVII.

PHIL VILLAPIANO

Oakland Raiders, linebacker, 6 feet 2, 225, Bowling Green. The starting left outside linebacker for the Raiders in Super Bowl XI, he literally used his head to prevent a touchdown in the 1st half. After the Minnesota Vikings had blocked a punt and had the ball on the

Oakland 3, Villapiano went in low and met Brent McClanahan, his helmet hitting the ball and knocking it loose. Oakland's Willie Hall recovered.

BOB VOGEL

Baltimore Colts, tackle, 6 feet 5, 250, Ohio State. Vogel started at left tackle for the Colts in both Super Bowls III and V.

STU VOIGT

Minnesota Vikings, tight end, 6 feet 1, 225, Wisconsin. Voigt started at tight end for the Vikings in three Super Bowls—SB VIII, SB IX, and SB XI. He scored the Vikings' final touchdown in SB XI, a 32–14 defeat by the Oakland Raiders, on a 13-yard pass from reserve quarterback Bob Lee. He finished the game with 4 receptions for 49 yards, with the longest 15 yards. In SB VIII, he caught 3 passes for 46 yards, with the longest 17 yards. In SB IX, he caught 2 passes for 31 yards, with the longest 28 yards.

RICK VOLK

Baltimore Colts, defensive back and safety, 6 feet 3, 195, Michigan. A starter in Super Bowls III and V, Volk caused a great deal of concern after SB III when he collapsed, went into con- vulsion, and had to be hospital- ized. It all began early in the game, when Volk was involved in a tackle on the NY Jets' Matt Snell. After the play, Volk remained on the ground, temporarily uncon- scious, then walked off the field groggily. He returned to play, but, with 3:19 left, was again knocked groggy and had to be helped from the field.

In his hotel room after the game, with his wife present, Volk collapsed, a doctor was called, and he was rushed to the hospital. He was checked out as fully re- covered two days later.

Volk returned with the Colts to SB V and played a key role in the team's victory over the Dallas Cowboys. Trailing, 13–6, in the 4th quarter, Dallas' Craig Morton threw a pass in the direction of back Walt Garrison. But one of the Colt defenders tipped the ball, and Volk picked it off, running it back 30 yards to the Dallas 3. Two plays later, Baltimore scored, and the game was tied with 6:35 left.

UWE VON SCHAMANN

Miami Dolphins, kicker, 6 feet, 188, Oklahoma. When Von Schamann lined up to attempt a 37-yard field goal early in Super Bowl XIX, Miami fans may have had a few doubts about him. After all, Von Schamann had made only 9 of 19 field-goal attempts during the regular season. But Von Scha- mann made the kick and his two other attempts—from 31 and 30 yards—that day and, along with his lone point-after-touchdown, accounted for 10 of Miami's 16 points in the 38–16 loss to San Francisco.

In fact, Von Schamann is perfect in SB play, since he made his lone field-goal attempt in SB XVII—from 20 yards—and both point-after-touchdowns.

BILLY WADDY

Los Angeles Rams, wide receiver, 5 feet 11, 180, Colorado. A starting wide receiver for the Rams in Super Bowl XIV, Waddy led the team in receiving with 3 receptions for 75 yards, including a long reception of 50 yards. The 50-yarder, in the 3rd quarter, keyed a drive that saw the Rams take a brief 19–17 lead, as it put Los Angeles on the Pittsburgh Steelers' 24-yard line. The Rams scored on the next play.

HENRY WAECHTER

Chicago Bears, defensive tackle, 6 feet 5, 275, Nebraska. A substitute in Super Bowl XX, Waechter finished off the scoring in the 46–10 Bears' romp by tackling New England quarterback Steve Grogan in the end zone with 5:36 left in the game for a safety.

MIKE WAGNER

Pittsburgh Steelers, safety, 6 feet 1, 210, Western Illinois. Starting left safety in Super Bowls IX and X and free safety in SB XIII. Wagner recorded interceptions in each of his first two SB appearances. In SB IX, Wagner helped end any hopes the Minnesota Vikings had as he picked off a first-down pass and returned it 26 yards to the Minnesota 41 with minutes remaining. In SB X, Wagner picked off a Roger Staubach pass intended for Drew Pearson and returned it 19 yards to help set up a field goal that gave the Steelers a 15–10 lead in the final quarter.

BOBBY WALDEN

Pittsburgh Steelers, punter, 6 feet, 190, Georgia. Walden handled the punting duties for the

Steelers in both Super Bowls IX and X and had punts blocked in both—each leading to a touchdown. In SB IX, with the Steelers leading, 9–0, Walden went back to punt deep in his own territory. Matt Blair, the Vikings' linebacker, broke through and blocked the kick; it bounced into the end zone and was recovered by the Vikings' Terry Brown for the team's only points in the game.

In SB X, Walden had an early punt attempt blocked, which led to a Dallas Cowboys' touchdown. Walden bobbled the snap from center, and by the time he recovered, he was tackled on his own 29. The Cowboys' ensuing touchdown gave them a 7–0 lead.

Walden finished SB IX with 7 punts for an average of 34.7 and finished SB X with 4 for 39.8.

FULTON WALKER

Miami Dolphins, corner back and kick returner, 5 feet 11, 193, West Virginia. Walker set a handful of records with a dazzling appearance in Super Bowl XVII, then added to career marks in SB XIX.

Walker helped the Dolphins to a 17–10 halftime lead in SB XVII, before his team folded in the 2nd half. After a Washington Redskin field goal, Walker took a 1st-half kickoff and went 42 yards to his own 47 to set his team up for a drive that led to a field goal and a 10–3 lead.

Then, after Washington tied the score at 10–10 near the end of the 2nd quarter, Walker took the kickoff and ran the ball back 98 yards for a record-setting touchdown.

In all, Walker returned 4 kickoffs for 190 yards, setting records for most yards gained in a game on kickoff returns and the longest return.

Walker began the 1984 season on the injured reserve list, then played mainly on special teams for the rest of the season. In SB XIX, he returned 2 punts for 15 yards and 4 kickoffs for 93 yards, with a long return of 28 yards. His career records include most yards gained, 283, and highest average, 35.4.

RICK WALKER

Washington Redskins, tight end, 6 feet 4, 235, UCLA. A free agent backup in Super Bowl XVII, Walker started at a tight end for the Redskins in SB XVIII. In SB XVII, Walker helped the Redskins come back from a 10–3 deficit late in the 1st half as he gained 27 yards on a pass reception, then ran for 6 more yards on a reverse on the next play as Washington headed for a tying touchdown. In SB XVIII, Walker did not record any individual statistics.

On a lighter note, Walker had the distinction of being the only dual member of the Redskins' many-nicknamed cliques. He was a member of the Hogs, the offensive line, and also of the Fun Bunch, whose members celebrated touchdowns with high fives in the end zone.

JACKIE WALLACE

Minnesota Vikings and Los Angeles Rams, corner back and kick returner, 6 feet 3, 197, Arizona. Wallace, a rookie, started at right corner back for the Vikings in Super Bowl IX and signaled for a fair catch on a lone punt return. In SB XIV, he played as a substitute.

MIKE WALTER

San Francisco 49ers, linebacker, 6 feet 3, 238, Oregon. A waiver-list pickup, Walter played as a substitute for the 49ers in Super Bowl XIX.

STAN WALTERS

Philadelphia Eagles, tackle, 6 feet 6, 275, Syracuse. Started at the left tackle position for the Eagles in Super Bowl XV.

BRUCE WALTON

Dallas Cowboys, tackle, 6 feet 6, 252, UCLA. Walton, on the Cowboys' roster for Super Bowl X, did not play.

SAM WALTON

New York Jets, tackle, 6 feet 5, 276, East Texas State. Walton

played as a substitute for the Jets in Super Bowl III.

JIM WARD

Baltimore Colts, quarterback, 6 feet 2, 195, Gettysburg. Ward, on the Colts' roster for Super Bowl III, did not play.

PAUL WARFIELD

Miami Dolphins, wide receiver, 6 feet, 185, Ohio State. A starting wide receiver and deep threat for the Dolphins in Super Bowls VI, VII, and VIII, he led his team in receiving in all three games. In SB VI, he pulled in 2 key receptions as the Dolphins drove to their only points—a 31-

Paul Warfield

yard field goal with just seconds left in the 1st half. He finished the game with 4 receptions for 39 yards, with a long reception of 23 yards. In SB VII, he caught 3 passes for 36 yards, with a long reception of 18 yards.

Warfield's status for SB VIII was in doubt, since he suffered a pulled hamstring shortly before the game. He ended up playing at less than full capacity, but still caught 2 passes for 33 yards, with a long reception of 27 yards. That reception helped key a drive that ended with the Dolphins' final touchdown, a 2-yard run by Larry Csonka.

DON WARREN

Washington Redskins, tight end, 6 feet 4, 242, San Diego State. Warren started at tight end in Super Bowls XVII and XVIII. He caught 5 passes for 28 yards in SB XVII and did not record any individual statistics in SB XVIII.

LONNIE WARWICK

Minnesota Vikings, linebacker, 6 feet 3, 235, Tennessee Tech. Starting middle linebacker for the Vikings in Super Bowl IV.

ANTHONY WASHINGTON

Washington Redskins, corner back, 6 feet 1, 204, Fresno State. Washington, obtained in a trade before the 1983 season, started at the right corner back position for the team in Super Bowl XVIII. He recovered one opponent's fumble in the game.

GENE WASHINGTON

Minnesota Vikings, wide receiver, 6 feet 3, 208, Michigan State. Washington, a starter at wide receiver, caught 1 pass for 9 yards in Super Bowl IV.

JOE WASHINGTON

Washington Redskins, running back, 5 feet 10, 179, Oklahoma. After an injury kept Washington from playing in Super Bowl XVII, he carried 3 times for 8 yards and caught 3 passes for 20 yards in SB XVIII.

MARK WASHINGTON

Dallas Cowboys, corner back, 5 feet 10, 188, Morgan State. Washington played as a substitute for the Cowboys in Super Bowls V and XII, started at left corner back for the team in SB X, and was on the Cowboys' roster but did not play in SB XIII.

In his first appearance, he ran past defender Tom Nowatzke, who was supposed to pick him up, and blocked Jim O'Brien's point-after-touchdown kick to leave the game knotted, at 6–6, in the 1st half. He was also involved in one of the most dramatic plays in SB history. In SB X, he covered Lynn Swann on the 64-yard touchdown play that proved to be the crucial point in the Pittsburgh Steelers' victory.

Washington had Swann covered on the early part of his route, but Swann broke away by a step late and caught the ball on the 5 and went into the end zone. The touchdown on which Steeler quarterback Terry Bradshaw was knocked unconscious helped give Pittsburgh a 21–10 lead on the way to victory.

In the 1st half of SB XII, Washington came up with one of 4 interceptions of Denver quarterback Craig Morton, taking in a pass with 17 seconds left in the period and running it back 27 yards.

CHARLIE WATERS

Dallas Cowboys, safety, 6 feet 1, 193, Clemson. Waters, a longtime stalwart in the defensive backfield for the Cowboys, started in four Super Bowls: at right safety in SB V; at left safety in SB X; and at strong safety in SB XII and SB XIII. He also played in SB VI as a substitute. His five appearances give him a share (with six others) of the SB record for service.

TED WATTS

Los Angeles Raiders, corner back and kick returner, 6 feet, 195, Texas Tech. Watts returned 1 punt in Super Bowl XVIII, and fumbled the ball away.

ROBERT WEATHERS

New England Patriots, running back, 6 feet 2, 222, Arizona State. Weathers played as a substitute in Super Bowl XX, carried 1 time for 3 yards and caught 1 pass for 3 yards.

JIM WEATHERWAX

Green Bay Packers, defensive tackle, 6 feet 7, 275, California State/Los Angeles. Weatherwax, a rookie, played as a substitute in Super Bowl I, then played in the same role a year later in SB II.

MIKE WEBSTER

Pittsburgh Steelers, center and guard, 6 feet 1, 232, Wisconsin. As a rookie, Webster played as a substitute in Super Bowl IX, played in the same role in SB X, then started at center for the team in SB XIII and SB XIV. After the Steelers' thrilling 35–31 victory over the Dallas Cowboys in SB XIII, Webster said, "I don't think there was a loser in this game. I think there are two champions."

NORRIS WEESE

Denver Broncos, quarterback, 6 feet 1, 193, Mississippi.

Weese was inserted into the Broncos' lineup early in the 2nd half of Super Bowl XII in relief of starter Craig Morton, who had thrown 4 interceptions in the 1st half and nearly threw his fifth early in the 2nd half.

Weese helped the team to their only touchdown of the game, in the 27–10 defeat. After Rick Upchurch's 67-yard kickoff return had given the Broncos the ball on the Dallas 26, and after Morton was pulled, Weese took Denver into the end zone in 4 plays, as Rob Lytle ran in from the 1-yard line.

Weese, however, provided the Cowboys with their clinching touchdown in the 4th period when he fumbled, attempting to pass. Dallas recovered, then scored on the next play, Robert Newhouse's 29-yard pass to Golden Richards.

Weese finished passing successfully 4 times in 10 attempts for 22 yards with no interceptions, 1 fumble, and 3 carries for 26 yards.

CLAXTON WELCH

Dallas Cowboys, running back, 5 feet 11, 203, Oregon. Welch played as a substitute for the Cowboys in Super Bowls V and VI but did not record any individual statistics.

WARREN WELLS

Oakland Raiders, end, 6 feet 1, 190, Texas Southern. A substitute in Super Bowl II, Wells caught 1 pass for 17 yards and fumbled the ball away once.

RAY WERSCHING

San Francisco 49ers, kicker, 5 feet 11, 210, California. A native of Austria, Wersching in two Super Bowl appearances kicked his way into the No. 2 spot among SB scoring, behind Pittsburgh's Franco Harris.

In SB XVI, he made all 4 of his field-goal attempts—from 22, 26, 40, and 23 yards.

Wersching made his only field-goal attempt in SB XIX, from 27 yards. He made both his point-after-touchdown kicks in SB XVI and all five in SB XIX, to give him a total of 22 points in the SB.

CHARLIE WEST

Minnesota Vikings, safety and kick returner, 6 feet 1, 190, Texas/El Paso. West's fumble in Super Bowl IV helped the Kansas City Chiefs jump off to a 16–0 lead the Vikings never recovered from. After Jan Stenerud's third field goal gave the Chiefs a 9–0 lead in the 2nd quarter, West waited at his goal line for the ensuing kickoff. But the ball slipped through his hands and was recovered by the Chiefs' Remi Prudhomme. Six plays later, Mike Garrett ran 5 yards over left tackle for a touchdown.

West finished SB IV with 2

punt returns for 18 yards and 3 kickoff returns for 46 yards. He finished SB VIII with 2 kickoff returns for 28 yards.

GREG WESTBROOKS

Los Angeles Rams, linebacker, 6 feet 3, 215, Colorado. Played in Super Bowl XIV as a substitute.

DANNY WHITE

Dallas Cowboys, quarterback and punter, 6 feet 2, 192, Arizona State. White handled punting duties for the Cowboys in Super Bowls XII and XIII, and played at the quarterback position in SB XII. Punting, he had 5 punts for an average of 41.6 yards with a long punt of 53 yards in SB XII. In that game, he completed 1 pass in 2 attempts for 5 yards and ran 1 time for 13 yards. In SB XIII, he punted 5 times for an average of 39.6 yards with a long punt of 50 yards.

DWIGHT WHITE

Pittsburgh Steelers, defensive end, 6 feet 4, 255, East Texas State. Starting right end—and member of the Steelers' Iron Curtain defense—for Super Bowls IX and X, and a substitute in SB XIII and SB XIV.

White played in SB IX despite spending most of the preceding week in the hospital with viral

Dwight White

pneumonia, which caused him to lose nearly 20 pounds. His return helped the Steelers hold the Minnesota Vikings to a record for the fewest net yards gained, 119. In the game, he scored the first safety in SB history midway through the 2nd quarter. When the Vikings' Fran Tarkenton fumbled a pitchout and slid into the end zone attempting to recover the ball, White calmly downed him for a safety.

ED WHITE

Minnesota Vikings, guard, 6 feet 3, 260, California. The starting right guard for the Vikings in Super Bowls VIII, IX, and XI and a substitute earlier in SB IV.

JAMES WHITE

Minnesota Vikings, defensive tackle, 6 feet 3, 263, Oklahoma State. A first-round draft choice, White, as a rookie, played as a substitute in Super Bowl XI.

JERIS WHITE

Washington Redskins, corner back, 5 feet 10, 188, Hawaii. White started at left corner back for the Redskins in Super Bowl XVII and was one of the backs covering Jimmy Cefalo on the 76-yard touchdown pass he caught from David Woodley in the 1st quarter, giving the Miami Dolphins a brief 7–0 lead.

RANDY WHITE

Dallas Cowboys, linebacker and defensive tackle, 6 feet 4, 245, Maryland. Denver quarterback Craig Morton got a view of Super Bowl XII similar to that of many fans—from the seat of his pants. That's because the Dallas Cowboys' defense kept the pressure on Morton, sacking him twice and forcing him into 4 interceptions, in just over half a game's play.

White, a former linebacker who played in that position as a substitute in SB X, was a key part of the Cowboys' defense in SB XII, and was named a co-MVP with defensive teammate Harvey Martin after the game, the only time the award has been shared.

Randy White

White's heroics started early as he and Martin pressured Morton into throwing a pass that went into the hands of safety Randy Hughes. Five plays later, the Cowboys scored the game's first touchdown. In all, the Cowboys held Denver to 156 net yards, and 8 completions in 25 attempts.

"We knew we had to pressure Morton," White said later. "It was part of our game plan."

White's role in SB XIII is one he'd probably like to forget, as he fumbled a kickoff in the final quarter, leading to the Steelers' final touchdown.

After Pittsburgh had scored to go ahead, 28–17, Ray Gerela's kick was a squibbler. White, in to block, picked the ball up, but was tackled and fumbled, and the Steelers' Dennis Winston recovered.

"I just picked it up and began to run, and a guy hit me, and the ball just popped out," White said. "I blame myself."

SAMMY WHITE

Minnesota Vikings, wide receiver and kickoff returner, 5 feet 11, 189, Grambling. A Pro Bowl pick after his first season, White started at wide receiver for the Vikings in Super Bowl XI, led the team in receiving and caught a touchdown pass.

White's 8-yard touchdown pass from Fran Tarkenton came with only minutes left in the 3rd quarter and concluded a 12-play, 68-yard drive. It pulled the Vikings to within 12 points of the Oakland Raiders, at 19–7. White finished with 5 receptions for 77 yards with a long catch of 20 yards and 1 carry for 7 yards. He also had 4 kickoff returns for 79 yards, with a long return of 26 yards.

WILSON WHITLEY

Cincinnati Bengals, nose tackle, 6 feet 3, 265, Houston. The starting nose tackle for the Bengals in Super Bowl XVI.

ARTHUR WHITTINGTON

Oakland Raiders, running back, 5 feet 11, 180, Southern Methodist. A substitute in Super Bowl XV, Whittington carried the ball 3 times for a loss of 2 yards.

RON WIDBY

Dallas Cowboys, punter, 6 feet 4, 210, Tennessee. Widby handled the punting duties for the Cowboys in Super Bowls V and VI. In his first appearance, he punted 9 times—an SB record—for an average of 41.9 yards and a long punt of 49 yards. In SB VI, he punted 5 times for an average of 37.2 and a long punt of 47.

JOHN WILBUR

Washington Redskins, guard, 6 feet 3, 251, Stanford. The starting right guard for the Redskins in Super Bowl VII.

REGGIE WILKES

Philadelphia Eagles, linebacker, 6 feet 4, 230, Georgia Tech. Wilkes, in his third year, played as a substitute for the Eagles in Super Bowl XV.

JERRY WILKINSON

Los Angeles Rams, defensive end, 6 feet 9, 255, Oregon State. The rookie played substitute for the Rams in Super Bowl XIV.

DARRYL (DOKIE) WILLIAMS

Los Angeles Raiders, wide receiver, 5 feet 11, 180, UCLA. As a rookie, Williams played in Super Bowl XVIII as a substitute, but did not record any individual statistics.

ED WILLIAMS

New England Patriots, linebacker, 6 feet 4, 244, Texas. Williams played as a substitute for the Patriots in Super Bowl XX, but did not record any statistics.

GREG WILLIAMS

Washington Redskins, safety, 5 feet 11, 185, Mississippi State. A top special-teams performer with the Redskins, Williams played in both Super Bowls XVII and XVIII, recovering a fumbled punt in SB XVIII.

HOWIE WILLIAMS

Oakland Raiders, defensive back, 6 feet 1, 186, Howard. The starting right safety for the Raiders in Super Bowl II, Williams was involved in the mixup in assignments that allowed Boyd Dowler to pull in a pass and run in for a 62-yard touchdown in the 2nd quarter that gave the Green Bay Packers a 13–0 lead. Williams and corner back Kent McCloughan said that they were crossed up on their signals, allowing Dowler to get free. "We were in a man-for-man coverage," said Williams. "I thought Kent would stay with Dowler, but he released him for me."

JOE WILLIAMS

Dallas Cowboys, running back, 6 feet, 193, Wyoming. Williams played as a substitute in Super Bowl VI, but did not record any individual statistics.

JOHN WILLIAMS

Baltimore Colts, guard, 6 feet 3, 256, Minnesota. A substitute in Super Bowl III, Williams started at right guard for the Colts in SB V.

LESTER WILLIAMS

New England Patriots, nose tackle, 6 feet 3, 272, Miami (Florida). The starting nose tackle for the Patriots in Super Bowl XX. Williams did not record any individual defensive statistics.

MIKE WILLIAMS

Washington Redskins, tight end, 6 feet 4, 251, Alabama A&M. Activated just two months before Super Bowl XVIII, after a knee injury, Williams played as a substitute in the game.

REGGIE WILLIAMS

Cincinnati Bengals, linebacker, 6 feet, 228, Dartmouth. The starting right outside linebacker for the Bengals in Super Bowl XVI.

SID WILLIAMS

Baltimore Colts, linebacker, 6 feet 2, 235, Southern University. Williams played as a substitute for the Colts in Super Bowl III.

TRAVIS WILLIAMS

Green Bay Packers, running back and kick returner, 6 feet 1, 210, Arizona State. The rookie speedster played as a substitute in Super Bowl II, carrying 8 times for 36 yards, with a long run of 18 yards, and returning 1 kickoff for 18 yards.

CARLTON WILLIAMSON

San Francisco 49ers, safety, 6 feet, 204, Pittsburgh. The starting strong safety for the 49ers in both Super Bowls XVI and XIX and part of one of the finest secondaries in the NFL in his time. He recorded an interception late in SB XIX, as the 49ers' defense stifled the strong Miami Dolphin passing attack. His unofficial playoff statistics—10 solo tackles, 6 assists, and half a sack—led the team that season.

FRED (THE HAMMER) WILLIAMSON

Kansas City Chiefs, defensive back, 6 feet 3, 209, Northwestern. As if there wasn't enough drama before Super Bowl I, the first meeting of the champions of the NFL and AFL, Williamson heightened the pregame scenario with a barrage of braggadocio, intimidation, and prediction. First, he went up and down the Packer lineup, comparing Green Bay players unfavorably with AFL greats. Then, he promised to deliver his "hammer"—a forearm blow to the head that put many an AFL player down—to Packer receivers who ventured his way. He wasn't nicknamed The Hammer for nothing.

And finally, he promised the Chiefs they would win.

They didn't. And the only player hurt in a collision with Williamson was Williamson, who had to be carried from the field in the 4th quarter.

On that play, Williamson came up to tackle the Packers' ball carrier, Donny Anderson. But he went in too low, caught what was apparently Anderson's knee, and was knocked cold.

Of course, the story has changed as time has gone on. After the game, Williamson said, "The next thing I knew, I was lying on a stretcher on the sideline, looking up at all that blue. I asked somebody, 'What the hell happened?' He said, 'You got knocked out cold.' Man, was I embarrassed."

But recently, Williamson has recalled it differently: "Somebody asked me if I was all right. I said, 'Sure I'm all right, but you've got to carry me off.' So they carried me off, and when they dumped me on the sideline, I got up and waved to the fans."

Williamson left football shortly after the Super Bowl and became an actor.

JOHN WILLIAMSON

Oakland Raiders, linebacker, 6 feet 2, 220, Louisiana Tech. A substitute in Super Bowl II, Williamson recovered a Raiders' fumble in the game.

CHESTER WILLIS

Los Angeles Raiders, running back, 5 feet 11, 195, Auburn. Willis played in Super Bowl XVIII in a reserve role and carried once for 7 yards. In special-teams capacity he recorded 2 tackles in the game.

LEN WILLIS

Minnesota Vikings, wide receiver and kick returner, 5 feet 10, 180, Ohio State. In Super Bowl XI, the rookie returned 3 punts for 14 yards, with a long

return of 8 yards, and returned 3 kickoffs for 57 yards, with a long return of 20 yards.

BEN WILSON

Green Bay Packers, running back, 6 feet 1, 230, Southern California. The Packers picked up Wilson in a trade in July of 1967, after he had spent the previous season as part of the LA Rams' taxi squad, and the move paid off when several regulars went down with injuries. Wilson was named to start in Super Bowl II just before gametime, without any explanation, and ended up with 17 carries for 62 yards, with a long run of 13 yards.

BRENARD WILSON

Philadelphia Eagles, safety, 6 feet, 175, Vanderbilt. The starting free safety for the Eagles in Super Bowl XV.

JERREL WILSON

Kansas City Chiefs, punter, 6 feet 4, 222, Southern Mississippi. Wilson, a member of the all-time AFL team, handled the Chiefs' punting duties in both Super Bowls I and IV. In SB I, Wilson punted 7 times for an average of 45.3 yards and a long punt of 61 yards. The 61-yarder stood as a record for the longest punt in the game until SB XX, when Rich

Camarillo of the New England Patriots kicked for 62 yards. In SB IV, Wilson punted 4 times for an average of 48.5 and a long punt of 59.

MARC WILSON

Oakland and Los Angeles Raiders, quarterback, 6 feet 5, 205, Brigham Young. Wilson, while on the Raiders' roster, did not play in Super Bowl XV. He played as a reserve in SB XVIII, but did not throw a pass.

MIKE WILSON

San Francisco 49ers, wide receiver, 6 feet 3, 210, Washington State. As a rookie, Wilson came up with his lone reception in Super Bowl XVI at a critical juncture to help the 49ers beat the Cincinnati Bengals. After Cincinnati had pulled to within 6 points, at 20–14, with about 10 minutes left, quarterback Joe Montana hit Wilson for a 22-yard completion that helped SF drive to an important field goal, putting Cincinnati more than a touchdown away from winning. He played as a reserve in SB XIX, but did not record any individual statistics.

MIKE WILSON

Cincinnati Bengals, tackle, 6 feet 5, 271, Georgia. The starting right tackle for the Bengals in Super Bowl XVI.

OTIS WILSON

Chicago Bears, linebacker, 6 feet 2, 232, Louisville. Starting left linebacker for the Bears in Super Bowl XX, he recorded 1 tackle, 1 assist, and 2 sacks for a total of 24 yards lost. One of his sacks sent New England starter Tony Eason down for an 11-yard loss and was Eason's final offensive play before being replaced by Steve Grogan. Wilson sacked Grogan for a 13-yard loss early in the 2nd half.

DENNIS WINSTON

Pittsburgh Steelers, linebacker, 6 feet, 228, Arkansas. A substitute in Super Bowl XIII, Winston started at left linebacker in SB XIV. In SB XIII, Winston came up with a fumble recovery on special teams that led to the Steelers' final points in the exciting game. Following a Pittsburgh touchdown, which gave the team a 28–17 lead with 7:10 left in the game, the Cowboys' Randy White tried to handle the kickoff. He was hit by the Steelers' Tony Dungy, and Winston recovered the ball at the Dallas 18. On the next play Terry Bradshaw hit Lynn Swann with a touchdown pass.

ROY WINSTON

Minnesota Vikings, linebacker, 5 feet 11, 226, Louisiana State. Starting left linebacker for the Vikings in Super Bowls IV, VIII, and IX, and substitute in SB XI.

JIM WOLF

Pittsburgh Steelers, defensive end, 6 feet 2, 230, Prairie View A&M. A rookie on the Steelers' roster, Wolf did not play in Super Bowl IX.

OTIS WONSLEY

Washington Redskins, running back and kick returner, 5 feet 10, 214, Alcorn State. Wonsley, a top special-teams performer, played in both Super Bowls XVII and XVIII. According to Redskins' press guide, he led John Riggins into the hole for his "Super Bowl-winning touchdown run of 1983." He also returned 1 kickoff for 13 yards in his first appearance.

WILLIE WOOD

Green Bay Packers, defensive back, 5 feet 10, 190, Southern California. A starter in the Packers' secondary in both Super Bowls I and II, Wood made a key interception in the first game, which helped the Packers break the game open.

The Packers led, 14–10, but the Chiefs were driving when Packer defensive linemen Henry Jordan and Willie Davis pressured Kansas City quarterback Len Dawson. Jordan hit Dawson's arm, and Wood picked the ball out of the air and returned it 50 yards to the Chiefs' 5. On the next play, the Packers' Elijah Pitts scored to

Willie Wood

push the Packer lead to 21–10 and break the game open.

Of the play, Chiefs' defensive back Fred Williamson said: "That was the game right there."

Wood, who had played college ball in the Los Angeles Coliseum (where SB I was played), said after the game, "This has to be my biggest thrill in Los Angeles."

DAVID WOODLEY

Miami Dolphins, quarterback, 6 feet 2, 204, Louisiana State. Woodley, the Dolphins' starter in Super Bowl XVII, must have wondered what hit his team at halftime. Miami went into the locker-room leading, 17–10, but came out to play a scoreless 2nd

215

half, in which the team did not complete a pass and made only 2 first downs in the period and lost, 27–17.

That was the same Miami team that charged into the lead on its second possession when Woodley hit wide receiver Jimmy Cefalo with a 76-yard scoring pass. Then a bit of disaster struck, as Woodley was hit on a later possession and fumbled, setting up a Redskins field goal. But the Dolphins came right back and drove to a field goal of their own. Then, after Washington tied up the score with a touchdown, Fulton Walker ran back the ensuing kickoff 98 yards for a touchdown to give the Dolphins' their 17–10 halftime lead.

But Woodley's 1st-half magic disappeared, he went 0 for 8 in the half and was finally pulled in favor of Don Strock. Woodley finished 4 for 14 for 97 yards with 1 interception. He also carried 4 times for 16 yards.

DWAYNE WOODRUFF

Pittsburgh Steelers, corner back, 5 feet 11, 189, Louisville. Woodruff, a rookie, played as a substitute in Super Bowl XIV.

ROLLY WOOLSEY

Dallas Cowboys, defensive back, 6 feet 1, 182, Boise State. A rookie, Woolsey played as a substitute in Super Bowl X.

RON WOOTEN

New England Patriots, guard, 6 feet 4, 273, North Carolina. Wooten started at right guard for the Patriots in Super Bowl XX.

ERIC WRIGHT

San Francisco 49ers, corner back, 6 feet 1, 180, Missouri. Starting right corner back for the 49ers in Super Bowls XVI and XIX. He made two key plays in SB XVI, first stripping the ball loose from receiver Cris Collinsworth at the SF 8 early in the 2nd quarter, then picking off a Ken Anderson pass intended for Collinsworth late in the game. He returned the interception 25 yards, helping to set up the 49ers' final field goal of the game.

Wright had no less a spectacular SB XIX. He broke up 3 passes, picking off a Dan Marino pass meant for Mark Clayton at the 49er 1, late in the 3rd quarter, as the 49ers' stellar secondary shut down Marino and receivers Clayton and Mark Duper.

GEORGE WRIGHT

Baltimore Colts, defensive tackle, 6 feet 3, 260, Sam Houston State. Wright, on the Colts' roster for Super Bowl V, did not play.

JEFF WRIGHT

Minnesota Vikings, safety, 5 feet 11, 190, Minnesota. The starting left safety for the Vikings in three Super Bowls—SB VIII, SB IX, and SB XI.

LOUIS WRIGHT

Denver Broncos, corner back, 6 feet 2, 195, San Jose State. The starting left corner back for the Broncos in Super Bowl XII.

NATE WRIGHT

Minnesota Vikings, corner back and kick returner, 5 feet 11, 180, San Diego State. Started at left corner back for the Vikings in Super Bowls VIII, IX, and XI. He returned 1 punt for 1 yard in SB IX.

RAYFIELD WRIGHT

Dallas Cowboys, tackle, 6 feet 6, 255, Fort Valley State. Started at right tackle for the Cowboys in Super Bowls V, VI, X, and XIII, and played as a substitute in SB XII. His five appearances gives

him a share (with six others) of the record for most games played.

STEVE WRIGHT

Green Bay Packers, tackle, 6 feet 6, 250, Alabama. Wright played as a substitute in Super Bowl I, but, although on the roster, did not play in SB II.

TIM WRIGHTMAN

Chicago Bears, tight end, 6 feet 3, 237, UCLA. A 1982 draft choice of the Bears, Wrightman was the first player to sign with the USFL, playing briefly with the Chicago Blitz. He joined the Bears in 1985 and played in Super Bowl XX as a substitute.

SAM WYCHE

Washington Redskins, quarterback, 6 feet 4, 218, Furman. Wyche, who played in Super Bowl VII, later became head coach at Indiana University and with the Cincinnati Bengals.

Y

☆ ☆ ☆

RON YARY

Minnesota Vikings, tackle, 6 feet 5, 265, Southern California. Yary, the top draft choice in the entire draft in 1968, played in four Super Bowls for the Vikings. He started at right tackle in SB IV, SB VIII, SB IX, and SB XI. After losing in SB XI, 32–14, to the Oakland Raiders, Yary was quoted as saying, "I don't know how you can play in four of these things and lose them all. Not only lose them all, but play bad football. I don't know how or why it happened, but for the first time in all the years that I've been playing football, I'm embarrassed."

GARO YEPREMIAN

Miami Dolphins, kicker, 5 feet 8, 175, no college. Yepremian's own Super Bowl footwork probably always will be overshadowed by what he tried to do with his arm—a goof that nearly put him in the league with such all-timers as Roy Riegels and Fred Merkle.

It was SB VII, one of three Yepremian performed in, and the Dolphins were seemingly on their way to their first title and an undefeated season as they led the Washington Redskins, 14–0, with just minutes remaining in the game. Yepremian was lined up to attempt a 42-yard field goal, which, if successful, would certainly put the game away.

But Yepremian's kick was blocked by the Redskins' Bill Brundige. Yepremian picked the ball up on a bounce, then cocked his arm as if to throw it. But the ball squirted out of his hand, he batted at it, but the Redskins' Mike Bass picked it off and ran 49 yards for his team's only touchdown.

"He should have fallen on it," said Miami Coach Don Shula.

Yepremian, who once was reported to have told a reporter he would like to "keek a touch-

Garo Yepremian

down," said, "I guess I should have fallen on it."

Luckily for Yepremian, the Redskins did not score again. But, still, there will always be a special place for the native of Cyprus in Super Bowl lore. "Well, I made a mistake," he was to say later.

Yepremian's attempt was the only one of the game, in which he made both of his point-after-touchdown kicks. Earlier, in SB VI, Yepremian was 1 of 2 in field goals, making a 31-yarder for Miami's only points of the game. In SB VIII, Yepremian was 1 of 1, hitting from 28 yards. He also made 3 point-after-touchdowns. He finished with 11 points.

CHARLE YOUNG

Los Angeles Rams and San Francisco 49ers, tight end, 6 feet 4, 234, Southern California. A first-round choice of the Philadelphia Eagles in 1973, Young was traded to the Rams in 1977 for quarterback Ron Jaworski. After playing as a substitute for the Rams in Super Bowl XIV, he was traded to the 49ers in 1980, and started at the tight end position for the 49ers in SB XVI. In that game, he caught 1 pass for 14 yards. The 14-yard reception keyed a 1st quarter drive and came on a trick play. With a third-and-1 on the Cincinnati 47, quarterback Joe Montana handed off to back Ricky Patton, who gave the ball to wide receiver Freddie Solomon, who pitched it back to Montana, who threw to Young for a first down.

CHARLEY YOUNG

Dallas Cowboys, running back, 6 feet 1, 210, North Carolina State. Young played as a substitute in Super Bowl X and caught 3 passes for 31 yards, with a long reception of 10 yards.

ROYNELL YOUNG

Philadelphia Eagles, corner back, 6 feet 1, 181, Alcorn State. A rookie, Young started at the left corner back position for the Eagles in Super Bowl XV. Young lost a match with Oakland receiver Cliff Branch that resulted in a 29-yard touchdown pass and a 21–3 Raider lead. On a second-down play, Jim

219

Plunkett passed toward Branch, and though Young stepped in front and had his hands on the ball, Branch pulled it away and fell into the end zone for a touchdown.

Young said later, "He just slipped around the side of me. I didn't know he was that close. All I know is I had the ball, and then I didn't."

The Raiders' Bob Chandler, who was running a pattern near the play, said, "That one was a classic. It was an interception, and [Branch] turned it into a touchdown."

JACK YOUNGBLOOD

Los Angeles Rams, defensive end, 6 feet 4, 243, Florida. One of the veterans who led the Rams into Super Bowl XIV. He started the game at defensive left end.

After the Steelers' hard-fought 31–19 victory, Youngblood said, "The Rams can play with anyone, anytime, anywhere. I'm not ashamed."

JIM YOUNGBLOOD

Los Angeles Rams, linebacker, 6 feet 3, 231, Tennessee Tech. Started at left linebacker for the Rams in Super Bowl XIV. He was no relation to Jack Youngblood, also a defensive starter on the Rams' Super Bowl team.

GODFREY ZAUNBRECHER

Minnesota Vikings, center, 6 feet 2, 240, Louisiana State. On the Vikings' roster for Super Bowl VIII, he did not play.

THE GAMES

☆ ☆ ☆

SUPER BOWL

I

Green Bay Packers 35, Kansas City Chiefs 10

Jan. 15, 1967
Los Angeles Memorial Coliseum
Attendance: 61,946

Kansas	0	10	0	0	—	10
Green Bay	7	7	14	7	—	35

Green Bay—McGee, 37, pass from Starr (Chandler kick).
Kansas City—McClinton, 7, pass from Dawson (Mercer kick).
Green Bay—Taylor, 14, run (Chandler kick).
Kansas City—Field goal, 31, Mercer.
Green Bay—Pitts, 5, run (Chandler kick).
Green Bay—McGee, 13, pass from Starr (Chandler kick).
Green Bay—Pitts, 1, run (Chandler kick).

Rushing: *Kansas City*—Dawson, 3 for 24; Garrett, 6 for 17; McClinton, 6 for 16; Beathard, 1 for 14; Coan, 3 for 1. *Green Bay*—J. Taylor, 16 for 53, 1 TD; Pitts, 11 for 45, 2 TD; D. Anderson, 4 for 30; Grabowski, 2 for 2.

Passing: *Kansas City*—Dawson, 16 of 27 for 211, 1 TD, 1 int.; Beathard, 1 of 5 for 17. *Green Bay*—Starr, 16 of 23 for 250, 2 TD, 1 int.; Bratkowski, 0 of 1.

Receiving: *Kansas City*—Burford, 4 for 67; O. Taylor, 4 for 57; Garrett, 3 for 28; McClinton, 2 for 34, 1 TD; Arbanas, 2 for 30; Carolan, 1 for 7; Coan, 1 for 5. *Green Bay*—McGee, 7 for 138, 2 TD; Dale, 4 for 59; Pitts, 2 for 32; Fleming, 2 for 22; J. Taylor, 1 for −1.

Punting: *Kansas City*—Wilson, 7 for 45.3 average. *Green Bay*—Chandler, 3 for 43.3 average; D. Anderson, 1 for 43.

Punt Returns: *Kansas City*—Garrett, 2 for 17; E. Thomas, 1 for 2. *Green Bay*—D. Anderson, 3 for 25; Wood, 1 for −2.

Kickoff Returns: *Kansas City*—Coan, 4 for 87; Garrett, 2 for 23. *Green Bay*—Adderley, 2 for 40; D. Anderson, 1 for 25.

Interceptions: *Kansas City*—Mitchell, 1 for 0. *Green Bay*—Wood, 1 for 50.

SUPER BOWL

Green Bay Packers 33, Oakland Raiders 14

Jan. 14, 1968
Orange Bowl, Miami
Attendance: 75,546

Green Bay	3	13	10	7	—	33
Oakland	0	7	0	7	—	14

Green Bay—Field goal, 39, Chandler.
Green Bay—Field goal, 20, Chandler.
Green Bay—Dowler, 62, pass from Starr (Chandler kick).
Oakland—Miller, 23, pass from Lamonica (Blanda kick).
Green Bay—Field goal, 43, Chandler.
Green Bay—Anderson, 2, run (Chandler kick).
Green Bay—Fieldgoal, 31, Chandler.
Green Bay—Adderley, 60, interception (Chandler kick).
Oakland—Miller, 23, pass from Lamonica (Blanda kick).

Rushing: *Green Bay*—Wilson, 17 for 62; Anderson, 14 for 48, 1 TD; Williams, 8 for 36; Starr, 1 for 14; Mercein, 1 for 0. *Oakland*—Dixon, 12 for 54; Todd, 2 for 37; Banaszak, 6 for 16.
Passing: *Green Bay*—Starr, 13 of 24 for 202, 1 TD. *Oakland*—Lamonica, 15 of 34 for 208, 2 TD, 1 int.
Receiving: *Green Bay*—Dale, 4 for 43; Fleming, 4 for 35; Anderson, 2 for 18; Dowler, 2 for 71, 1 TD; McGee, 1 for 35. *Oakland*—Miller, 5 for 84, 2 TD; Banaszak, 4 for 69; Cannon, 2 for 25; Biletnikoff, 2 for 10; Wells, 1 for 17; Dixon, 1 for 3.
Punting: *Green Bay*—Anderson, 6 for 39.0 average. *Oakland*—Eischeid, 6 for 44.
Punt Returns: *Green Bay*—Wood, 5 for 35. *Oakland*—Bird, 2 for 12.
Kickoff Returns: *Green Bay*—Adderley, 1 for 24; Williams, 1 for 18; Crutcher, 1 for 7. *Oakland*—Todd, 3 for 63; Grayson, 2 for 61; Hawkins, 1 for 3; Kocourek, 1 for 0, Kocourek lateraled to Grayson who returned 11 yards.
Interceptions: *Green Bay*—Adderley, 1 for 60, 1 TD. *Oakland*—None.

SUPER BOWL

New York Jets 16, Baltimore Colts 7

Jan. 12, 1969
Orange Bowl, Miami
Attendance: 75,389

New York	0	7	6	3	—	16
Baltimore	0	0	0	7	—	7

New York—Snell, 4, run (Turner kick).
New York—Field goal, 32, Turner.
New York—Field goal, 30, Turner.
New York—Field goal, 9, Turner.
Baltimore—Hill, 1, run (Michaels kick).

Rushing: *New York*—Snell, 30 for 121, 1 TD; Boozer, 10 for 19; Mathis, 3 for 2. *Baltimore*—Matte, 11 for 116; Hill, 9 for 29, 1 TD; Unitas, 1 for 0; Morrall, 2 for −2.

Passing: *New York*—Namath, 17 of 28 for 206; Parilli, 0 of 1. *Baltimore*—Morrall, 6 of 17 for 71, 3 int.; Unitas, 11 of 24 for 110, 1 int.

Receiving: *New York*—Sauer, 8 for 133; Snell, 4 for 40; Mathis, 3 for 20; Lammons, 2 for 13. *Baltimore*—Richardson, 6 for 58; Orr, 3 for 42; Mackey, 3 for 35; Matte, 2 for 30; Hill, 2 for 1; Mitchell, 1 for 15.

Punting: *New York*—Johnson, 4 for 38.8 average. *Baltimore*—Lee, 3 for 44.3.

Punt Returns: *New York*—Baird, 1 for 0. *Baltimore*—Brown, 4 for 34.

Kickoff Returns: *New York*—Christy, 1 for 25. *Baltimore*—Pearson, 2 for 59; Brown, 2 for 46.

Interceptions: *New York*—Beverly, 2 for 0; Hudson, 1 for 9; Sample, 1 for 0. *Baltimore*—None.

SUPER BOWL
IV

Kansas City Chiefs 23, Minnesota Vikings 7

Jan. 11, 1970
Tulane Stadium, New Orleans
Attendance: 80,562

Minnesota	0	0	7	0	—	7
Kansas City	3	13	7	0	—	23

Kansas City—Field goal, 48, Stenerud.
Kansas City—Field goal, 32, Stenerud.
Kansas City—Field goal, 25, Stenerud.
Kansas City—Garrett, 5, run (Stenerud kick).
Minnesota—Osborn, 4, run (Cox kick).
Kansas City—Taylor, 46, pass from Dawson (Stenerud kick).

Rushing: *Minnesota*—Brown, 6 for 26; Reed, 4 for 17; Osborn, 7 for 15, 1 TD; Kapp, 2 for 9. *Kansas City*—Garrett, 11 for 39, 1 TD; Pitts, 3 for 37; Hayes, 8 for 31; McVea, 12 for 26; Dawson, 3 for 11; Holmes, 5 for 7.

Passing: *Minnesota*—Kapp, 16 of 25 for 183, 2 int.; Cuozzo, 1 of 3 for 16, 1 int. *Kansas City*—Dawson, 12 of 17 for 142, 1 TD, 1 int.

Receiving: *Minnesota*—Henderson, 7 for 111; Brown, 3 for 11; Beasley, 2 for 41; Reed, 2 for 16; Osborn, 2 for 11; Washington, 1 for 9. *Kansas City*—Taylor, 6 for 81, 1 TD; Pitts, 3 for 33; Garrett, 2 for 25; Hayes, 1 for 3.

Punting: *Minnesota*—Lee, 3 for 37 average. *Kansas City*—Wilson, 4 for 48.5.

Punt Returns: *Minnesota*—West, 2 for 18. *Kansas City*—Garrett, 1 for 0.

Kickoff Returns: *Minnesota*—West, 3 for 46; Jones, 1 for 33. *Kansas City*—Hayes, 2 for 36.

Interceptions: *Minnesota*—Krause, 1 for 0. *Kansas City*—Lanier, 1 for 9; Robinson, 1 for 9; Thomas, 1 for 6.

SUPER BOWL
V

Baltimore Colts 16, Dallas Cowboys 13

Jan. 17, 1971
Orange Bowl, Miami
Attendance: 79,204

Baltimore	0	6	0	10	—	16
Dallas	3	10	0	0	—	13

Dallas—Field goal, 14, Clark.
Dallas—Field goal, 30, Clark.
Baltimore—Mackey, 75, pass from Unitas (kick blocked).
Dallas—Thomas, 7, pass from Morton (Clark kick).
Baltimore—Nowatzke, 2, run (O'Brien kick).
Baltimore—Field goal, 32, O'Brien.

Rushing: *Baltimore*—Nowatzke, 10 for 33, 1 TD; Bulaich, 18 for 28; Unitas, 1 for 4; Havrilak, 1 for 3; Morrall, 1 for 1. *Dallas*—Garrison, 12 for 65; Thomas, 18 for 35; Morton, 1 for 2.

Passing: *Baltimore*—Unitas, 3 of 9 for 88, 1 TD, 2 int.; Morrall, 7 of 15 for 147, l int.; Havrilak, 1 of 1 for 25. *Dallas*—Morton, 12 of 26 for 127, 1 TD, 3 int.

Receiving: *Baltimore*—Jefferson, 3 for 52; Mackey, 2 for 80, 1 TD; Hinton, 2 for 51; Havrilak, 2 for 27; Nowatzke, 1 for 45; Bulaich, 1 for 5. *Dallas*—Reeves, 5 for 46; Thomas, 4 for 21, 1 TD; Garrison, 2 for 19; Hayes, 1 for 41.

Punting: *Baltimore*—Lee, 4 for 41.5 average. *Dallas*—Widby, 9 for 41.9.

Punt Returns: *Baltimore*—Logan, 1 for 8; Gardin, 4 for 4. *Dallas*—Hayes, 3 for 9.

Kickoff Returns: *Baltimore*—Duncan, 4 for 90. *Dallas*—Harris, 1 for 18; Hill, 1 for 14; Kiner, 1 for 2.

Interceptions: *Baltimore*—Volk, 1 for 30; Logan, 1 for 14; Curtis, 1 for 13. *Dallas*—Howley, 2 for 22; Renfro, 1 for 0.

SUPER BOWL
VI

Dallas Cowboys 24, Miami Dolphins 3

Jan. 16, 1972
Tulane Stadium, New Orleans
Attendance: 81,023

Dallas	3	7	7	7	—	24
Miami	0	3	0	0	—	3

Dallas—Field goal, 9, Clark.
Dallas—Alworth, 7, pass from Staubach (Clark kick).
Miami—Field goal, 31, Yepremian.
Dallas—D. Thomas, 3, run (Clark kick).
Dallas—Ditka, 7, pass from Staubach (Clark kick).

Rushing: *Dallas*—D. Thomas, 19 for 95, 1 TD; Garrison, 14 for 74; Hill, 7 for 25; Staubach, 5 for 18; Ditka, 1 for 17; Hayes, 1 for 16; Reeves, 1 for 7. *Miami*—Csonka, 9 for 40; Kiick, 10 for 40; Griese, 1 for 0.

Passing: *Dallas*—Staubach, 12 of 19 for 119, 2 TD. *Miami*—Griese, 12 of 23 for 134, 1 int.

Receiving: *Dallas*—D. Thomas, 3 for 17; Alworth, 2 for 28, 1 TD; Ditka, 2 for 28, 1 TD; Hayes, 2 for 23; Garrison, 2 for 11; Hill, 1 for 12. *Miami*—Warfield, 4 for 39; Kiick, 3 for 21; Csonka, 2 for 18; Fleming, 1 for 27; Twilley, 1 for 20; Mandich, 1 for 9.

Punting: *Dallas*—Widby, 5 for 37.2 average. *Miami*—Seiple, 5 for 40.0.

Punt Returns: *Dallas*—Hayes, 1 for −1. *Miami*—Scott, 1 for 21.

Kickoff Returns: *Dallas*—I. Thomas, 1 for 23; Waters, 1 for 11. *Miami*—Morris, 4 for 90; Ginn, 1 for 32.

Interceptions: *Dallas*—Howley, 1 for 41. *Miami*—None.

SUPER BOWL
VII

Miami Dolphins 14, Washington Redskins 7

Jan. 14, 1973
Los Angeles Memorial Coliseum
Attendance: 90,182

Miami	7	7	0	0	—	14
Washington	0	0	0	7	—	7

Miami—Twilley, 28, pass from Griese (Yepremian kick).
Miami—Kiick, 1, run (Yepremian kick).
Washington—Bass, 49, fumble return (Knight kick).

Rushing: *Miami*—Csonka, 15 for 112; Kiick, 12 for 38, 1 TD; Morris, 10 for 34. *Washington*—Brown, 22 for 72; Harraway, 10 for 37; Kilmer, 2 for 18; C. Taylor, 1 for 8; Smith, 1 for 6.

Passing: *Miami*—Griese, 8 of 11 for 88, 1 TD, 1 int. *Washington*—Kilmer, 14 of 28 for 104, 3 int.

Receiving: *Miami*—Warfield, 3 for 36; Kiick, 2 for 6; Twilley, 1 for 28, 1 TD; Mandich, 1 for 19; Csonka, 1 for −1. *Washington*—Jefferson, 5 for 50; Brown, 5 for 26; C. Taylor, 2 for 20; Smith, 1 for 11; Harraway, 1 for −3.

Punting: *Miami*—Seiple, 7 for 43.0 average. *Washington*—Bragg, 5 for 31.2.

Punt Returns: *Miami*—Scott, 2 for 4. *Washington*—Haymond, 4 for 9.

Kickoff Returns: *Miami*—Morris, 2 for 33. *Washington*—Haymond, 2 for 30; Mul-Key, 1 for 15.

Interceptions: *Miami*—Scott, 2 for 63; Buoniconti, 1 for 32. *Washington*—Owens, 1 for 0.

SUPER BOWL
VIII

Miami Dolphins 24, Minnesota Vikings 7

Jan. 13, 1974
Rice Stadium, Houston
Attendance: 68,142

Minnesota	0	0	0	7	—	7
Miami	14	3	7	0	—	24

Miami—Csonka, 5, run (Yepremian kick).
Miami—Kiick, 1, run (Yepremian kick).
Miami—Field goal, 28, Yepremian.
Miami—Csonka, 2, run (Yepremian kick).
Minnesota—Tarkenton, 4, run (Cox kick).

Rushing: *Minnesota*—Reed, 11 for 32; Foreman, 7 for 18; Tarkenton, 4 for 17, 1 TD; Marinaro, 1 for 3; B. Brown, 1 for 2. *Miami*—Csonka, 33 for 145, 2 TD; Morris, 11 for 34; Kiick, 7 for 10, 1 TD; Griese, 2 for 7.

Passing: *Minnesota*—Tarkenton, 18 of 28 for 182, 1 int. *Miami*—Griese, 6 of 7 for 73.

Receiving: *Minnesota*—Foreman, 5 for 27; Gilliam, 4 for 44; Voigt, 3 for 46; Marinaro, 2 for 39; B. Brown, 1 for 9; Kingsriter, 1 for 9; Lash, 1 for 9; Reed, 1 for − 1. *Miami*—Warfield, 2 for 33; Mandich, 2 for 21; Briscoe, 2 for 19.

Punting: *Minnesota*—Eischeid, 5 for 42.2 average. *Miami*—Seiple, 3 for 39.7.

Punt Returns: *Minnesota*—Bryant, 0 for 0. *Miami*—Scott, 3 for 20.

Kickoff Returns: *Minnesota*—Gilliam, 2 for 41; West, 2 for 28. *Miami*—Scott, 2 for 47.

Interceptions: *Minnesota*—None. *Miami*—Johnson, 1 for 10.

SUPER BOWL
IX

Pittsburgh Steelers 16, Minnesota Vikings 6

Jan. 12, 1975
Tulane Stadium, New Orleans
Attendance: 80,997

Pittsburgh	0	2	7	7	—	16
Minnesota	0	0	0	6	—	6

Pittsburgh—Safety, White downed Tarkenton in end zone.
Pittsburgh—Harris, 9, run (Gerela kick).
Minnesota—T. Brown recovered blocked punt in end zone (kick failed).
Pittsburgh—L. Brown, 4, pass from Bradshaw (Gerela kick).

Rushing: *Pittsburgh*—Harris, 34 for 158, 1 TD; Bleier, 17 for 65; Bradshaw, 5 for 33; Swann, 1 for −7. *Minnesota*—Foreman, 12 for 18; Tarkenton, 1 for 0; Osborn, 8 for −1.

Passing: *Pittsburgh*—Bradshaw, 9 of 14 for 97, 1 TD. *Minnesota*—Tarkenton, 11 of 26, for 102, 3 int.

Receiving: *Pittsburgh*—Brown, 3 for 49, 1 TD; Stallworth, 3 for 24; Bleier, 2 for 11; Lewis, 1 for 12. *Minnesota*—Foreman, 5 for 50; Voigt, 2 for 31; Osborn, 2 for 7; Gilliam, 1 for 16; Reed, 1 for −2.

Punting: *Pittsburgh*—Walden, 7 for 34.7 average. *Minnesota*—Eischeid, 6 for 37.2.

Punt Returns: *Pittsburgh*—Swann, 3 for 34; Edwards, 2 for 2. *Minnesota*—McCullum, 3 for 11; N. Wright, 1 for 1.

Kickoff Returns: *Pittsburgh*—Harrison, 2 for 17; Pearson, 1 for 15. *Minnesota*—McCullum, 1 for 26; McClanahan, 1 for 22; B. Brown, 1 for 2.

Interceptions: *Pittsburgh*—Wagner, 1 for 26; Blount, 1 for 10; Greene, 1 for 10. *Minnesota*—None.

SUPER BOWL

Pittsburgh Steelers 21, Dallas Cowboys 17

Jan. 18, 1976
Orange Bowl, Miami
Attendance: 80,187

| Dallas | 7 | 3 | 0 | 7 | — | 17 |
| Pittsburgh | 7 | 0 | 0 | 14 | — | 21 |

Dallas—D. Pearson, 29, pass from Staubach (Fritsch kick).
Pittsburgh—Grossman, 7, pass from Bradshaw (Gerela kick).
Dallas—Field goal, 36, Fritsch.
Pittsburgh—Safety, Harrison blocked Hoopes' punt through end zone.
Pittsburgh—Field goal, 36, Gerela.
Pittsburgh—Field goal, 18, Gerela.
Pittsburgh—Swann, 64, pass from Bradshaw (kick failed).
Dallas—P. Howard, 34, pass from Staubach (Fritsch kick).

Rushing: *Dallas*—Newhouse, 16 for 56; Staubach, 5 for 22; Dennison, 5 for 16; Pearson, 5 for 14. *Pittsburgh*—Harris, 27 for 82; Bleier, 15 for 51; Bradshaw, 4 for 16.

Passing: *Dallas*—Staubach, 15 of 24 for 204, 2 TD, 3 int. *Pittsburgh*—Bradshaw, 9 of 19 for 209, 2 TD.

Receiving: *Dallas*—P. Pearson, 5 for 53; Young, 3 for 31; D. Pearson, 2 for 59, 1 TD; Newhouse, 2 for 12; P. Howard, 1 for 34, 1 TD; Fugett, 1 for 9; Dennison, 1 for 6. *Pittsburgh*—Swann, 4 for 161, 1 TD; Stallworth, 2 for 8; Harris, 1 for 26; Grossman, 1 for 7; L. Brown, 1 for 7.

Punting: *Dallas*—Hoopes, 7 for 35.0 average. *Pittsburgh*—Walden, 4 for 39.8.

Punt Returns: *Dallas*—Richards, 1 for 5. *Pittsburgh*—D. Brown, 3 for 14; Edwards, 2 for 17.

Kickoff Returns: *Dallas*—T. Henderson, 48, after lateral; P. Pearson, 4 for 48. *Pittsburgh*—Blount, 3 for 64; Collier, 1 for 25.

Interceptions: *Dallas*—None. *Pittsburgh*—Edwards, 1 for 35; Thomas, 1 for 35; Wagner, 1 for 19.

SUPER BOWL
XI

Oakland Raiders 32, Minnesota Vikings 14

Jan. 9, 1977
Rose Bowl, Pasadena, Calif.
Attendance: 100,421

Oakland	0	16	3	13	—	32
Minnesota	0	0	7	7	—	14

Oakland—Field goal, 24, Mann.
Oakland—Casper, 1, pass from Stabler (Mann kick).
Oakland—Banaszak, 1, run (kick failed).
Oakland—Field goal, 40, Mann.
Minnesota—S. White, 8, pass from Tarkenton (Cox kick).
Oakland—Banaszak, 2, run (Mann kick).
Oakland—Brown, 75, interception return (kick failed).
Minnesota—Voigt, 13, pass from Lee (Cox kick).

Rushing: *Oakland*—Davis, 16 for 137; van Eeghen, 18 for 73; Garrett, 4 for 19; Banaszak, 10 for 19, 2 TD; Ginn, 2 for 9; Rae, 2 for 9. *Minnesota*—Foreman, 17 for 44; Johnson, 2 for 9; S. White, 1 for 7; Lee, 1 for 4; Miller, 2 for 4; McClanahan, 3 for 3.

Passing: *Oakland*—Stabler, 12 of 19 for 180, 1 TD. *Minnesota*—Tarkenton, 17 of 35 for 205, 2 TD, 1 int.; Lee, 7 of 9 for 81, 1 TD.

Receiving: *Oakland*—Biletnikoff, 4 for 79; Casper, 4 for 70, 1 TD; Branch, 3 for 20; Garrett, 1 for 11. *Minnesota*—S. White, 5 for 77, 1 TD; Foreman, 5 for 62; Voigt, 4 for 49, 1 TD; Miller, 4 for 19; Rashad, 3 for 53; Johnson, 3 for 26.

Punting: *Oakland*—Guy, 4 for 40.5 average. *Minnesota*—Clabo, 7 for 37.9.

Punt Returns: *Oakland*—Colzie, 4 for 43. *Minnesota*—Willis, 3 for 14.

Kickoff Returns: *Oakland*—Garrett, 2 for 47; Siani, 1 for 0. *Minnesota*—Willis, 3 for 57; S. White, 4 for 79.

Interceptions: *Oakland*—Brown, 1 for 75, 1 TD; Hall, 1 for 16. *Minnesota*—None.

SUPER BOWL XII

Dallas Cowboys 27, Denver Broncos 10

Jan. 15, 1978
Louisiana Superdome, New Orleans
Attendance: 75,583

Dallas	10	3	7	7	—	27
Denver	0	0	10	0	—	10

Dallas—Dorsett, 3, run (Herrera kick).
Dallas—Field goal, 35, Herrera.
Dallas—Field goal, 43, Herrera.
Denver—Field goal, 47, Turner.
Dallas—Johnson, 45, pass from Staubach (Herrera kick).
Denver—Lytle, 1, run (Turner kick).
Dallas—Richards, 29, pass from Newhouse (Herrera kick).

Rushing: *Dallas*—Dorsett, 15 for 66, 1 TD; Newhouse, 14 for 55; White, 1 for 13; P. Pearson, 3 for 11; Staubach, 3 for 6; Laidlaw, 1 for 1; Johnson, 1 for −9. *Denver*—Lytle, 10 for 35, 1 TD; Armstrong, 7 for 27; Weese, 3 for 26; Jensen, 1 for 16; Keyworth, 5 for 9; Perrin, 3 for 8.

Passing: *Dallas*—Staubach, 17 of 25 for 183, 1 TD; Newhouse, 1 of 1 for 29, 1 TD; White, 1 of 2 for 5. *Denver*—Morton, 4 of 15 for 39, 4 int.; Weese, 4 of 10 for 22.

Receiving: *Dallas*—P. Pearson, 5 for 37; DuPree, 4 for 66; Newhouse, 3 for −1; Johnson, 2 for 53, 1 TD; Richards, 2 for 38, 1 TD; Dorsett, 2 for 11; D. Pearson, 1 for 13. *Denver*—Dolbin, 2 for 24; Odoms, 2 for 9; Moses, 1 for 21; Upchurch, 1 for 9; Jensen, 1 for 5; Perrin, 1 for −7.

Punting: *Dallas*—White, 5 for 41.6 average. *Denver*—Dilts, 4 for 38.2.

Punt Returns: *Dallas*—Hill, 1 for 1. *Denver*, Upchurch, 3 for 22; Schultz, 1 for 0.

Kickoff Returns: *Dallas*—Johnson, 2 for 29; Brinson, 1 for 22. *Denver*—Upchurch, 3 for 94; Schultz, 2 for 62; Jensen, 1 for 17.

Interceptions: *Dallas*—Washington, 1 for 27; Kyle, 1 for 19; Barnes, 1 for 0; Hughes, 1 for 0. *Denver*—None.

SUPER BOWL

XIII

Pittsburgh Steelers 35, Dallas Cowboys 31

Jan. 21, 1979
Orange Bowl, Miami
Attendance: 79,484

Pittsburgh	7	14	0	14	—	35
Dallas	7	7	3	14	—	31

Pittsburgh—Stallworth, 28, pass from Bradshaw (Gerela kick).
Dallas—Hill, 39, pass from Staubach (Septien kick).
Dallas—Hegman, 37, fumble recovery return (Septien kick).
Pittsburgh—Stallworth, 75, pass from Bradshaw (Gerela kick).
Pittsburgh—Bleier, 7, pass from Bradshaw (Gerela kick).
Dallas—Field goal, 27, Septien.
Pittsburgh—Harris, 22, run (Gerela kick).
Pittsburgh—Swann, 18, pass from Bradshaw (Gerela kick).
Dallas—DuPree, 7, pass from Staubach (Septien kick).
Dallas—Johnson, 4, pass from Staubach (Septien kick).

Rushing: *Pittsburgh*—Harris, 20 for 68, 1 TD; Bleier, 2 for 3; Bradshaw, 2 for −5. *Dallas*—Dorsett, 16 for 96; Staubach, 4 for 37; Laidlaw, 3 for 12; P. Pearson, 1 for 6; Newhouse, 8 for 3.
Passing: *Pittsburgh*—Bradshaw, 17 of 30 for 318, 4 TD, 1 int. *Dallas*—Staubach, 17 of 30 for 228, 3 TD, 1 int.
Receiving: *Pittsburgh*—Swann, 7 for 124, 1 TD; Stallworth, 3 for 115, 2 TD; Grossman, 3 for 29; Bell, 2 for 21; Harris, 1 for 22; Bleier, 1 for 7, 1 TD. *Dallas*—Dorsett, 5 for 44; D. Pearson, 4 for 73; Hill, 2 for 49, 1 TD; Johnson, 2 for 30, 1 TD; DuPree, 2 for 17, 1 TD; P. Pearson, 2 for 15.
Punting: *Pittsburgh*—Colquitt, 3 for 43.0 average. *Dallas*—D. White, 5 for 39.6.
Punt Returns: *Pittsburgh*—Bell, 4 for 27. *Dallas*—Johnson, 2 for 33.
Kickoff Returns: *Pittsburgh*—L. Anderson, 3 for 45. *Dallas*—Johnson, 3 for 63; Brinson, 2 for 41; R. White, 1 for 0.
Interceptions: *Pittsburgh*—Blount, 1 for 13. *Dallas*—Lewis, 1 for 21.

SUPER BOWL
XIV

Pittsburgh Steelers 31, Los Angeles Rams 19

Jan. 20, 1980
Rose Bowl, Pasadena, Calif.
Attendance: 103,985

Los Angeles	7	6	6	0	—	19
Pittsburgh	3	7	7	14	—	31

Pittsburgh—Field goal, 41, Bahr.
Los Angeles—Bryant, 1, run (Corral kick).
Pittsburgh—Harris, 1, run (Bahr kick).
Los Angeles—Field goal, 31, Corral.
Los Angeles—Field goal, 45, Corral.
Pittsburgh—Swann, 47, pass from Bradshaw (Bahr kick).
Los Angeles—R. Smith, 24, pass from McCutcheon (kick failed).
Pittsburgh—Stallworth, 73, pass from Bradshaw (Bahr kick).
Pittsburgh—Harris, 1, run (Bahr kick).

Rushing: *Los Angeles*—Tyler, 17 for 60; Bryant, 6 for 30, 1 TD; McCutcheon, 5 for 10; Ferragamo, 1 for 7. *Pittsburgh*—Harris, 20 for 46, 2 TD; Bleier, 10 for 25; Bradshaw, 3 for 9; Thornton, 4 for 4.

Passing: *Los Angeles*—Ferragamo, 15 of 25 for 212, 1 int.; McCutcheon, 1 of 1 for 24, 1 TD. *Pittsburgh*—Bradshaw, 14 of 21 for 309, 2 TD, 3 int.

Receiving: *Los Angeles*—Waddy, 3 for 75; Bryant, 3 for 21; Tyler, 3 for 20; Dennard, 2 for 32; Nelson, 2 for 20; D. Hill, 1 for 28; Smith, 1 for 24, 1 TD; McCutcheon, 1 for 16. *Pittsburgh*—Swann, 5 for 79, 1 TD; Stallworth, 3 for 121, 1 TD; Harris, 3 for 66; Cunningham, 2 for 21; Thornton, 1 for 22.

Punting: *Los Angeles*—Clark, 5 for 44.0 average. *Pittsburgh*—Colquitt, 2 for 42.5.

Punt Returns: *Los Angeles*—Brown, 1 for 4. *Pittsburgh*—Bell, 2 for 17; Smith, 2 for 14.

Kickoff Returns: *Los Angeles*—E. Hill, 3 for 47; Jodat, 2 for 32; Andrews, 1 for 0. *Pittsburgh*—L. Anderson, 5 for 162.

Interceptions: *Los Angeles*—Elmendorf, 1 for 10; Brown, 1 for 6; Perry, 1 for −1; Thomas, 0 for 6. *Pittsburgh*—Lambert, 1 for 16.

SUPER BOWL XV

Oakland Raiders 27, Philadelphia Eagles 10

Jan. 25, 1981
Louisiana Superdome, New Orleans
Attendance: 76,135

Oakland	14	0	10	3	—	27
Philadelphia	0	3	0	7	—	10

Oakland—Branch, 2, pass from Plunkett (Bahr kick).
Oakland—King, 80, pass from Plunkett (Bahr kick).
Philadelphia—Field goal, 30, Franklin.
Oakland—Branch, 29, pass from Plunkett (Bahr kick).
Oakland—Field goal, 46, Bahr.
Philadelphia—Krepfle, 8, pass from Jaworski (Franklin kick).
Oakland—Field goal, 35, Bahr.

Rushing: *Oakland*—van Eeghen, 19 for 80; King, 6 for 18; Jensen, 3 for 12; Plunkett, 3 for 9; Whittington, 3 for − 2. *Philadelphia*—Montgomery, 16 for 44; Harris, 7 for 14; Giamonna, 1 for 7; Harrington, 1 for 4; Jaworski, 1 for 0.

Passing: *Oakland*—Plunkett, 13 of 21 for 261, 3 TD. *Philadelphia*—Jaworski, 18 of 38 for 291, 1 TD, 3 int.

Receiving: *Oakland*—Branch, 5 for 67, 2 TD; Chandler, 4 for 77; King, 2 for 93, 1 TD; Chester, 2 for 24. *Philadelphia*—Montgomery, 6 for 91; Carmichael, 5 for 83; Smith, 2 for 59; Krepfle, 2 for 16, 1 TD; Spagnola, 1 for 22; Parker, 1 for 19; Harris, 1 for 1.

Punting: *Oakland*—Guy, 3 for 42.0 average. *Philadelphia*—Runager, 3 for 36.7.

Punt Returns: *Oakland*—Matthews, 2 for 1. *Philadelphia*—Sciarra, 2 for 18; Henry, 1 for 2.

Kickoff Returns: *Oakland*—Matthews, 2 for 29; Moody, 1 for 19. *Philadelphia*—Campfield, 5 for 87; Harrington, 1 for 0.

Interceptions: *Oakland*—Martin, 3 for 4. *Philadelphia*—None.

SUPER BOWL
XVI

San Francisco 49ers 26, Cincinnati Bengals 21

Jan. 24, 1982
Pontiac (Mich.) Silverdome
Attendance: 81,270

San Francisco	7	13	0	6	—	26
Cincinnati	0	0	7	14	—	21

San Francisco—Montana, 1, run (Wersching kick).
San Francisco—Cooper, 11, pass from Montana (Wersching kick).
San Francisco—Field goal, 22, Wersching.
San Francisco—Field goal, 26, Wersching.
Cincinnati—Anderson, 5, run (Breech kick).
Cincinnati—Ross, 4, pass from Anderson (Breech kick).
San Francisco—Field goal, 40, Wersching.
San Francisco—Field goal, 23, Wersching.
Cincinnati—Ross, 3, pass from Anderson (Breech kick).

Rushing: *San Francisco*—Patton, 17 for 55; Cooper, 9 for 34; Montana, 6 for 18, 1 TD; Ring, 5 for 17; Davis, 2 for 5; Clark, 1 for −2. *Cincinnati*—Johnson, 14 for 36; Alexander, 5 for 17; Anderson, 4 for 15, 1 TD; A. Griffin, 1 for 4.

Passing: *San Francisco*—Montana, 14 of 22 for 157, 1 TD. *Cincinnati*—Anderson, 25 of 34 for 300, 2 TD, 2 int.

Receiving: *San Francisco*—Solomon, 4 for 52; Clark, 4 for 45; Cooper, 2 for 15, 1 TD; Wilson, 1 for 22; Young, 1 for 14; Patton, 1 for 6; Ring, 1 for 3. *Cincinnati*—Ross, 11 for 104, 2 TD; Collinsworth, 5 for 107; Curtis, 3 for 42; Kreider, 2 for 36; Johnson, 2 for 8; Alexander, 2 for 3.

Punting: *San Francisco*—Miller, 4 for 46.3 average. *Cincinnati*—McInally, 3 for 43.7.

Punt Returns: *San Francisco*—Hicks, 1 for 6. *Cincinnati*—Fuller, 4 for 35.

Kickoff Returns: *San Francisco*—Hicks, 1 for 23; Lawrence, 1 for 17; Clark, 1 for 0. *Cincinnati*—Verser, 5 for 52; A. Griffin, 1 for 0; Frazier, 1 for 0.

Interceptions: *San Francisco*—Hicks, 1 for 27; Wright, 1 for 25. *Cincinnati*—None.

SUPER BOWL
XVII

Washington Redskins 27, Miami Dolphins 17

Jan. 30, 1983
Rose Bowl, Pasadena, Calif.
Attendance: 103,667

Miami	7	10	0	0	—	17
Washington	0	10	3	14	—	27

Miami—Cefalo, 76, pass from Woodley (von Schamann kick).
Washington—Field goal, 31, Moseley.
Miami—Field goal, 20, von Schamann.
Washington—Garrett, 4, pass from Theismann (Moseley kick).
Miami—Walker, 98, kickoff return (von Schamann kick).
Washington—Field goal, 20, Moseley.
Washington—Riggins, 43, run (Moseley kick).
Washington—Brown, 6, pass from Theismann (Moseley kick).

Rushing: *Miami*—Franklin, 16 for 49; Woodley, 4 for 16; Nathan, 7 for 26; Harris, 1 for 1; Vigorito, 1 for 4. *Washington*—Riggins, 38 for 166, 1 TD; Harmon, 9 for 40; Walker, 1 for 6; Theismann, 3 for 20; Garrett, 1 for 44.

Passing: *Miami*—Woodley, 4 of 14 for 97, 1 TD, 1 int.; Strock, 0 of 3 for 0. *Washington*—Theismann, 15 of 23 for 143, 2 TD, 2 int.

Receiving: *Miami*—Cefalo, 2 for 82, 1 TD; Harris, 2 for 15. *Washington*—Brown, 6 for 60, 1 TD; Warren, 5 for 28; Walker, 1 for 27; Riggins, 1 for 15; Garrett, 2 for 13, 1 TD.

Punting: *Miami*—Orosz, 6 for 37.8 average. *Washington*—Hayes, 4 for 42.

Punt Returns: *Miami*—Vigorito, 2 for 22. *Washington*—Nelms, 6 for 52.

Kickoff Returns: *Miami*—L. Blackwood, 2 for 32; Walker, 4 for 190. *Washington*—Nelms, 2 for 44; Wonsley, 1 for 13.

Interceptions: *Miami*—Duhe, 1 for 0; L. Blackwood, 1 for 0. *Washington*—Murphy, 1 for 0.

SUPER BOWL
XVIII

Los Angeles Raiders 38, Washington Redskins 9

Jan. 22, 1984
Tampa Stadium
Attendance: 72,920

Washington	0	3	6	0	—	9
Los Angeles	7	14	14	3	—	38

Los Angeles—Jensen recovered blocked punt in end zone (Bahr kick).
Los Angeles—Branch, 12, pass from Plunkett (Bahr kick).
Washington—Field goal, 24, Moseley.
Los Angeles—Squirek, 5, interception return (Bahr kick).
Washington—Riggins, 1, run (kick blocked).
Los Angeles—Allen, 5, run (Bahr kick).
Los Angeles—Allen, 74, run (Bahr kick).
Los Angeles—Field goal, 21, Bahr.

Rushing: *Washington*—Riggins, 26 for 64, 1 TD; Theismann, 3 for 18; J. Washington, 3 for 8. *Los Angeles*—Allen, 20 for 191, 2 TD; King, 3 for 12; Hawkins, 3 for 6; Pruitt, 5 for 17; Plunkett, 1 for −2; Willis, 1 for 7.

Passing: *Washington*—Theismann, 16 of 35 for 243, 2 int. *Los Angeles*—Plunkett, 16 of 25 for 172, 1 TD.

Receiving: *Washington*—Didier, 5 for 65; J. Washington, 3 for 20; Garrett, 1 for 17; Brown, 3 for 93; Giaquinto, 2 for 21; Monk, 1 for 26; Riggins, 1 for 1. *Los Angeles*—Allen, 2 for 18; King, 2 for 8; Christensen, 4 for 32; Branch, 6 for 94, 1 TD; Hawkins, 2 for 20.

Punting: *Washington*—Hayes, 7 for 37 average. *Los Angeles*—Guy, 7 for 42.7.

Punt Returns: *Washington*—Green, 1 for 34; Giaquinto, 1 for 1. *Los Angeles*—Watts, 1 for 0; Pruitt, 1 for 8.

Kickoff Returns: *Washington*—Garrett, 5 for 100; Grant, 1 for 32; Kimball, 1 for 0. *Los Angeles*—Pruitt, 1 for 17.

Interceptions: *Washington*—None. *Los Angeles*—Squirek, 1 for 5, 1 TD; Haynes, 1 for 0.

SUPER BOWL
XIX

San Francisco 49ers 38, Miami Dolphins 16

Jan. 20, 1985
Stanford Stadium, Palo Alto, Calif.
Attendance: 84,059

Miami	10	6	0	0	—	16
San Francisco	7	21	10	0	—	38

Miami—Field goal, 37, von Schamann.
San Francisco—Monroe, 33, pass from Montana (Wersching kick).
Miami—D. Johnson, 2, pass from Marino (von Schamann kick).
San Francisco—Craig, 8, pass from Montana (Wersching kick).
San Francisco—Montana, 6, run (Wersching kick).
San Francisco—Craig, 2, run (Wersching kick).
Miami—Field goal, 31, von Schamann.
Miami—Field goal, 30, von Schamann.
San Francisco—Field goal, 27, Wersching.
San Francisco—Craig, 16, pass from Montana (Wersching kick).

Rushing: *Miami*—Bennett, 3 for 7; Nathan, 5 for 18; Marino, 1 for 0. *San Francisco*—Tyler, 13 for 65; Craig, 15 for 58; 1 TD; Montana, 5 for 59, 1 TD; Harn, 5 for 20; Cooper, 1 for 4; Solomon, 1 for 5.

Passing: *Miami*—Marino, 29 of 50 for 318, 1 TD, 2 int. *San Francisco*—Montana, 24 of 35 for 331, 3 TD.

Receiving: *Miami*—Nathan, 10 for 83; D. Johnson, 3 for 28, 1 TD; Clayton, 6 for 92; Duper, 1 for 11; Rose, 6 for 73; Moore, 2 for 17; Cefalo, 1 for 14. *San Francisco*—Tyler, 4 for 70; D. Clark, 6 for 77; Craig, 7 for 77, 2 TD; Monroe, 1 for 33, 1 TD; Francis, 5 for 60; Solomon, 1 for 14.

Punting: *Miami*—Roby, 6 for 39.3 average. *San Francisco*—Runager, 3 for 32.7.

Punt Returns: *Miami*—Walker, 2 for 15. *San Francisco*—McLemore, 5 for 51.

Kickoff Returns: *Miami*—Hardy, 2 for 31; Walker, 4 for 93; Hill, 1 for 16. *San Francisco*—Harmon, 2 for 24; Monroe, 1 for 16; McIntyre, 1 for 0.

Interceptions: *Miami*—None. *San Francisco*—Wright, 1 for 0; Williamson, 1 for 0.

SUPER BOWL
XX

Chicago Bears 46, New England Patriots 10

Jan. 26, 1986
Louisiana Superdome, New Orleans
Attendance: 73,818

Chicago	13	10	21	2	—	46
New England	3	0	0	7	—	10

New England—Field goal, 36, Franklin.
Chicago—Field goal, 28, Butler.
Chicago—Field goal, 24, Butler.
Chicago—Suhey, 11, run (Butler kick).
Chicago—McMahon, 2, run (Butler kick).
Chicago—Field goal, 24, Butler.
Chicago—McMahon, 1, run (Butler kick).
Chicago—Phillips, 28, interception return (Butler kick).
Chicago—Perry, 1, run (Butler kick).
New England—Fryar, 8, pass from Grogan (Franklin kick).
Chicago—Safety, Grogan tackled in end zone by Waechter.

Rushing: *Chicago*—Payton, 22 for 61; Suhey, 11 for 52, 1 TD; McMahon, 5 for 14, 2 TD; Thomas, 2 for 8; Gentry, 3 for 15; Perry, 1 for 1, 1 TD; Fuller, 1 for 1; Sanders, 4 for 15. *New England*—C. James, 5 for 1; Hawthorne, 1 for −4; Collins, 3 for 4; Weathers, 1 for 3; Grogan, 1 for 3.

Passing: *Chicago*—McMahon, 12 of 20 for 256; Fuller, 0 of 4; Perry, 0 of 0. *New England*—Eason, 0 of 6; Grogan, 17 of 30 for 177, 1 TD, 2 int.

Receiving: *Chicago*—Gault, 4 for 129; Moorehead, 2 for 22; Thomas, 1 for 4; Suhey, 1 for 24; Gentry, 2 for 41; Margerum, 2 for 36. *New England*—Collins, 2 for 19; C. James, 1 for 6; Morgan, 7 for 70; Starring, 2 for 39; Ramsey, 2 for 16; Weathers, 1 for 3; Fryar, 2 for 24, 1 TD.

Punting: *Chicago*—Buford, 4 for 43.3 average. *New England*—Camarillo, 6 for 43.8.

Punt Returns: *Chicago*—Ortego, 2 for 20. *New England*—Fryar, 2 for 22.

Kickoff Returns: *Chicago*—Gault, 4 for 49. *New England*—Starring, 7 for 153.

Interceptions: *Chicago*—Phillips, 1 for 18, 1 TD; Morrissey, 1 for 47. *New England*—None.

GAME RECORDS

INDIVIDUAL RECORDS

SCORING

Most Points, Game
18 Roger Craig, San Francisco vs. Miami, 1985 (3-td)
15 Don Chandler, Green Bay vs. Oakland, 1968 (3-pat, 4-fg)
Most Touchdowns, Game
3 Roger Craig, San Francisco vs. Miami, 1985 (1-r, 2-p)
2 Max McGee, Green Bay vs. Kansas City, 1967 (2-p)
Elijah Pitts, Green Bay vs. Kansas City, 1967 (2-r)
Bill Miller, Oakland vs. Green Bay, 1968 (2-p)
Larry Csonka, Miami vs. Minnesota, 1974 (2-r)
Pete Banaszak, Oakland vs. Minnesota, 1977 (2-r)
John Stallworth, Pittsburgh vs. Dallas, 1979 (2-p)
Franco Harris, Pittsburgh vs. Los Angeles, 1980 (2-r)
Cliff Branch, Oakland vs. Philadelphia, 1981 (2-p)
Dan Ross, Cincinnati vs. San Francisco, 1982 (2-p)
Marcus Allen, L.A. Raiders vs. Washington, 1984 (2-r)
Jim McMahon, Chicago vs. New England, 1986 (2-r)
Most Points After Touchdown, Game
5 Don Chandler, Green Bay vs. Kansas City, 1967 (5 att)
Roy Gerela, Pittsburgh vs. Dallas, 1979 (5 att)
Chris Bahr, L.A. Raiders vs. Washington, 1984 (5 att)
Ray Wersching, San Francisco vs. Miami, 1985 (5 att)
Kevin Butler, Chicago vs. New England, 1986 (5 att)
4 Rafael Septien, Dallas vs. Pittsburgh, 1979 (4 att)
Matt Bahr, Pittsburgh vs. Los Angeles, 1980 (4 att)
Most Field Goals Attempted, Game
5 Jim Turner, N.Y. Jets vs. Baltimore, 1969
Efren Herrera, Dallas vs. Denver, 1978

4 Don Chandler, Green Bay vs. Oakland, 1968
  Roy Gerela, Pittsburgh vs. Dallas, 1976
  Ray Wersching, San Francisco vs. Cincinnati, 1982

Most Field Goals, Game
4 Don Chandler, Green Bay vs. Oakland, 1968
  Ray Wersching, San Francisco vs. Cincinnati, 1982
3 Jim Turner, N.Y. Jets vs. Baltimore, 1969
  Jan Stenerud, Kansas City vs. Minnesota, 1970
  Uwe von Schamann, Miami vs. San Francisco, 1985
  Keven Butler, Chicago vs. New England, 1986.

Longest Field Goal
48 Jan Stenerud, Kansas City vs. Minnesota, 1970
47 Jim Turner, Denver vs. Dallas, 1978
46 Chris Bahr, Oakland vs. Philadelphia, 1981

Most Safeties, Game
1 Dwight White, Pittsburgh vs. Minnesota, 1975
  Reggie Harrison, Pittsburgh vs. Dallas, 1976
  Henry Waechter, Chicago vs. New England, 1986

RUSHING

Most Attempts, Game
38 John Riggins, Washington vs. Miami, 1983
34 Franco Harris, Pittsburgh vs. Minnesota, 1975
33 Larry Csonka, Miami vs. Minnesota, 1974

Most Yards Gained, Game
191 Marcus Allen, L.A. Raiders vs. Washington, 1984
166 John Riggins, Washington vs. Miami, 1983
158 Franco Harris, Pittsburgh vs. Minnesota, 1975

Longest Run From Scrimmage
74 Marcus Allen, L.A. Raiders vs. Washington, 1984 (TD)
58 Tom Matte, Baltimore vs. N.Y. Jets, 1969
49 Larry Csonka, Miami vs. Washington, 1973

Highest Average Gain, Game (10 attempts)
10.5 Tom Matte, Baltimore vs. N.Y. Jets, 1969 (11-116)
9.6 Marcus Allen, L.A. Raiders vs. Washington, 1984 (20-191)
8.6 Clarence Davis, Oakland vs. Minnesota, 1977 (16-137)

Most Touchdowns, Game
2 Elijah Pitts, Green Bay vs. Kansas City, 1967
2 Larry Csonka, Miami vs. Minnesota, 1974
  Pete Banaszak, Oakland vs. Minnesota, 1977
  Franco Harris, Pittsburgh vs. Los Angeles, 1980
  Marcus Allen, L.A. Raiders vs. Washington, 1984
  Jim McMahon, Chicago vs. New England, 1986.

PASSING

Most Passes Attempted, Game
  50 Dan Marino, Miami vs. San Francisco, 1985
  38 Ron Jaworski, Philadelphia vs. Oakland, 1981
  36 Fran Tarkenton, Minnesota vs. Oakland, 1977
      Joe Theismann, Washington vs. L.A. Raiders, 1984
      Joe Montana, San Francisco vs. Miami, 1985

Most Passes Completed, Game
  29 Dan Marino, Miami vs. San Francisco, 1985
  25 Ken Anderson, Cincinnati vs. San Francisco, 1982
  24 Joe Montana, San Francisco vs. Miami, 1985

Most Consecutive Completions, Game
   8 Len Dawson, Kansas City vs. Green Bay, 1967
      Joe Theismann, Washington vs. Miami, 1983

Highest Completion Percentage, Game (20 attempts)
  73.5 Ken Anderson, Cincinnati vs. San Francisco, 1982 (34–25)
  69.6 Bart Starr, Green Bay vs. Kansas City, 1967 (23–16)
  68.6 Joe Montana, San Francisco vs. Miami, 1985 (35–24)

Most Yards Gained, Game
  331 Joe Montana, San Francisco vs. Miami, 1985
  318 Terry Bradshaw, Pittsburgh vs. Dallas, 1979
       Dan Marino, Miami vs. San Francisco, 1985
  309 Terry Bradshaw, Pittsburgh vs. Los Angeles, 1980

Longest Pass Completion
  80 Jim Plunkett (to King), Oakland vs. Philadelphia, 1981 (TD)
  76 David Woodley (to Cefalo), Miami vs. Washington, 1983 (TD)
  75 Johnny Unitas (to Mackey), Baltimore vs. Dallas, 1971 (TD)
      Terry Bradshaw (to Stallworth), Pittsburgh vs. Dallas, 1979
      (TD)

Most Touchdown Passes, Game
  4 Terry Bradshaw, Pittsburgh vs. Dallas, 1979
  3 Roger Staubach, Dallas vs. Pittsburgh, 1979
     Jim Plunkett, Oakland vs. Philadelphia, 1981
     Joe Montana, San Francisco vs. Miami, 1985
  2 By many players

Most Attempts, Without Interception, Game
  36 Joe Montana, San Francisco vs. Miami, 1985
  28 Joe Namath, N.Y. Jets vs. Baltimore, 1969
  25 Roger Staubach, Dallas vs. Denver, 1978
      Jim Plunkett, L.A. Raiders vs. Washington, 1984

Most Passes Had Intercepted, Game
  4 Craig Morton, Denver vs. Dallas, 1978
  3 By seven players

PASS RECEIVING

Most Receptions, Game
  11 Dan Ross, Cincinnati vs. San Francisco, 1982
  10 Tony Nathan, Miami vs. San Francisco, 1985
  8 George Sauer, N.Y. Jets vs. Baltimore, 1969
Most Yards Gained, Game
  161 Lynn Swann, Pittsburgh vs. Dallas, 1976
  138 Max McGee, Green Bay vs. Kansas City, 1967
  133 George Sauer, N.Y. Jets vs. Baltimore, 1969
Longest Reception
  80 Kenny King (from Plunkett), Oakland vs. Philadelphia, 1981 (TD)
  76 Jimmy Cefalo (from Woodley), Miami vs. Washington, 1983 (TD)
  75 John Mackey (from Unitas), Baltimore vs. Dallas, 1971 (TD)
  John Stallworth (from Bradshaw), Pittsburgh vs. Dallas, 1979 (TD)
Most Touchdowns, Game
  2 Max McGee, Green Bay vs. Kansas City, 1967
  Bill Miller, Oakland vs. Green Bay, 1968
  John Stallworth, Pittsburgh vs. Dallas, 1979
  Cliff Branch, Oakland vs. Philadelphia, 1981
  Dan Ross, Cincinnati vs. San Francisco, 1982
  Roger Craig, San Francisco vs. Miami, 1985

INTERCEPTIONS BY

Most Interceptions By, Game
  3 Rod Martin, Oakland vs. Philadelphia, 1981
  2 Randy Beverly, N.Y. Jets vs. Baltimore, 1969
  Chuck Howley, Dallas vs. Baltimore, 1971
  Jake Scott, Miami vs. Washington, 1973
Most Yards Gained, Game
  75 Willie Brown, Oakland vs. Minnesota, 1977
  63 Jake Scott, Miami vs. Washington, 1973
  60 Herb Adderley, Green Bay vs. Oakland, 1968
Longest Return
  75 Willie Brown, Oakland vs. Minnesota, 1977 (TD)
  60 Herb Adderley, Green Bay vs. Oakland, 1968 (TD)
  55 Jake Scott, Miami vs. Washington, 1973
Most Touchdowns, Game
  1 Herb Adderley, Green Bay vs. Oakland, 1968

Willie Brown, Oakland vs. Minnesota, 1977
Jack Squirek, L.A. Raiders vs. Washington, 1984
Reggie Phillips, Chicago vs. New England, 1986

PUNTING

Most Points, Game
   9 Ron Widby, Dallas vs. Baltimore, 1971
   7 By seven players
Longest Punt
   62 Rich Camarillo, New England vs. Chicago, 1986
   61 Jerrel Wilson, Kansas City vs. Green Bay, 1967
   59 Jerrel Wilson, Kansas City vs. Minnesota, 1970
      Bobby Walden, Pittsburgh vs. Dallas, 1976
      Ken Clark, Los Angeles vs. Pittsburgh, 1980
Highest Average, Punting, Game (4 punts)
   48.5 Jerrel Wilson, Kansas City vs. Minnesota, 1970 (4–194)
   46.3 Jim Miller, San Francisco vs. Cincinnati, 1982 (4–185)
   45.3 Jerrel Wilson, Kansas City vs. Green Bay, 1967 (7–317)

PUNT RETURNS

Most Punt Returns, Game
   6 Mike Nelms, Washington vs. Miami, 1983
   5 Willie Wood, Green Bay vs. Oakland, 1968
      Dana McLemore, San Francisco vs. Miami, 1985
   4 By six players

KICKOFF RETURNS

Most Kickoff Returns, Game
   7 Stephen Starring, New England vs. Chicago, 1986
   5 Larry Anderson, Pittsburgh vs. Los Angeles, 1980
      Billy Campfield, Philadelphia vs. Oakland, 1981
      David Verser, Cincinnati vs. San Francisco, 1982
      Alvin Garrett, Washington vs. L.A. Raiders, 1984
Most Yards Gained, Game
   190 Fulton Walker, Miami vs. Washington, 1983
   162 Larry Anderson, Pittsburgh vs. Los Angeles, 1980
   153 Stephen Starring, New England vs. Chicago, 1986

Longest Return

98 Fulton Walker, Miami vs. Washington, 1983 (TD)

67 Rick Upchurch, Denver vs. Dallas, 1978

48 Thomas Henderson, Dallas vs. Pittsburgh, 1976 (lateral)

Most Touchdowns, Game

1 Fulton Walker, Miami vs. Washington, 1983

FUMBLES

Most Fumbles, Game

3 Roger Staubach, Dallas vs. Pittsburgh, 1976

2 Franco Harris, Pittsburgh vs. Minnesota, 1975

Butch Johnson, Dallas vs. Denver, 1978

Terry Bradshaw, Pittsburgh vs. Dallas, 1979

Most Fumbles Recovered, Game

2 Jack Scott, Miami vs. Minnesota, 1974 (1 own, 1 opp)

Roger Staubach, Dallas vs. Pittsburgh, 1976 (2 own)

Randy Hughes, Dallas vs. Denver, 1978 (2 opp)

Butch Johnson, Dallas vs. Denver, 1978 (2 own)

Mike Singletary, Chicago vs. New England, 1986 (2 opp)

Most Yards Gained, Game

49 Mike Bass, Washington vs. Miami, 1973 (opp)

37 Mike Hegman, Dallas vs. Pittsburgh, 1979 (opp)

21 Randy Hughes, Dallas vs. Denver, 1978 (opp)

Longest Return

49 Mike Bass, Washington vs. Miami, 1973 (TD)

37 Mike Hegman, Dallas vs. Pittsburgh, 1979 (TD)

19 Randy Hughes, Dallas vs. Denver, 1978

Most Touchdowns, Game

1 Mike Bass, Washington vs. Miami, 1973 (opp 49 yds)

Mike Hegman, Dallas vs. Pittsburgh, 1979 (opp 37 yds)

COMBINED NET YARDS GAINED

Most Yards Gained, Game

209 Marcus Allen, L.A. Raiders vs. Washington, 1984

192 Stephen Starring, New England vs. Chicago, 1986

190 Fulton Walker, Miami vs. Washington, 1983

181 John Riggins, Washington vs. Miami, 1983

TEAM RECORDS

SCORING

Most Points, Game
    46 Chicago vs. New England, 1986
    38 L.A. Raiders vs. Washington, 1984
       San Francisco vs. Miami, 1985
    35 Green Bay vs. Kansas City, 1967
       Pittsburgh vs. Dallas, 1979

Fewest Points, Game
    3 Miami vs. Dallas, 1972
    6 Minnesota vs. Pittsburgh, 1975
    7 By four teams

Most Points, Both Teams, Game
    66 Pittsburgh (35) vs. Dallas (31), 1979
    56 Chicago (46) vs. New England (10), 1986
    54 San Francisco (38) vs. Miami (16), 1985
    50 Pittsburgh (31) vs. Los Angeles (19), 1980

Fewest Points, Both Teams, Game
    21 Washington (7) vs. Miami (14), 1973
    22 Minnesota (6) vs. Pittsburgh (16), 1975
    23 Baltimore (7) vs. N.Y. Jets (16), 1969

Largest Margin of Victory, Game
    36 Chicago vs. New England, 1986 (46–10)
    29 L.A. Raiders vs. Washington, 1984 (38–9)
    25 Green Bay vs. Kansas City, 1967 (35–10)

Most Points, Each Half
1st:
    28 San Francisco vs. Miami, 1985
2nd:
    23 Chicago vs. New England, 1986
    21 Green Bay vs. Kansas City, 1967
       Pittsburgh vs. Los Angeles, 1980
       Cincinnati vs. San Francisco, 1982

Most Touchdowns, Game
    5 Green Bay vs. Kansas City, 1967
      Pittsburgh vs. Dallas, 1979
      L.A. Raiders vs. Washington, 1984
      San Francisco vs. Miami, 1985
      Chicago vs. New England, 1986
    4 Oakland vs. Minnesota, 1977
      Dallas vs. Pittsburgh, 1979

Pittsburgh vs. Los Angeles, 1980

3 By many teams

Fewest Touchdowns, Game

0 Miami vs. Dallas, 1972

1 By 13 teams

Most Touchdowns, Both Teams, Game

9 Pittsburgh (5) vs. Dallas (4), 1979

6 Green Bay (5) vs. Kansas City (1), 1967

Oakland (4) vs. Minnesota (2), 1977

Pittsburgh (4) vs. Los Angeles (2), 1980

L.A. Raiders (5) vs. Washington (1), 1984

San Francisco (5) vs. Miami (1), 1985

Chicago (5) vs. New England (1), 1986

Fewest Touchdowns, Both Teams, Game

2 Baltimore (1) vs. N.Y. Jets (1), 1969

3 In five games

Most Field Goals Attempted, Game

5 N.Y. Jets vs. Baltimore, 1969

Dallas vs. Denver, 1978

4 Green Bay vs. Oakland, 1968

Pittsburgh vs. Dallas, 1976

San Francisco vs. Cincinnati, 1982

Most Field Goals Attempted, Both Teams, Game

7 N.Y. Jets (5) vs. Baltimore (2), 1969

6 Dallas (5) vs. Denver (1), 1978

5 Green Bay (4) vs. Oakland (1), 1968

Pittsburgh (4) vs. Dallas (1), 1976

Oakland (3) vs. Philadelphia (2), 1981

Fewest Field Goals Attempted, Both Teams, Game

1 Minnesota (0) vs. Miami (1), 1974

2 Green Bay (0) vs. Kansas City (2), 1967

Miami (1) vs. Washington (1), 1973

Dallas (1) vs. Pittsburgh (1), 1979

Most Field Goals, Game

4 Green Bay vs. Oakland, 1968

San Francisco vs. Cincinnati, 1982

3 N.Y. Jets vs. Baltimore, 1969

Kansas City vs. Minnesota, 1970

Miami vs. San Francisco, 1985

Chicago vs. New England, 1986

Most Field Goals, Both Teams, Game

4 Green Bay (4) vs. Oakland (0), 1968

San Francisco (4) vs. Cincinnati (0), 1982

Miami (3) vs. San Francisco (1), 1985

Chicago (3) vs. New England (1), 1986
　　3 In seven games
Fewest Field Goals, Both Teams, Game
　　0 Miami vs. Washington, 1973
　　　Pittsburgh vs. Minnesota, 1975
　　1 Green Bay (0) vs. Kansas City (1), 1967
　　　Minnesota (0) vs. Miami (1), 1974
　　　Pittsburgh (0) vs. Dallas (1), 1979
Most Safeties, Game
　　1 Pittsburgh vs. Minnesota, 1975; vs. Dallas, 1976
　　　Chicago vs. New England, 1986

FIRST DOWNS

Most First Downs, Game
　　31 San Francisco vs. Miami, 1985
　　24 Cincinnati vs. San Francisco, 1982
　　　Washington vs. Miami, 1983
　　23 Dallas vs. Miami, 1972
Fewest First Downs, Game
　　9 Minnesota vs. Pittsburgh, 1975
　　　Miami vs. Washington, 1983
　　10 Dallas vs. Baltimore, 1971
　　　Miami vs. Dallas, 1972
　　11 Denver vs. Dallas, 1978
Most First Downs, Both Teams, Game
　　50 San Francisco (31) vs. Miami (19), 1985
　　44 Cincinnati (24) vs. San Francisco (20), 1982
　　41 Oakland (21) vs. Minnesota (20), 1977
Fewest First Downs, Both Teams, Game
　　24 Dallas (10) vs. Baltimore (14), 1971
　　26 Minnesota (9) vs. Pittsburgh (17), 1975
　　27 Pittsburgh (13) vs. Dallas (14), 1976
Most First Downs, Rushing, Game
　　16 San Francisco vs. Miami, 1985
　　15 Dallas vs. Miami, 1972
　　14 Washington vs. Miami, 1983
Fewest First Downs, Rushing, Game
　　1 New England vs. Chicago, 1986
　　2 Minnesota vs. Kansas City, 1970
　　　Minnesota vs. Pittsburgh, 1975
　　　Minnesota vs. Oakland, 1977
　　　Pittsburgh vs. Dallas, 1979

Miami vs. San Francisco, 1985
3 Miami vs. Dallas, 1972
Philadelphia vs. Oakland, 1981

Most First Downs, Rushing, Both Teams, Game
21 Washington (14) vs. Miami (7), 1983
18 Dallas (15) vs. Miami (3), 1972
Miami (13) vs. Minnesota (5), 1974
San Francisco (16) vs. Miami (2), 1985
17 N.Y. Jets (10) vs. Baltimore (7), 1969

Fewest First Downs, Rushing, Both Teams, Game
8 Baltimore (4) vs. Dallas (4), 1971
Pittsburgh (2) vs. Dallas (6), 1979
9 Philadelphia (3) vs. Oakland (6), 1981
10 Minnesota (2) vs. Kansas City (8), 1970

Most First Downs, Passing, Game
17 Miami vs. San Francisco, 1985
15 Minnesota vs. Oakland, 1977
Pittsburgh vs. Dallas, 1979
San Francisco vs. Miami, 1985
14 Philadelphia vs. Oakland, 1981

Fewest First Downs, Passing, Game
1 Denver vs. Dallas, 1978
2 Miami vs. Washington, 1983
4 Miami vs. Minnesota, 1974

Most First Downs, Passing, Both Teams, Game
32 Miami (17) vs. San Francisco (15), 1985
28 Pittsburgh (15) vs. Dallas (13), 1979
24 Philadelphia (14) vs. Oakland (10), 1981

Fewest First Downs, Passing, Both Teams, Game
9 Denver (1) vs. Dallas (8), 1978
10 Minnesota (5) vs. Pittsburgh (5), 1975
11 Dallas (5) vs. Baltimore (6), 1971
Miami (2) vs. Washington (9), 1983

Most First Downs, Penalty, Game
4 Baltimore vs. Dallas, 1971
Miami vs. Minnesota, 1974
Cincinnati vs. San Francisco, 1982
3 Kansas City vs. Minnesota, 1970
Minnesota vs. Oakland, 1977

Most First Downs, Penalty, Both Teams, Game
6 Cincinnati (4) vs. San Francisco (2), 1982
5 Baltimore (4) vs. Dallas (1), 1971
Miami (4) vs. Minnesota (1), 1974
4 Kansas City (3) vs. Minnesota (1), 1970

Fewest First Downs, Penalty, Both Teams, Game
    0 Dallas vs. Miami, 1972
        Miami vs. Washington, 1973
        Dallas vs. Pittsburgh, 1976
        Miami vs. San Francisco, 1985
    1 Green Bay (0) vs. Kansas City (1), 1967
        Miami (0) vs. Washington (1), 1983

INTERCEPTIONS BY

Most Interceptions By, Game
    4 N.Y. Jets vs. Baltimore, 1969
        Dallas vs. Denver, 1978
    3 By eight teams
Most Interceptions by, Both Teams, Game
    6 Baltimore (3) vs. Dallas (3), 1971
    4 In five games
Most Yards Gained, Game
    95 Miami vs. Washington, 1973
    91 Oakland vs. Minnesota, 1977
    89 Pittsburgh vs. Dallas, 1976
Most Yards Gained, Both Teams, Game
    95 Miami (95) vs. Washington (0), 1973
    91 Oakland (91) vs. Minnesota (0), 1977
    89 Pittsburgh (89) vs. Dallas (0), 1976
Most Touchdowns, Game
    1 Green Bay vs. Oakland, 1968
        Oakland vs. Minnesota, 1977
        L.A. Raiders vs. Washington, 1984
        Chicago vs. New England, 1986

PUNTING

Most Punts, Game
    9 Dallas vs. Baltimore, 1971
    8 Washington vs. L.A. Raiders, 1984
    7 By six teams
Fewest Punts, Game
    2 Pittsburgh vs. Los Angeles, 1980
    3 By eight teams
Most Punts, Both Teams, Game
    15 Washington (8) vs. L.A. Raiders (7), 1984

13 Dallas (9) vs. Baltimore (4), 1971
   Pittsburgh (7) vs. Minnesota (6), 1975
12 In three games

Fewest Punts, Both Teams, Game
   6 Oakland (3) vs. Philadelphia (3), 1981
   7 In four games

PUNT RETURNS

Most Punt Returns, Game
   6 Washington vs. Miami, 1983
   5 By five teams
Fewest Punt Returns, Game
   0 Minnesota vs. Miami, 1974
   1 By eight teams
Most Punt Returns, Both Teams, Game
   9 Pittsburgh (5) vs. Minnesota (4), 1975
   8 Green Bay (5) vs. Oakland (3), 1968
     Baltimore (5) vs. Dallas (3), 1971
     Washington (6) vs. Miami (2), 1983
   7 Green Bay (4) vs. Kansas City (3), 1967
     Oakland (4) vs. Minnesota (3), 1977
     San Francisco (5) vs. Miami (2), 1985
Fewest Punt Returns, Both Teams, Game
   2 Dallas (1) vs. Miami (1), 1972
   3 Kansas City (1) vs. Minnesota (2), 1970
     Minnesota (0) vs. Miami (3), 1974
Most Yards Gained, Game
   52 Washington vs. Miami, 1983
   51 San Francisco vs. Miami, 1985
   43 Oakland vs. Minnesota, 1977
Fewest Yards Gained, Game
   1 Dallas vs. Miami, 1972
   0 By four teams
Most Yards Gained, Both Teams, Game
   74 Washington (52) vs. Miami (22), 1983
   66 San Francisco (51) vs. Miami (15), 1985
   60 Dallas (33) vs. Pittsburgh (27), 1979
Fewest Yards Gained, Both Teams, Game
   13 Miami (4) vs. Washington (9), 1973
   18 Kansas City (0) vs. Minnesota (18), 1970
   20 Dallas (−1) vs. Miami (21), 1972
     Minnesota (0) vs. Miami (20), 1974

KICKOFF RETURNS

Most Kickoff Returns, Game
7 Oakland vs. Green Bay, 1968
Minnesota vs. Oakland, 1977
Cincinnati vs. San Francisco, 1982
Washington vs. L.A. Raiders, 1984
Miami vs. San Francisco, 1985
New England vs. Chicago, 1986
6 By six teams
Fewest Kickoff Returns, Game
1 N.Y. Jets vs. Baltimore, 1969
L.A. Raiders vs. Washington, 1984
2 By six teams
Most Kickoff Returns, Both Teams, Game
11 Los Angeles (6) vs. Pittsburgh (5), 1980
Miami (7) vs. San Francisco (4), 1985
New England (7) vs. Chicago (4), 1986
10 Oakland (7) vs. Green Bay (3), 1968
9 In seven games
Fewest Kickoff Returns, Both Teams, Game
5 N.Y. Jets (1) vs. Baltimore (4), 1969
Miami (2) vs. Washington (3), 1973
6 In three games
Most Yards Gained, Game
222 Miami vs. Washington, 1983
173 Denver vs. Dallas, 1978
162 Pittsburgh vs. Los Angeles, 1980
Fewest Yards Gained, Game
17 L.A. Raiders vs. Washington, 1984
25 N.Y. Jets vs. Baltimore, 1969
32 Pittsburgh vs. Minnesota, 1975
Most Yards Gained, Both Teams, Game
279 Miami (222) vs. Washington (57), 1983
231 Pittsburgh (162) vs. Los Angeles (79), 1980
224 Denver (173) vs. Dallas (51), 1978
Fewest Yards Gained, Both Teams, Game
78 Miami (33) vs. Washington (45), 1973
82 Pittsburgh (32) vs. Minnesota (50), 1975
92 San Francisco (40) vs. Cincinnati (52), 1982
Most Touchdowns, Game
1 Miami vs. Washington, 1983

PENALTIES

Most Penalties, Game
   12 Dallas vs. Denver, 1978
   10 Dallas vs. Baltimore, 1971
    9 Dallas vs. Pittsburgh, 1979
Fewest Penalties, Game
    0 Miami vs. Dallas, 1972
      Pittsburgh vs. Dallas, 1976
    1 Green Bay vs. Oakland, 1968
      Miami vs. Minnesota, 1974; vs. San Francisco, 1985
    2 By four teams
Most Penalties, Both Teams, Game
   20 Dallas (12) vs. Denver (8), 1978
   16 Cincinnati (8) vs. San Francisco (8), 1982
   14 Dallas (10) vs. Baltimore (4), 1971
      Dallas (9) vs. Pittsburgh (5), 1979
Fewest Penalties, Both Teams, Game
    2 Pittsburgh (0) vs. Dallas (2), 1976
    3 Miami (0) vs. Dallas (3), 1972
      Miami (1) vs. San Francisco (2), 1985
    5 Green Bay (1) vs. Oakland (4), 1968
Most Yards Penalized, Game
  133 Dallas vs. Baltimore, 1971
  122 Pittsburgh vs. Minnesota, 1975
   94 Dallas vs. Denver, 1978
Fewest Yards Penalized, Game
    0 Miami vs. Dallas, 1972
      Pittsburgh vs. Dallas, 1976
    4 Miami vs. Minnesota, 1974
   10 Miami vs. San Francisco, 1985
      San Francisco vs. Miami, 1985
Most Yards Penalized, Both Teams, Game
  164 Dallas (133) vs. Baltimore (31), 1971
  154 Dallas (94) vs. Denver (60), 1978
  140 Pittsburgh (122) vs. Minnesota (18), 1975
Fewest Yards Penalized, Both Teams, Game
   15 Miami (0) vs. Dallas (15), 1972
   20 Pittsburgh (0) vs. Dallas (20), 1976
      Miami (10) vs. San Francisco (10), 1985
   43 Green Bay (12) vs. Oakland (31), 1968

FUMBLES

Most Fumbles, Game
    6 Dallas vs. Denver, 1978
    5 Baltimore vs. Dallas, 1971
    4 In four games
Fewest Fumbles, Game
    0 In six games
Most Fumbles, Both Teams, Game
    10 Dallas (6) vs. Denver (4), 1978
    8 Dallas (4) vs. Pittsburgh (4), 1976
       New England (4) vs. Chicago (3), 1986
    7 Pittsburgh (4) vs. Minnesota (3), 1975
       New England (4) vs. Chicago (3), 1986
Fewest Fumbles, Both Teams, Game
    0 Los Angeles vs. Pittsburgh, 1980
    1 Oakland (0) vs. Minnesota (1), 1977
       Oakland (0) vs. Philadelphia (1)), 1981
    2 In three games
Most Fumbles Lost, Game
    4 Baltimore vs. Dallas, 1971
       Denver vs. Dallas, 1978
       New England vs. Chicago, 1986
    2 In many games
Most Fumbles Recovered, Game
    8 Dallas vs. Denver, 1978 (4 own, 4 opp)
    5 Chicago vs. New England, 1986 (1 own, 4 opp)
    4 Pittsburgh vs. Minnesota, 1975 (2 own, 2 opp)
       Dallas vs. Pittsburgh, 1976 (4 own)

TURNOVERS

(Number of times losing the ball on interceptions and fumbles)

Most Turnovers, Game
    8 Denver vs. Dallas, 1978
    7 Baltimore vs. Dallas, 1971
    6 New England vs. Chicago, 1986
Fewest Turnovers, Game
    0 Green Bay vs. Oakland, 1968
       Miami vs. Minnesota, 1974
       Pittsburgh vs. Dallas, 1976
       Oakland vs. Minnesota, 1977; vs. Philadelphia, 1981
    1 By many teams

Most Turnovers, Both Teams, Game
    11 Baltimore (7) vs. Dallas (4), 1971
    10 Denver (8) vs. Dallas (2), 1978
    7 New England (6) vs. Chicago (2), 1986
Fewest Turnovers, Both Teams, Game
    2 Green Bay (1) vs. Kansas City (1), 1967
      Miami (0) vs. Minnesota (2), 1974
    3 Green Bay (0) vs. Oakland (3), 1968
      Pittsburgh (0) vs. Dallas (3), 1976
      Oakland (0) vs. Minnesota (3), 1977
    4 In five games

NET YARDS GAINED RUSHING & PASSING

Most Yards Gained, Game
    537 San Francisco vs. Miami, 1985
    429 Oakland vs. Minnesota, 1977
    408 Chicago vs. New England, 1986
Fewest Yards Gained, Game
    119 Minnesota vs. Pittsburgh, 1975
    123 New England vs. Chicago, 1986
    156 Denver vs. Dallas, 1978
Most Yards Gained, Both Teams, Game
    851 San Francisco (537) vs. Miami (314), 1985
    782 Oakland (429) vs. Minnesota (353), 1977
    737 Oakland (377) vs. Philadelphia (360), 1981
Fewest Yards Gained, Both Teams, Game
    452 Minnesota (119) vs. Pittsburgh (333), 1975
    481 Washington (228) vs. Miami (253), 1973
        Denver (156) vs. Dallas (325), 1978
    497 Minnesota (238) vs. Miami (259), 1974

RUSHING

Most Attempts, Game
    57 Pittsburgh vs. Minnesota, 1975
    53 Miami vs. Minnesota, 1974
    52 Oakland vs. Minnesota, 1977
       Washington vs. Miami, 1983
Fewest Attempts, Game
    9 Miami vs. San Francisco, 1985
    11 New England vs. Chicago, 1986

19 Kansas City vs. Green Bay, 1967
   Minnesota vs. Kansas City, 1970

Most Attempts, Both Teams, Game
81 Washington (52) vs. Miami (29), 1983
78 Pittsburgh (57) vs. Minnesota (21), 1975
   Oakland (52) vs. Minnesota (26), 1977
77 Miami (53) vs. Minnesota (24), 1974
   Pittsburgh (46) vs. Dallas (31), 1976

Fewest Attempts, Both Teams, Game
49 Miami (9) vs. San Francisco (40), 1985
52 Kansas City (19) vs. Green Bay (33), 1967
56 Pittsburgh (24) vs. Dallas (32), 1979

Most Yards Gained, Game
276 Washington vs. Miami, 1983
266 Oakland vs. Minnesota, 1977
252 Dallas vs. Miami, 1972

Fewest Yards Gained, Game
 7 New England vs. Chicago, 1986
17 Minnesota vs. Pittsburgh, 1975
25 Miami vs. San Francisco, 1985

Most Yards Gained, Both Teams, Game
372 Washington (276) vs. Miami (96), 1983
337 Oakland (266) vs. Minnesota (71), 1977
332 Dallas (252) vs. Miami (80), 1972

Fewest Yards Gained, Both Teams, Game
171 Baltimore (69) vs. Dallas (102), 1971
174 New England (7) vs. Chicago (167), 1986
186 Philadelphia (69) vs. Oakland (117), 1981

Most Touchdowns, Game
4 Chicago vs. New England, 1986
3 Green Bay vs. Kansas City, 1967
   Miami vs. Minnesota, 1974
2 Oakland vs. Minnesota, 1977
   Pittsburgh vs. Los Angeles, 1980
   L.A. Raiders vs. Washington, 1984
   San Francisco vs. Miami, 1985

Fewest Touchdowns, Game
0 By 13 teams

Most Touchdowns, Both Teams, Game
4 Miami (3) vs. Minnesota (1), 1974
   Chicago (4) vs. New England (0), 1986
3 Green Bay (3) vs. Kansas City (0), 1967
   Pittsburgh (2) vs. Los Angeles (1), 1980
   L.A. Raiders (2) vs. Washington (1), 1984

Fewest Touchdowns, Both Teams, Game
    0 Pittsburgh vs. Dallas, 1976
      Oakland vs. Philadelphia, 1981
    1 In seven games

PASSING

Most Passes Attempted, Game
    50 Miami vs. San Francisco, 1985
    44 Minnesota vs. Oakland, 1977
    41 Baltimore vs. N.Y. Jets, 1969
Fewest Passes Attempted, Game
    7 Miami vs. Minnesota, 1974
    11 Miami vs. Washington, 1973
    14 Pittsburgh vs. Minnesota, 1975
Most Passes Attempted, Both Teams, Game
    85 Miami (50) vs. San Francisco (35), 1985
    70 Baltimore (41) vs. N.Y. Jets (29), 1969
    63 Minnesota (44) vs. Oakland (19), 1977
Fewest Passes Attempted, Both Teams, Game
    35 Miami (7) vs. Minnesota (28), 1974
    39 Miami (11) vs. Washington (28), 1973
    40 Pittsburgh (14) vs. Minnesota (26), 1975
      Miami (17) vs. Washington (23), 1983
    24 Minnesota (14) vs. Oakland (32), 1977
      San Francisco (38) vs. Miami (16), 1985
Most Passes Completed, Game
    29 Miami vs. San Francisco, 1985
    25 Cincinnati vs. San Francisco, 1982
    24 Minnesota vs. Oakland, 1977
      San Francisco vs. Miami, 1985
Fewest Passes Completed, Game
    4 Miami vs. Washington, 1983
    6 Miami vs. Minnesota, 1974
    8 Miami vs. Washington, 1973
      Denver vs. Dallas, 1978
Most Passes Completed, Both Teams, Game
    53 Miami (29) vs. San Francisco (24), 1985
    39 Cincinnati (25) vs. San Francisco (14), 1982
    36 Minnesota (24) vs. Oakland (12), 1977
Fewest Passes Completed, Both Teams, Game
    19 Miami (4) vs. Washington (15), 1983

20 Pittsburgh (9) vs. Minnesota (11), 1975

22 Miami (8) vs. Washington (14), 1973

Most Yards Gained, Game

326 San Francisco vs. Miami, 1985

309 Pittsburgh vs. Los Angeles, 1980

291 Pittsburgh vs. Dallas, 1979

Philadelphia vs. Oakland, 1981

Fewest Yards Gained, Game

35 Denver vs. Dallas, 1978

63 Miami vs. Minnesota, 1974

69 Miami vs. Washington, 1973

Most Yards Gained, Both Teams, Game

615 San Francisco (326) vs. Miami (289), 1985

551 Philadelphia (291) vs. Oakland (260), 1981

503 Pittsburgh (309) vs. Los Angeles (194), 1980

Fewest Yards Gained, Both Teams, Game

156 Miami (69) vs. Washington (87), 1973

186 Pittsburgh (84) vs. Minnesota (102), 1975

205 Dallas (100) vs. Miami (105), 1972